INTRAPRENEURSHIP

Managing Ideas within Your Organizaition

As an employee, you suspect that your best ideas are valuable and could greatly benefit your organization. Management also recognizes that the company's ability to compete is contingent on how well it leverages its employees' ideas. So why are individuals at all levels of organizations typically poor advocates for new ideas? *Intrapreneurship* provides an engaging guide for both managers and employees on how to direct the flow of ideas and foster a culture of entrepreneurship within their company's existing structure.

Based on Kevin C. Desouza's research and experience consulting with thirty global organizations, *Intrapreneurship* outlines ways to mobilize all types of ideas – including blockbusters with the potential to create radically new external products and services, and more incremental innovations for improving internal processes. With practical frameworks and real-life examples for both employees and managers, *Intrapreneurship* will help you to identify the value in your own ideas and those of others to ultimately benefit your organization.

KEVIN C. DESOUZA is a Foundation Professor in the School of Public Affairs at Arizona State University and a Nonresident Senior Fellow in the Governance Studies program at the Brookings Institution.

KEVIN C. DESOUZA

Intrapreneurship

Managing Ideas within Your Organization

UNIVERSITY OF TORONTO PRESS
Toronto Buffalo London

© University of Toronto Press 2011
Rotman-UTP Publishing
University of Toronto Press
Toronto Buffalo London
utorontopress.com
Printed in the U.S.A.

Reprinted in paperback 2017

ISBN 978-1-4426-4143-3 (cloth)   ISBN 978-1-4875-2283-4 (paper)

∞ Printed on acid-free, 100% post-consumer recycled paper.

Library and Archives Canada Cataloguing in Publication

Desouza, Kevin C., 1979–
Intrapreneurship : managing ideas within your organization / Kevin C. Desouza.

Includes bibliographical references and index.
ISBN 978-1-4426-4143-3 (bound).   ISBN 978-1-4875-2283-4 (softcover)

1. Creative ability in business – Management.   2. Entrepreneurship
I. Title.

HD53.D48 2011   658.4'03   C2011-905852-9

University of Toronto Press acknowledges the financial assistance to its
publishing program of the Canada Council for the Arts and the Ontario Arts
Council, an agency of the Government of Ontario.

Canada Council   Conseil des Arts
for the Arts   du Canada

ONTARIO ARTS COUNCIL
CONSEIL DES ARTS DE L'ONTARIO
an Ontario government agency
un organisme du gouvernement de l'Ontario

Funded by the   Financé par le
Government   gouvernement
of Canada   du Canada   Canadä

To my lovely wife, Sally

Contents

Foreword

THOMAS H. DAVENPORT

President's Distinguished Professor of Information Technology
and Management, Babson College

This book is about ideas, and it contains plenty of great ideas within
its covers. But I would argue that there are three very important ideas
at its core that merit particular attention. While they may not seem
earth shattering, having worked with companies and organizations
for over twenty years on innovation and intrapreneurship issues, I can
testify to the fact that few have mastered even one of them.

1) *Growth and innovation arise from the systematic pursuit of ideas.*

I suspect most senior executives would agree with this statement, but
you wouldn't know it from how their organizations operate. Almost
every innovative thing an organization does can be traced to an idea
that was generated, modified, or borrowed by an individual or group.
So if an organization desires innovation, why would it not have programs, processes, and systems in place to systematically pursue ideas?

As Kevin Desouza describes in this book, this systematic pursuit is
absolutely necessary but is not easy to pull off. Ideas don't grow like
crops, in specified fields during specified seasons. They can come
from anyone at any time. But like crops, they do need to be nurtured.
Creating them is often the easy part. Capturing them accurately, deciding which ones to pursue, determining whether they work, and
adopting the innovations they describe – those are tough. Desouza describes these processes in the second half of the book – don't even
think about skipping them! I am a particular fan of chapter 5, on
experimentation. I feel strongly that organizations desiring to be innovative must be very good at experimentation and at learning from
both success and failure.

2) *Everybody's ideas matter.*

Unfortunately, Western business cultures have historically taken the view that some people are much more innovative than others, and that we need to segregate the innovators in R&D organizations while everyone else just executes. This is a really bad idea, and you see it operating even in the smartest organizations. For example, while I am generally a big fan of Google's approaches to innovation, they grant '20 percent time' for innovation only to engineers and managers. Isn't it likely that employees in advertising sales, public relations, and facilities management have some good ideas to share?

The 'democratization of innovation' – a core principle of this book – is a no-brainer if your definition of innovation is sufficiently broad. Again, historically we have viewed innovation as something very narrow that applies only to the invention of new products. Product innovation is still important, of course, but there are many other types: process innovation, service innovation, business model innovation, and marketing innovation, to name a few. These other types of innovation are particularly critical in service-oriented businesses (and service-oriented organizations such as government), and leading economies are rapidly becoming service economies. Who is the best person to identify an innovation in customer service, for example? You guessed it – the person who provides customer service and knows the strengths and weaknesses of the existing process. You'll be leaving a lot of great ideas that can help your business on the table if you restrict your idea-driven intrapreneurship to product innovation and the R&D department.

3) *Ideas and the knowledge they embody can be successfully managed.*

Some people think of ideas as ephemeral thoughts that cannot be managed. To put a bureaucracy around idea management, they might say, is to kill the good ideas. Not true. There is plenty of evidence that ideas – the initial revelation, the supporting evidence, the refining of the idea in a filtering process, and the status of its implementation – can be managed as well as debits and credits in an accounting ledger.

Why such confidence that this is so? There has been a movement to manage knowledge – an even more potentially ephemeral topic than ideas – for a couple of decades now. For the organizations that were serious about it, knowledge management has worked quite well. Those that treated it seriously received – and are still receiving – considerable value. Ideas for doing things better are only one form of knowledge, but they are a particularly valuable type. There are many technologies that can help with idea management, but it still requires a large dose of cultural and behavioral change – as this book wisely notes.

I first met Kevin Desouza through our mutual work on knowledge management, and that movement informs this book. But it has also been nurtured by Kevin's first job as a software engineer, his work on information management in the intelligence community, and now his most recent work on the incentive prizes for innovation to solve societal grand challenges. He possesses an uncommon combination of expertise and perspectives, and *Intrapreneurship* is a unique book. If you care about ideas, innovation, engaged employees, or better organizational performance, you have come to the right place.

INTRAPRENEURSHIP

Managing Ideas within Your Organization

1 Introduction

Think back to the last time you had a brilliant idea at work. How did your manager and peers react to your idea? Were you able to communicate the idea effectively and demonstrate its business value? Did the organization support your efforts to experiment and bring the idea to fruition as a product or service? If you're like most employees, your answer to all these questions is a resounding 'no.' Most employees struggle to move their ideas from initial conception to outputs that have organizational value.

We can't blame anyone but ourselves for how ideas get managed in our organizations. After all, any organization is an expression of the individual employees who work to influence, and who are influenced by, its structures, processes, and goals. Think of the last time a peer or a subordinate came to you to discuss an idea. How did you react? Were you able to support his or her idea and help develop it? Were you able to connect the employee with people who might be advocates or sponsors for the idea? Did you help articulate a business case for the idea? Despite our good intentions, most of us are poor supporters of ideas.

Individuals have many reasons for being reluctant to support new ideas. Most of us have daily assignments that take up too much of our cognitive energies for us to consider other endeavors. We may ask ourselves, 'Why should I take the time to support someone else's idea when I may not be rewarded for it?' or, worse, 'Will the idea threaten my own position and authority in this organization?' Because we have time constraints or are just plain insecure, we're more likely to kill ideas than nurture them.

This response – or lack of response – hurts both individuals and their organizations: idea creators are frustrated when a work environment stifles their imagination, and organizations suffer when they lose their greatest human asset – the inventive zeal of their employees. An organization's ability to compete and continuously renew itself is contingent upon how well it leverages the idea creators in its midst. When organizations fail to leverage their employees' ideas and when employees stumble in their ability to effectively manage those ideas, the loss of energy at all levels – from individuals to organizations and even to society – is tremendous.

Intrapreneurship is especially challenging for large established organizations.[1] As organizations grow and become 'incumbents' (established players) in their industry, managers shrink from radical ideas. Firms become comfortable doing what they do – a condition that leads to myopia and discourages risk taking. Furthermore, organizations' values and structures can become rigid over time, resulting in a narrow focus on operations and core mission. As a result, they lose the qualities that got them to where they are – creative energy, drive, and openness to experimentation. New ideas are often perceived as threats to the status quo rather than opportunities. Instead of welcoming new ideas, the organization grows increasingly intolerant of risk, tending to promote only *incremental* innovation that aligns with existing structures. Once organizations have deep knowledge in particular domains, they concentrate on ideas within this space, devaluing outside ideas. Microsoft fell prey to this type of thinking when it continued to pour resources into the Windows operating system and the Office suite of products even as the Internet was revolutionizing the industry. As a result, they missed out on the search engine market that was quickly dominated by Google.

Most incumbents focus on preserving their market position rather than on advancing it or entering new markets. Consider the case of Intuit, where a third to even a half of the firm's operating income goes into developing products and services that are unproven – even unprofitable. QuickBooks, one of Intuit's blockbusters, took more than three years to develop, and then another three to become profitable.[2] Most incumbent organizations would have 'cut their losses' early on with a product like QuickBooks. In their pursuit of stability, incumbents focus on standardization of internal systems and structures. This pursuit of efficiency leads to steady-state equilibrium. Rigid structures evolve in the form of departments or 'silos' that provide economies of scale and efficiencies. Myopic managers within organizations focus internally rather than externally – they look neither outside the organization nor outside their own units. Incentives for collaboration are lacking; there is competition for resources and, in economic downturns, little training on how to be innovative.

In established organizations, resources tend to be locked in or invested in large-scale efforts, limiting investment choices and hampering the flexible allocation of resources. Non-incumbents, however, can be swift and flexible. Consider the case of Ryanair, a disruptive organization in the airline industry. They established new relationships with airports, in which the airports actually pay the airline to bring passengers to them, while national carriers (the incumbents) have to pay for landing slots. In this way Ryanair ignored the standard industry practice of committing to long-term contracts, instead negotiating demand-driven ones. Established carriers were unable to respond to Ryanair's challenge because of the complex power structures that drove their resource allocation and legacy accounting systems that were hard to change. While incumbents face an uphill battle when it comes to supporting intrapreneurship, they can't afford to sit idle.

I define intrapreneurship as an individual's ability to be inventive and entrepreneurial within the parameters of an organization. Being inventive requires the freedom to pursue ideas and develop them, while being intrapreneurial requires a focus on commercializing ideas to arrive at solutions that customers value. In this chapter, I outline critical factors that make intrapreneurship a strategic imperative within an organization. The chapter will situate this book's perspective on how to manage ideas for intrapreneurship within the literature on corporate entrepreneurship.

The Concept of Intrapreneurship

The term *intrapreneurship* is not new.[3] Management scholars have a rich history of studying the concept of intrapreneurship; they do so with the intention of studying how large, mainly well-established firms renew themselves through innovation in order to continue to stay relevant in the marketplace.[4] In the academic literature, the concept of intrapreneurship is seen as a subset of the larger concept of *corporate entrepreneurship*.[5]

Corporate entrepreneurship can be realized through a number of mechanisms, such as supporting the creation of new internal ventures, facilitating the redefinition of capabilities and strategies, and even supporting innovation from within, all of which may expand a firm's operations into new markets or redefine their focus in current markets.[6] To facilitate corporate entrepreneurship, an organization needs to have a process that allows employees to leverage their ideas toward these ends.

Currently, most of the literature on intrapreneurship focuses on why corporate entrepreneurship is strategically valuable and how the presence of corporate entrepreneurship programs is correlated with financial benefits to the organization.[7] Unfortunately, little guidance is provided to employees and managers about how to implement intrapreneurship. This book will outline a process for leveraging ideas within the organization. It will outline how ideas should be managed over their life cycle, from conception to commercialization, and then to diffusion and implementation in their intended marketplace. The implementation of solutions (products, services, or practices) gives rise to new ideas and/or identifies spaces that are ripe for reflection and investigation, encouraging the continuation of the iterative intrapreneurship process.

Most studies also take a traditional, top-down view of innovation. The organization, as instantiated by the corporate strategy, drives innovation, and consequently any form of intrapreneurship.[8] The senior executives of the organization meet, discuss, and arrive at the organization's strategic goals, which in turn determine the areas of innovation that will be targeted and influence budgets, product offerings, customer interactions, and so on. Employees are supposedly asked to concentrate on predetermined focus areas. This top-down thinking limits creativity, among other things, and can lead to problems such as being blindsided by developments outside the areas of focus. In addition, most of the literature places a great emphasis on encouraging innovation for external constituents – most notably the customers of an organization. While there is no doubting the importance of innovation for customers, many employees (for example, those in the human resources department) do not interact directly with external customers of the firm. Does this mean they have nothing to offer in terms of innovation? Absolutely not! These employees have ideas, and many of these ideas can help an organization be more successful if they are optimally managed toward improving internal business processes – that is, serving internal customers of the organization (for example, through a more effective employee-retention program).

Organizations must have the capacity to support intrapreneurship from the bottom up to transform ideas into products and services that have value in their internal and external environments. This book describes a process whereby intrapreneurship leverages the collective intelligence of employees, allowing an organization to take advantage of emergent ideas that do not fall neatly within organizationally sanctioned priorities for innovation or that may not have immediate customer applicability. While only a few leaders define strategic innovation priorities, every employee has ideas. An organization that recognizes and supports these ideas can tap into the creativity of all its employees. One way to think about this is in terms of the commonly used framing of the 80–20 dichotomy: in most organizations, 80 percent of the innovation focus is on the 20 percent of ideas that are externally oriented. What would happen if we could change this dynamic and give due attention to the ideas that have value to our internal customers?

All employees have the ability to contribute to the improvement of the organization's internal processes. One of the most important yet basic reasons why employees do not contribute to the innovation and intrapreneurship agenda of the firm is that most organizations conspicuously lack sanctioned processes for leveraging ideas. Simply put, employees do not know what do with their ideas. As one CEO I interviewed at a biotechnology company put it,

> We are in the idea business. [Our] scientists and researchers drive our existence and excellence . . . we must get better at taking their ideas to the next level. We have some of the brightest minds on this floor working on the most complex problems in the health sciences. Yet, we struggle and do so often . . . ideas get lost, ideas do not get shared, ideas are poorly experimented with, and at the end ideas die . . . if left uncorrected . . . we lose our ideas, the bright minds, and eventually we are extinct.

While many organizations recognize the transformative power of intrapreneurship, few have processes to support it. It's hard to imagine a world without Google. Headquartered in Mountain View, California, the organization employs more than 16,000 individuals in over forty global locations. Google's mission is to organize the world's information and make it universally accessible. Google News (http://news.google.com), for example, was created by Krishna Bharat, now a principal scientist at Google. After the attacks of 11 September 2001, Bharat became a news junkie, tracking information from several news sites. He came up with an idea of creating a tool that could crawl and parse different news sites to cluster the type of information he wanted to read. Google magnified his idea to form a complete news service on their site. Not surprisingly, the company has several technology-enabled solutions to foster intrapreneurship among its employees. Google Ideas, one such tool, acts as a repository for innovative ideas. The tool enables employees to share new ideas on products and services and to comment on the ideas of other employees. The tool also allows employees to rate one another's ideas on a scale of zero to five, zero meaning 'Dangerous or harmful if implemented' and five meaning 'Great idea! Make it so.'

Why Intrapreneurship Is Important Now

As Google has become larger and taken on the role of an incumbent in its industry, some might argue that even Google is beginning to lose its entrepreneurial edge. Think for a moment – what was the last blockbuster idea you heard out of Google? Don't despair if you can't list a major product after Google Maps or Gmail. Google has had a series of major product flops in recent history, including Buzz, Wave, and Google Answers, among others.[9] Building an environment where intrapreneurship thrives is vital for capitalizing on an organization's most vital asset – its human energy and ideas.

Human energy and ideas are the most critical assets of an organization today. Organizations must find ways to leverage human potential at the highest levels. Consider the case of pfizerWorks, which allows Pfizer employees to outsource mundane tasks such as creating presentation slides or basic data analysis.[10] This simple effort helped Pfizer give back more than 65,000 hours to employees to be used for more value-added work. Such support systems are vital to building intrapreneurship.

While organizations can buy two of anything and duplicate the technical infrastructure of their competitors, they can't duplicate an employee's knowledge or ideas. Organizations spend an inordinate amount of resources on recruiting talented employees, especially for knowledge workers such as scientists, engineers, management consultants, and project managers. Time and energy are spent in identifying the best fit for the organization's culture – on finding the candidate with the best ideas who can help the organization grow and will commit to a future with the organization. Once recruitment is complete, further resources are expelled on orientation and training programs. Given all the energy and resources that are expended in recruiting the best and brightest, it would be a shame if the employee did not (1) stick around the organization for a while, (2) contribute ideas to the organization, and (3) improve the internal or external operations of the organization. But even the brightest new minds will be unable to fulfill these three functions unless their organization supports intrapreneurship in a broad sense. As a recent postgraduate hire in a major technology organization remarked, 'they hire the best . . . from [the] top business and engineering schools in the world . . . once we get here, though, we are told how things "are" and are indoctrinated to follow procedures rather than trying out the great ideas we talked about during the interviews . . . I am frustrated by the job, waiting for the right opportunity to leave . . .' In order to develop an environment conducive to sharing ideas, the organization needs to ensure that employees feel a sense of belonging to the organization and see and feel that their ideas matter and can help strengthen the organization. In short, the organization needs to engage employees in the innovation agenda of the organization.

In today's business world, four converging trends are putting great pressure on firms to recognize the changing dynamics of how ideas and energy are managed within and across organizations.

Trend 1: Decentralization of Ideas

Ideas used to be centrally controlled and managed within the organization. Today, we are seeing a movement toward decentralization of ideas, in terms of who has ideas and of how ideas are shared. Traditionally, innovation has been the purview of a few select people who work in research and development (R&D) labs. This is where 'innovation' has always been done; sometimes these institutions are called innovation labs and institutes. Yet in two ways the traditional R&D structure often impedes new ideas:

1 Ideas are sanitized and people become more risk-averse as they move up the organizational hierarchy (i.e., risk tolerance and risk amplification occur across hierarchical levels).
2 Ideas are blocked as they move spatially through the organization, preventing cross-fertilization of ideas.

More effective than an R&D structure is a networked, community-centered innovation model that includes employees of all ranks. This decentralized focus makes sense given the economics of supply and demand: only a few people work in an R&D lab, but intrapreneurship broadens the base of idea development. In addition, the organization as a whole can focus on a larger number of ideas rather than being restricted by the disciplined and focused top-down approach in an R&D lab. A bottom-up, decentralized platform will engage a broad range of employees, while an R&D lab can execute focused research projects. In many organizations, also, the R&D labs are working on 'grand ideas' that may shape the future; these ideas are from five to ten years ahead of their time. Simply focusing on innovation in this context is risky, as it undermines the innovations that need to be made to solve the problems and opportunities of today, including the ones that are internal to the organization. Ultimately, if an organization can't be successful in the present, its chances of being around to take advantage of the future are slim.

The failure of the Xerox Palo Alto Research Center (PARC) to capitalize on its innovations in computing in the 1970s perfectly illustrates the negative fallout when an organization's research arm is not integrated with the rest of the company. In the 1970s, Xerox PARC was a leader in innovation, developing many of the fundamental computing technologies that were later commercialized by Silicon Valley companies such as Apple Computer, Adobe, and 3M.[11] Xerox provided PARC with the resources and financial backing to hire top engineering talent but failed to grasp the significance of their employees' inventions and watched as other companies commercialized them first.[12] PARC learned from its mistake and later enjoyed success in the 1990s. John Seely Brown reflects on the company's recovery: 'the problem is, few companies know how to learn from this local innovation and how to use it to improve their overall effectiveness. At PARC, we are studying this process of local innovation with employees on the front lines of Xerox's business and developing technologies to harvest its lessons for the company as a whole.'[13] To capture returns on its employees' diverse set of experiences, expertise, capabilities, and perspectives, the organization must invite them into its innovation agenda.

Trend 2: Empowering the Front Lines

As idea generation is decentralized, organizations need to be structured so as to empower employees on the front lines to leverage ideas as part of their work assignments. Rather than confining decision-making authority to the higher echelons of the organization, empowering the front lines enables the organization to become more agile – more responsive to new ideas and able to act on information in a timely manner. Real-time organizations need to be able to sense, recognize, and act on signals in their environments in a time-sensitive and cost-effective manner. Employees must be encouraged and enabled to react to situations, seek out ideas, develop new ideas as needed, and find ways of incorporating these into the fabric of the organization.

The U.S. Department of Defense (DoD), traditionally a hierarchical organization, has begun to embrace the concepts of decentralization of idea generation and empowering the front lines. Within DoD circles, the concept of the 'edge organization' (EO) is gaining traction.[14] The EO sharply contrasts with how the DoD currently operates. The EO proposes a networked structure rather than a hierarchical setup and stresses the need to push information, knowledge, and decision-making authority to the 'edges' (i.e., the front lines) of the organization. The nodes (the soldiers, devices, etc.) on the front lines need to generate real-time situational awareness of their environment and be able to take action not only to address their local challenges and opportunities but also to contribute to advancing the global mission. The days of having the front lines simply work in response to orders from the top are coming to an end. Organizations of the future, including the DoD, will have network-based work structures, where authority is granted and respected, based not on tenure or age but on expertise, know-how, and the ability to develop innovative solutions for problems and opportunities as they arise. With respect to the DoD, innovations are developed to meet local conditions, and much of the planning is done locally rather than at headquarters. To this end, there is a big push within the DoD to enhance their knowledge about processes and systems that can optimize the flow of information and knowledge within networked environments. They see the necessity of preparing the next generation of their workforce to work in a collaborative and empowered environment.

With increasing pressure to flatten organizational structures, the need to empower the front lines has never been greater. Employees often see entrepreneurship as something that people from the outside do. Moreover, they falsely believe that entrepreneurship calls for working from scratch and building *new* organizations. As a result, they often associate entrepreneurship only with glamorous success stories such as Groupon or Facebook. In the end they see their role as just executing tasks in a routine manner, without realizing how they might be entrepreneurial within their organization. While the front lines have normally been used to executing strict orders from above, the new challenge faced by front-line workers is to think creatively and recognize and respond promptly and with ingenuity to problems and opportunities. To this end they absolutely must know how to manage their ideas and creative potential. The ideal organization will know how to engage their front-line workforce and leverage the ideas being created at the leading edge of the organization.

Trend 3: User-Driven Innovation

By empowering the front lines, an organization can build a culture in which employees see their work and tasks in the context of meeting the needs of a customer. Work that gets done in an organization, across all levels, needs to have a customer focus. This requires employees to pay attention to how outputs and work processes impact both the immediate stakeholders and the end customers. If employees are empowered and supported to adopt such an approach, they stand a better chance of relating ideas to customer needs and working with those ideas to make the lives of their internal and external customers better.

The customers themselves also have valuable ideas to offer. We are seeing a shift from manufacturer-driven innovation to user-driven innovation. Studies on user innovation have shown that anywhere from 10 percent to 40 percent of users modify products.[15] Users who engage with products most often employ them in ways that were not intended by the product's original designers. In addition, through extended use, users uncover limitations and shortcomings in the product. When the product fails to meet their needs, users create workarounds and modifications to the original design.

User-driven innovation has been shown to be more effective than traditional, manufacturer-driven innovation for several reasons. First, user-driven innovation provides us with a mechanism to address the 'sticky information'[16] problem. Users are seldom able to communicate their needs to developers because much of the information needed for innovation is difficult for users to articulate. Developers then have to work with incomplete and sometimes flawed requirements when trying to innovate. Second, since designers are not 'living' in the shoes of the users, they have a hard time seeing the world from the users' vantage point. Third, given a chance, users may be better innovators because they know how products actually perform rather than how they were designed to perform. Fourth, there is the 'absorptive capacity' factor.[17] To appreciate ideas fully, one must have the requisite knowledge to process the idea. For example, without an advanced degree in chemistry, a person will probably not be able to appreciate a new method for protein synthesis. Similarly, an outside designer will probably not adequately understand ideas that originate from, or have an impact on, an unfamiliar environment such as a factory assembly line or a retail store.

One way to solve the problem is to push responsibility for innovation to the edges of the organization. Organizations can empower users to innovate by deploying toolkits and tapping into their core users' ideas. The individuals who are at the edges of the organization are accustomed to receiving information in the form of orders and directives, and are seldom seen as sources of innovation. However, an organization that values intrapreneurship wants these individuals to innovate and work in an entrepreneurial fashion. They can capture information at its source, enabling the idea creators (the employees) to learn by doing,[18] and then refine and improve new prototypes. Employees can work on ideas by taking information from the sources, combining it with the tacit knowledge they possess, and then designing solutions directly and determining whether they are workable.

Trend 4: The Digital Generation

The Internet has fundamentally altered how we seek out, process, and share information in multiple contexts. For example, the Internet has dramatically changed the way in which we engage with customers about products and services. Today, organizations receive real-time feedback from customers not only through channels the organizations devise (e.g., surveys) but also through customer-centered platforms (e.g., blogs, wikis, and even tweets about products). This change in the way knowledge is created, shared, and applied is profoundly important. Apple has been highly innovative in taking advantage of such trends as decentralized idea generation, a customer focus, and user-driven innovation through the 'App Store' for the iPhone and iPod Touch. For a nominal fee, Apple provides their Software Developer Kit

(SDK) to anyone who wishes to develop an application for the iPhone and sell it in the iTunes Store. Developers even set their own price, of which Apple takes a small percentage for each transaction. In its first year, the App Store had more than 1.5 billion downloads, offered upwards of 65,000 applications, and registered more than 100,000 developers in the iPhone developer program.[19] The App Store brought unprecedented success to Apple, with the result that companies like Microsoft, Google, and Palm have adopted the model by creating their own app stores. It's interesting to note that Microsoft created the original platform for more open application development – the Windows operating system – which led to a massive amount of democratization in software development, as users could now easily develop and launch their own applications. Apple took a page out of Microsoft's strategy book and just beat them at it in the mobile space.

Another critical and related trend is how organizations deal with the next generation of workers. Organizations must prepare to welcome the next generation of workers – people who grew up in an environment of social networking. Members of the next generation thrive on sharing knowledge and expertise and are more likely than their parents to consult external knowledge sources for solutions to their problems. They gladly share knowledge that is 'half-baked' and use their networks to advance their causes. They enjoy collaborative work and seek out expert advice from positions of power within their social networks. To them, the most impressive positions of power are earned by achieving goals and by innovating, and they may resent authority that has been imposed upon them for any other reason. In addition, these young people like to multi-task and are easily distracted; hence, giving them single tasks in the workplace will not be productive. They are likely to 'invent' their own (possibly counterproductive) mechanisms for sharing ideas. For example, if employees do not have a sanctioned process for sharing and mobilizing ideas, they may resort to sharing ideas using unauthorized platforms (e.g., on public forums) or channels (e.g., through instant messaging conversations). These may evolve as a means to seek feedback from other employees and can be valuable, but they could also have costs in terms of information leaks and loss of intellectual property. The organization must have, as a matter of pure necessity, a viable platform for intrapreneurship so as to prevent individuals from airing their ideas in spaces that the organization may not control. Most importantly, the digital generation loves playing with ideas. And, if you are to attract the best and brightest from this generation to your organization, you must be able to give them a platform on which to engage. An intrapreneurial environment is vital to retain the workforce's next generation. Chances are high that the best and brightest young minds in your organization will invent (and reinvent) products and services that fundamentally alter the future of your organization and the market at large. The question you have to ask is, do you want them to do this under the auspices of the organization or from the outside?

Realizing the Promise of Intrapreneurship

Most organizations will acknowledge the impact of the above trends on the pressure to be innovative. Yet too often organizations talk about the strategic need for innovation, creativity, and new product development but fail to follow up with tangible actions that help employees and managers on the front line to leverage their ideas. Consider the following comment:[20]

> Innovation is a must to survive in our environment . . . All of my [executive] colleagues understand the need for innovation and are a hundred percent supportive of employees who innovate . . . Yet, I cannot say that we have an organizational process for innovation . . . innovation happens, but I cannot outline the process to you because I do not think we have one. (CEO of an information technology organization)

Imagine an organization that fosters a disciplined approach to innovating from within: employees who help each other refine and advocate ideas, a robust experimentation and commercialization process that tests those ideas, and a feedback process that helps generate new ideas. This is possible – if you believe in the power of *intrapreneurship* and have a process to leverage ideas towards it.

Leading organizations retain their talent by creating just this sort of environment. Google, for example, has instituted practices that support intrapreneurship, such as the '70/20/10 rule.' Employees spend 70 percent of their time working on their core projects, 20 percent on ideas that are closely related to their projects, and 10 percent on any other ideas they would like to pursue. Two of Google's best-known products, Gmail and Google News, grew out of employees' 20 percent space.[21] Google's method for organizing employee time isn't completely novel. Decades ago, 3M developed a policy whereby employees could spend up to 15 percent of their time developing ideas that weren't directly related to their work assignments but that might be beneficial to 3M.

Intrapreneurship-focused organizations give employees resources, time, and budgets to work on their own ideas because they know that creating space for their employees to be inventive may yield the most valuable contributions. Moreover, these organizations do not simply give employees space and then forget about them. They know how to hold employees accountable for their ideas, support employees in their efforts to develop and commercialize ideas, and encourage the intrapreneurial spirit.

Whether you are an employee or a manager, this book is written to help you leverage ideas within your organization. Its sole goal is to make you realize the promise of intrapreneurship by taking you through the process of managing ideas in an optimal manner, from the time they are conceived, through the commercialization process, and ultimately to a point of implementation and diffusion in their intended market, whether internal or external to the organization. I'll focus on ideas of all kinds, from the blockbusters that have the potential to create radically new products and services to the more common incremental ideas that offer tangible ways to improve current products, services, and practices.

Lens and Perspective

Every author brings a unique perspective. A researcher sees things differently from a practicing line manager or executive, whose perspective, in turn, differs from that of a student or a journalist. My own perspective is that of an 'insider': I have been part of intrapreneurship programs as an employee, a manager, and a researcher.

As an employee – a software engineer – I saw great potential in the product I was working on and grew frustrated when the project manager and even the higher-ups in my organization packaged the module as a 'free' product offering. The company insisted that it had no additional value above the fees that the client was already paying. To prove them wrong, I used a series of creative end runs: talking directly to the customers and convincing them to try out versions of my idea informally. Without my manager's knowledge, I worked with one client to fully exploit the tool's potential. In the end, this client was the one who suggested that my boss should add a line in the contract for the price of the tool, and, as they say, the rest is history!

As a manager, I spent a lot of energy trying (often failing, then retrying) to build an intrapreneurial organization. I opened up several small management consulting outfits, all of which eventually morphed into the Engaged Enterprise (EE). EE was formed on the premise that organizations had tangible and intangible assets that needed to be leveraged through creative mechanisms that engaged the spirit of intrapreneurship in each employee. Along with several colleagues, I had the good fortune to help leading organizations bolster their information- and knowledge-management capabilities. While leading EE, I learned at first hand – through multiple episodes of trial and error – how to engage the intrapreneurial spirit of my own employees. The success of EE can be directly attributed to the successful practice of true intrapreneurship in several organizations that supported, enhanced, and harnessed the creativity of their employees. It was innovative ideas from employees that helped us compete against the bigger and more established management-consulting firms – and win. In this book, I will share lessons I learned as a manager and owner of the Engaged Enterprise.

Most recently, I have studied – and experienced at first hand – the concerns of researchers building innovative enterprises within academia. Along with several colleagues at the University of Washington, I created the Institute for Innovation in Information Management (I3M) in late 2005 (In August 2011, I decided to move from the University of Washington to Virginia Tech). I3M has received continuous support from private organizations to research critical information-management problems. Two I3M research projects have examined organizational innovation processes. Much of what I share with the reader in this book comes from the examination of organizational innovation processes in more than thirty leading global organizations. These organizations are headquartered in more than ten countries and span the Asian, European, North American, and Australian continents. We studied everything from prominent Fortune 100 companies, to small-to-medium sized companies, to non-profit and government organizations. In addition, I share lessons learned while trying to innovate in the academic environment. Over the course of five years at the University of Washington, I have been director of two Institutes, have created one, and have co-led one. Each of these experiences has given me the necessary environment to reflect on and refine lessons learned about intrapreneurship from the private sector.

My cognitive focus is on information. This is how I see both problems and opportunities. Information helps us arrive at decisions, take advantage of opportunities, and resolve problems. Organizations falter when information is trapped, unattended to, or misused – all problems that emerge from brittle information-management processes and lack of strategic foresight in managing the information space. In this book, I'll consider ideas as information and focus on how organizations manage information about, from, and through ideas. Like other information nuggets, ideas must be attended to effectively and efficiently if they are to enable decision making or secure competitive advantages. Just as information needs to be identified, distinguished from noise, evaluated, applied, and learned from via feedback within a system (or environment), ideas need to be managed within the context of an organization. This book will outline a process for managing ideas as seeds of information from their planting (conception), to their growth (commercialization), and finally their flowering (diffusion and implementation) within a given environment.

I've engaged in and observed intrapreneurship from multiple perspectives throughout my career, yet this book represents the first time I've synthesized my experiences in written form. It is my sincere hope that this book will provide you, regardless of your role within an organization, with an applied information-management – based perspective on leveraging ideas within your organization.

Roadmap

This book looks at the many ways in which intrapreneurship can benefit an organization. It begins with a discussion of the concept of intrapreneurship. It then examines the stages of the intrapreneurship process and concludes with some guiding principles for designing a sustainable process. These topics are examined from the perspectives of both the organization – the formal structures and managers – and the employee. Too often, business ideas are discussed on only one side of the employee-management dynamic. The goal here is to engage both managers *and* employees in the discussion, so that both sides can appreciate the roles everyone can play in practicing intrapreneurship within their organization.

Chapter 2 examines the concepts or ideas, the key ingredients of the intrapreneurship process. It then explores the roles played by various entities in fostering intrapreneurship. Next, it presents an overview of the five stages of the intrapreneurship process. The process described is cyclical, beginning with the generation of ideas and ending with their diffusion and implementation, which then feeds back into the generation of new ideas. The chapter concludes with a look at the key organizational actors and the roles they play in building an intrapreneurial enterprise.

Beginning with chapter 3, we will see the intrapreneurial process in action by examining its various stages. Chapter 3 investigates in detail the first stage of the intrapreneurial process, exploring how ideas are generated and mobilized in organizations. We see that some ideas are created from scratch, but most are mobilized across domains. The focus is on encouraging employees to think about spaces of interest to the organization rather than simply generating a lot of ideas. Equally important is encouraging managers to pay attention to ideas that do not fall within predefined areas of interest. In addition, organizations need to devise mechanisms that facilitate easy transfer of ideas from one part of the organization to another.

Chapter 4 talks about advocating and screening ideas. All organizations face the traditional economic challenge of having unlimited wants that need to be satisfied with limited resources. Difficult decisions will need to be made about which ideas receive funding and attention. It is critical to have robust and transparent screening procedures for ideas. Equally important is the need for organizations to develop and support people who can advocate for ideas. Idea advocates help refine the ideas and get them in front of the people who can implement them. Employees need to find strong advocates who can support their ideas, and organizations need to remove the barriers that stifle idea advocacy, instead putting reward structures in place.

Once an idea has been screened, it goes through the experimentation phase, where its suitability is gauged through prototyping and testing. Chapter 5 explores how organizations can build robust processes for experimentation. Too often, organizations keep experimentation locked up in their research and development labs. Employees should know how to run experiments on their ideas, how to gather and analyze data from experiments, and how best to present the results from these efforts. The organization should seek to capture the results of experiments that are conducted by employees in the course of their work.

Once ideas are developed within a context, the next step is to make them appealing to the intended audience through the act of commercialization. Chapter 6 offers guidelines for introducing new ideas within the organization through packaging, pricing, and promotion. While a multitude of articles and books examine how to commercialize ideas externally, relatively few resources discuss how to commercialize ideas within an organization. In my opinion, it is harder to get ideas commercialized within the organization because organizations are highly skeptical about home-grown ideas.

Employees who want to persuade organizational decision makers to accept their ideas should operate like management consultants to intervene in work settings, engage their internal customers, and get management to believe in their ideas. Chapter 7 discusses the diffusion and implementation stage, in which an idea creator achieves buy-in for the innovation and sets up a structure for utilizing it. As an idea is used and reused, individuals will have a chance to identify the idea's shortcomings, gauge its elasticity, and learn the boundaries of its applicability. Gathering good feedback from the marketplace and using this information strategically to guide new idea development is vital at this stage. This is why intrapreneurship is circular rather than linear.

Chapter 8 outlines key design principles to bear in mind as you embark on building an intrapreneurial organization. It describes how to take intrapreneurship from a concept to a source of sustainable, competitive advantage for your organization through four principles: (1) creating dialogue and building a network of believers; (2) simplifying mechanisms for capturing and communicating feedback; (3) measuring the maturity of the intrapreneurship process; and (4) keeping an eye out for complacency.

The End Game

In today's competitive environment, an organization is only as good as its ability to manage ideas. Successful organizations will be able to design, build, implement, and sustain intrapreneurship processes that are superior to those of their competitors. It is through these processes that organizations will be able to act quickly and effectively to introduce new products and services, avoid blind spots, and attract and retain the best minds around.

In describing how to become intrapreneurial using a process perspective, my goals are to:

1 provide organizations with a simple yet reliable and comprehensive framework within which to think about leveraging ideas. My hope is that organizations will take up the challenge of building environments that support intrapreneurship;
2 provide managers with an understanding of the challenges that employees face when trying to manage ideas within each of the stages of the intrapreneurship process. To this end, it is my hope that organizations will seriously consider engineering a robust intrapreneurship process;
3 provide employees with an operational framework that can guide them as they seek to be entrepreneurial within the organization;
4 provide the manager and the employee with a framework that will facilitate dialogue between them.

This book has been a long time in the making, and it is my hope that you will find it interesting and worthwhile. I decided that this book had to be written after I shared with several dozen organizations what it takes to be intrapreneurial and realized that I had no documentation to leave with them. We live and die by our ideas. We advance people who are willing to leverage their ideas toward a positive end. Organizations thrive on their ability to leverage ideas. And, ultimately, societies are transformed by great ideas.

We are now ready to explore the three key ingredients needed to make intrapreneurship a reality in organizations – ideas, roles, and the process.

2 Ideas, Roles, and Process

Intrapreneurship is both a science and an art. The *science* arises from a systematic implementation of the principles laid out in this book. Rules and practices dictate innovation. As we have seen, Google and 3M regulate how employees divide their time among core tasks, related tasks, and development of new ideas. Likewise, Procter and Gamble has set up infrastructures for promoting the exchange of problems (and solutions) with trusted entities beyond the organization through its 'Connect and Develop' program. Microsoft, Johnson & Johnson, and Intel all sponsor 'Idea Fests' where employees can showcase their works-in-progress and get feedback from internal reviewers and, in some cases, external stakeholders. These organizations engage in their innovation-centered efforts mindfully: activities are diligently managed and organized so they generate business value – thus, the *science* is in the design, evaluation, and continuous improvement of their intrapreneurship management process.

The *art* arises from the reality that no matter how much you plan, organize, and control these efforts, the business of intrapreneurship is chaotic. It's hard, if not impossible, to predict when an employee might come up with a good idea. It's also challenging to identify initially which ideas are going to be accepted by the marketplace, or when to launch a given product or service. As with a work of art, the beauty of an idea is often in the eye of the beholder. And the old adage that one person's trash is another person's treasure is true of ideas as well. Organizations must perfect the art of flexibility to allow for creative agility around established intrapreneurship processes. The processes must not be static but dynamic: as an organization matures in its practice of intrapreneurship, it must continuously update and overhaul its programs to keep them relevant and optimized for the current business environment. Furthermore, just as every artist has a unique vision, no two innovation programs or set of best practices will work or should be implemented in exactly the same way.

Given that intrapreneurship is an art and a science, we would benefit from taking a process view of how it works within an organization. Process models and frameworks abound in business literature. Most of them can be reduced to a simple input-process-output model: add 'a' to process 'b' and you end up with 'c.' I find these quite appealing as explanatory tools since they are not only simple to understand but also provide us with an approach to management. Managing processes, quite simply, comes down to two things: (1) ensuring that the process (i.e., the capturing of inputs, the transformation of capacities, and the delivery of outputs) is effective and efficient, and (2) ensuring that outputs are valuable to the organization's stakeholders. Pundits have long called attention to the fact that organizational processes need to be deliberately managed, as they are a source of business value. The concept of business process re-engineering originated in the 1990s.[1] Unfortunately, many organizations embraced the concept to redesign and optimize processes around their structured business operations (e.g., sales, production, etc.) but didn't apply it to processes affecting intrapreneurship and innovation in general. As a result, even today many organizations lack a clear process to move ideas from conception to commercialization. Consider the following comments:[2]

> A process for innovation is missing in this organization . . . One reason why I have been harping on setting up a process, or at least a template, is the need to measure our efforts . . . we spend money on [R&D] workshops, brainstorming retreats, experimentation, and a million other things; some of these work and some don't . . . I could not tell you where are the strengths and weaknesses of our innovation capacities . . . I can guess that we are very good at getting ideas from our employees, and not so good at the ways we commercialize the ideas . . . but these are my guesses . . . It is difficult to manage with guesswork.' (VP of Research for an information technology organization)

Comments such as these are not uncommon. While most senior executives express the need for entrepreneurship within the organization, few can point to a business process that could help them meet that need. Even fewer have processes that are managed with the same care and effort as the operational processes found in traditional departments such as accounting, finance, and operations. Intrapreneurship, for the most part, remains 'informal' or occurs by 'happenstance.' It's common to find localized processes for soliciting and screening ideas within departments. In most cases, ideas are solicited periodically, commonly during the preparation of the annual budget and when charting out major initiatives. As a result, most managers face the usual glut of submissions, with limited resources to support them and even less time to give serious consideration to all of them. Moreover, local ideas remain isolated, and there's limited cross-pollination of ideas across vertical silos or even hierarchical layers. What's even more troubling is the fact that limited organizational learning takes places in terms of how to improve the underlying processes used to manage ideas.

Any good manager knows that unless you specify a process, chances are you're not actively managing it. And if you're not measuring the viscosity, efficiency, and effectiveness of the process, you won't be able to improve it or benchmark how your process compares to those of your competitors and business partners. Few organizations have taken the time to articulate a process for intrapreneurship and communicate it to their employees. As a result, there are few employees who know how to take their ideas from initial concept to artifacts that have business value.

Let's examine the ramifications of this shortcoming using energy as an analogy. Most management gurus talk in terms of managing tasks, managing resources, and even managing time. All of these are valid topics, but making organizations successful and motivating employees to do things that others think are impossible comes down to the management of energy. Physics teaches us that energy cannot be created or destroyed, but simply transforms states. Moreover, we know that when we engage in work, some energy is lost as heat. Now, consider how this applies to an organization. Robust organizations know how to use their employees' energy in an effective and efficient manner. Employee energy drives the organization to do work that transforms resources into products and services. But organizations that lack a robust, well-articulated process for intrapreneurship will see their employees expend great amounts of energy without actually creating anything of value. As a result, the organization as a whole wastes energy when it doesn't efficiently manage the flow of ideas. Energy wasted in mismanaging ideas leaves less energy available for other matters such as operational tasks, with a negative impact on day-to-day business operations. Finally, physics also teaches us that unless living systems have continuous inputs of energy, they die (this draws on the second law of thermodynamics that specifies how energy is lost, as heat, in the conduct of work). The most important source of energy for competitive advantage in an organization is its *employees,* and more specifically the *ideas* and *know-how* of its employees. To put it another way, the immature organization will not only lose energy as it fails to adequately transform ideas into value; it will also lose new sources of energy. As a result, the organization can be assured of only one outcome – failure and eventual extinction. Organizations that use a systematic process for leveraging ideas fare significantly better than organizations that do not.

Ideas are the critical ingredients that move through the intrapreneurship process. The intrapreneurship quest begins with ideas, which are its key input. Ideas, strangely enough, are not easy to describe. They can be random thoughts, products of our imagination, concepts, images, and the list goes on. Ideas can originate from planned efforts, such as problem-solving engagements, or at random moments, such as during your morning shower. Most of us admit it's difficult to control the flow of ideas in our minds. Sometimes, the most creative ideas come to us when we least expect them. At other times, we spend hours puzzling over a problem with no solution in sight. And not all ideas have the same shelf life. Ideas may be useful for a limited time or during a narrow window of opportunity, or they may last longer. Some ideas are persistent; they emerge time and time again, while others are transient; they spring up then disappear without trace. Ideas also differ in their scope – from a quick fix to a problem to a broad reconsideration of a foundational purpose, direction, or behavior.

In addition to considering ideas themselves, we must also be aware of the various roles that members of the organization can play as part of the intrapreneurship process. Roles in the intrapreneurship process are not static or fixed. At times you may be the intrapreneur struggling to get an idea across. At other times, you may find yourself in the role of a manager who is trying to guide and harness the energy of an intrapreneur, or you may be an observer who is called upon to sponsor other intrapreneurs' efforts. It's quite conceivable that during a given work day you will find yourself oscillating among these various roles. Thus, it's vital to understand the intrapreneurship process from each of these vantage points.

The rest of this chapter explores three main topics. First, it explores the concept of *ideas*. After all, it is ideas that we are going to focus on in this book, from concept to refinement, experimentation, and eventual transformation into solutions that are valued by customers. Second, it examines the *roles* played by various organizational members throughout the intrapreneurship process. Third, it provides an overview of the intrapreneurship *process*. In successive chapters, each stage of the process is explored in depth. Taken as a collection, these three things – ideas, roles, and process – are the critical components that need to be managed to realize the promise of intrapreneurship.

Ideas

> An idea is nothing more nor less than a new combination of old elements.
>
> – James Webb Young

> An idea is a feat of association.
>
> – Robert Frost

The former president and founder of Xerox, Joseph Chamberlain Wilson, enjoyed using words like 'creativity,' 'ideas,' 'risk,' 'innovation,' and 'change' in his speeches. The following is an excerpt from a new employee orientation speech delivered in 1960:

> We are a company which pays a premium on imagination and the use of creativity and the use of brains to think of new ideas. We don't want to do things the same old way. We suspect the same old way. Therefore, as you come here, I hope you come here with an attitude that change will be a way of life for you. You will not be doing things tomorrow the way you have been doing them today. And if you do, we will feel that somehow the momentum that has taken years and years to build up is perhaps slowing down, and I assure you that we will bend every effort to keep it from slowing down. Therefore, we are seeking people who are willing to accept risks, who are willing to try new ideas, who have new ideas of their own, who are not afraid to change what they are doing from one day to the next or one year to the next, who welcome new challenges, who welcome new people, who welcome new positions, and if you are that sort of person you will be very welcome here at Xerox.

Love for new ideas and innovation led to the creation of Xerox PARC (Palo Alto Research Center), an interdisciplinary research institute chartered to create the 'Office of the Future' in 1970. Xerox PARC remains one of the most inventive institutes of recent times, having created things like the first object-oriented programming language (Smalltalk), the first graphical user interface (GUI), the first WYSIWYG text editor, and laser printing.

Here's a simple exercise. Find twenty people from various hierarchical levels and functional departments in your organization. Ask them two simple questions: 'How would you define a good idea?' and 'How do you recognize a good idea?' If you work in a typical organization, you'll probably get twenty different answers! Some of your colleagues may not even be able to articulate their responses. Is this a problem? You bet it is!

Organizations face a common challenge: the lack of a definition for what constitutes a good idea. Some take the position that a good idea is in the eye of the beholder, or that they'll recognize it when they see it. Most organizations lack a process to recognize good ideas. As one manager put it, 'employees might not recognize a good idea if it smacked them right in their face.' Ideas come in all different shapes and sizes. Ideas have varying degrees of novelty. Ideas may come from different sources. It's important to appreciate the diversity of ideas if we are going to manage them. Different ideas require different management resources and approaches. Defining the concept of an idea might best be left to philosophers,[3] but we must try to do so in the interest of understanding intrapreneurship.

Scaling Ideas

One of the best approaches I have found is for organizations to take a developmental approach to scaling the various types of thoughts that represent ideas at different levels (see figure 2.1). The scale can range from *raw*, or unprocessed, to *refined*, or processed.

In the rawest form, ideas can be simple random thoughts that pass through employees' minds as they conduct work: wouldn't it be nice if we did things this way? Or, why was this customer not happy? These *random thoughts and musings* may not have a lot of value in their present form, but, if processed, they point to valuable new developments for an organization to pay attention to. One way to think of these, from an information management perspective, is as the signals that employees receive from agents (other employees, customers, etc.)

Figure 2.1: Scaling ideas

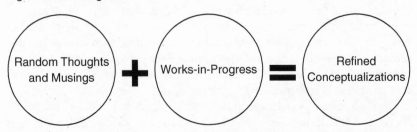

and objects (machinery, computers, artificial processes, etc.) as they conduct their work. We might dismiss such signals as isolated thoughts, but if several employees share similar notions, we might be onto an area that an organization should investigate.

The level after raw thoughts includes ideas that have had some *processing*. These ideas are essentially casual thoughts that have been subjected to some analysis. For example, employees may collect data about how an idea could work or find case studies about how the idea was deployed in another organization. Hence, they convert their raw thoughts into *works-in-progress*. You'll be surprised to find how many of these nuggets employees store away. Most of us are natural investigators, so if a casual thought seems to have some significance, we explore it further. Today, with the convenience of the Internet, it is becoming easier for employees to research and refine their thoughts. At this level, managers may gauge just how invested an employee is in an idea.

At the third level, the works-in-progress are further processed to become somewhat *refined*. They become logical and take on the physical manifestation of prototypes. Employees build models that can be deployed. These models still need to be put through rigorous experimentation and testing, but employees have something that in their opinion 'works.' Front-line employees build models like workarounds for business processes or technology solutions on a regular basis. The reason for this is simple: as employees conduct their work they notice things that don't work as they want; yet requesting formal changes is impractical or slow. Firms such as SPSS have long taken advantage of customer ideas and included them in successive versions of their products. Users of statistical packages often have to come up with workarounds and even create their own scripts to get the program to do what they want. These companies have realized that the add-ins and scripts might be valuable to other users as well.

Scope of Ideas

We've described the scale of ideas; now let's turn to their scope, or range of impact. In this category, we might identify them as having either *operational, tactical,* or *strategic* importance (see figure 2.2). *Operational* ideas are those that affect current business operations: for example, how to address current operational challenges or engineering problems.

At the next level, *tactical,* are ideas that may have a longer-term impact, say over the next one to three years. These ideas require significant changes to the organization or the organization's external environment. For example, an employee might have an idea about how to deploy a new product in a new market segment, but the organization may be preoccupied with getting its current customers to adopt and believe in the product, so it cannot act on the idea immediately. Tactical ideas can also include methods for improving how the organization conducts the functions of middle management: such things as managing projects, incentivizing employees, and improving information and communication protocols.

Ideas at the final, *strategic* level normally relate to the business model of the organization. They are big and broad, and may call into question the very essence of how the organization earns its current resources and how they are deployed to attain the overall mission. Microsoft, for example, clearly missed the Internet revolution, especially when compared to Google. Microsoft could have dominated the search engine market, yet, as many former employees have told me (who had the ear and attention of Bill Gates), the company didn't leverage ideas at the strategic level because many of these ideas threatened or cannibalized their main sources of revenue, the Windows operating system and the Microsoft Office Suite. About 98 percent of the time, ideas at the strategic level originate from individuals who are a few layers removed from the front lines. This is not to say that all these ideas originate from the C-suite. Middle managers who have responsibility for profit and loss statements (P&Ls) are good sources of these ideas, and so are the individuals they report to. Yet to truly generate ideas at the strategic level, the individual must have a good understanding of the strategic posture of the organization and the nature of the organization's competitive marketplace. A global rather than a local view of the organization is necessary to generate these ideas.

Figure 2.2: Hierarchy of ideas

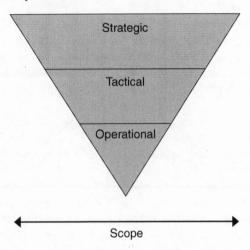

Degree of Change of Ideas

We can also classify ideas as *incremental* or *radical* based on the degree to which they call for changes to existing products, processes, and strategies of the organization (see table 2.1). A summary of the characteristics of incremental ideas and radical ideas follows.

Incremental ideas are those that build on existing frameworks, processes, products, and services. These ideas are normally add-ons to existing infrastructure. Incremental ideas may call for the replacement of small components within an existing infrastructure. These ideas are well-defined in scope, require only tweaks or adjustments to the existing infrastructure, and have limited impact. These ideas improve existing process and output measures. For example, an incremental idea might help improve a process's performance by increasing product throughput or reducing error rates. Or, it might improve how a product is displayed, or transported from the organization to the customer, or reconfigured to appeal to new business partners in an existing customer channel. More often than not, it's easy to get support for these low-risk, incremental ideas. Consider the recent prize offered by the X-Prize Foundation: a $10 million prize for creating a car that can get 100 miles to the gallon, or its energy equivalent, sponsored by the insurance agency Progressive. Since there are already cars on the road

Table 2.1
Characteristics of incremental and radical ideas

Type	Characteristics / Description
Incremental	• Well-defined in scope
	• Related to improving existing processes
	• Limited impact and risk
Radical	• Broad in scope
	• Invoke new ways of thinking and novel approaches
	• Higher payoff and risk

that get up to 50 miles per gallon, the prize for a car that gets 100 miles per gallon would be an incremental innovation. The traditional mechanics of a car, such as having wheels, a gear box, a steering system, and so on, are not undergoing a fundamental change.

By contrast, radical ideas have a greater impact and scope, ranging from redesigning an entire business process to changing the organization's strategic orientation, or even to restructuring a firm's current organizational setup. Radical ideas have a longer time horizon and are higher risk but potentially more profitable than incremental ideas. Radical ideas emerge from 'outside-the-box' thinking. As one executive told me, 'of course, we love out-of-the box thinking . . . but to be truly radical and novel, you need to think as though there was no box.' Radical ideas call for individuals to take on different mindsets. As Einstein once noted, 'The significant problems we face cannot be solved at the same level of thinking we were at when we created them.' Radical ideas normally call for individuals to take a step back, leave their current thinking behind, and re-examine problems and opportunities. These ideas call into question deeply held assumptions about how and why certain things occur, and may even challenge long-held myths about how things are 'supposed' to be done versus the way things 'can' be done. Radical ideas require a great amount of energy to secure organizational or political support. These ideas are often shot down before they've been given a fair chance to be heard.

The SpaceShipOne team sponsored by Burt Rutan and his team at Scaled Composites, with funding from Microsoft co-founder Paul Allen, won an X-Prize Foundation award for the first private space flight in 2006. This innovation was not only the first of its kind but also opened up space to private citizens, a radical change for a realm exclusively explored by governments up to that point. Today, the outgrowth from the SpaceShipOne innovation has created a multibillion dollar private space industry. Radical ideas are difficult to appreciate at first because they don't fall neatly into pre-existing categories and can't be subjected to the same scrutiny as incremental ideas. Radical ideas are often cross-cutting; they span multiple domains or functional areas. Hence, to truly appreciate them, one has to converse with individuals from diverse backgrounds and embrace unfamiliar experiences and attitudes. Moreover, since radical ideas are by default more risky both in how they are conceived and how they might be executed, organizations need to elevate their risk thresholds if these ideas are going to have a chance. Furthermore, these ideas comprise many unknowns. Hence articulating a project plan initially might not be feasible, or even desirable. A fluid management approach is needed for these ideas, which must be cultivated without hard or narrow preconceptions of what fruits might emerge. The seeds need to be given care and attention, with ongoing consideration of how to grow them better.

Orientation of Ideas

You can also classify ideas as internally or externally oriented. Internal ideas optimize business processes. External ideas are incorporated into products or services of value to customers. Both types of ideas can be leveraged through the intrapreneurship process. Most employees don't have ideas that are going to turn out to be the next product blockbusters, but they do have ideas that can help an organization optimize its operations and also ideas that can point the way to redesigning existing business practices and procedures. These ideas are not to be taken for granted or shunned. If you were to survey the ideas held by most non-managerial employees, I estimate that 80 percent of their ideas are internally focused. These employees make up 80 percent of most organizations. A focus on only the 20 percent of ideas that are externally focused means that most likely you are listening to ideas from only 20 percent of your employees, and are missing out on many ideas that may benefit the organization.

Navigating the Idea Space

You can classify, slice, and dice ideas across multiple dimensions. For example, combining the dimensions of scale and scope, you have a

Table 2.2
Categorizing ideas

	Operational	Tactical	Strategic
Random thoughts and musings			
Works-in-progress			
Refined conceptualizations			

three-by-three matrix (see table 2.2) that may be quite valuable for understanding what represents an idea and how to encourage the development of an idea across your organization.

A critical step towards understanding the range of ideas you're interested in, either as an organization or as an individual employee, is to map out the *idea space*. Mapping the range of ideas, much like creating an organizational chart for ideas, is important for understanding the range and scope of ideas that one needs to manage. A common strategy used successfully in organizations is to create illustrative examples that employees can relate to as they visualize the idea space of their organization. For example, what does an incremental idea at the operational level, focused on an internal customer, look like? If you are a management consulting house this might be a solution to information sharing between two departments that can bolster business process efficiency. It's vital to know how to classify and categorize an idea so that it can be attended to adequately. Identifying the idea space is vital, akin to making the organizational chart visible to all. As will be shown, each class of ideas needs slightly different attention and care as it's managed. For example, the screening processes for incremental ideas differ from those that work best for radical ideas.

Roles

Hierarchical organizations tend to cast us in different roles in the employee-manager dynamic: a software engineer might report to a project manager, who might then report to a director, who in turn reports to a division head, who is accountable to a vice-president, who reports to a C-level executive, who ultimately reports to the CEO of the organization. Similar dynamics play out in government and non-profit organizations. At nearly every layer, a person can be a manager or an employee. From an organization perspective, only managers can create an intrapreneurial environment. For the purposes of this book, the term 'manager' will be used to signify individuals who may hear ideas from employees they are responsible for.

Having seen hundreds of intrapreneurs at work, and having heard the glory (and horror) stories of managers who have had to hold these individuals accountable, one thing is clear to me: energy across the intrapreneurship process is wasted and confusion ensues when both the intrapreneur and the manager lack empathy for the other's position. It's my hope that, as you read this book, you will get a deep appreciation for the roles and responsibilities of each party in the intrapreneurship process and that, through this, you will be able to work collaboratively for the betterment of your organization.

The Intrapreneur

Intrapreneurs share the drive and zeal of entrepreneurs, but they don't want to leave their organization, preferring to work within an established framework and with resources provided by the organization. Organizations have a lot to offer intrapreneurs: marketing firepower, technology resources such as expensive instruments and tools, financial resources, known and trusted networks, and an existing client base. A smart organization will allow employees to take advantage of these resources by letting them come in and use labs, computers, and other facilities or resources during off-hours – for example, software engineers may come in on the weekend to solve problems and write notes on a whiteboard.

Often, intrapreneurs have strong ties to their organizations, enjoying deep social networks and relationships. In one of my meetings with a very accomplished product development engineer at a large software engineering firm in the Pacific Northwest, I asked, 'Why have you not left the organization and opened up your own business?' The engineer paused a moment and then answered, 'I've thought about leaving countless times. I've received many offers, from our competitors to venture capitalist colleagues who want me to jump ship . . . but at the end of the day, I can't seem to make myself leave . . . I've hired 90 percent of the people that work in my division . . . They are my friends, some are even the sons and daughters of my college classmates . . . I love it here . . .' Many intrapreneurs are genuinely concerned with the organizational mission and want to make a difference where they are. Their goal is often to improve their own work processes. They want to get rid of their pain points and invent things that will increase quality.

Intrapreneurs are also motivated by how they can contribute to customer growth, market growth, and creation of new innovations. They understand how to take calculated risks, often because they are quick learners and have gone through numerous iterations of trial-and-error learning. And they understand how to undertake risks that have a good chance of paying off within the organization. Intrapreneurs are some of the most productive employees in their day jobs because they don't want their performance on their everyday tasks to distract them from their preferred activity: pursuing their ideas. Managers may incorrectly see intrapreneurs as arrogant and selfish, always talking about their ideas and working on them; a good manager will understand why they are doing so and view intrapreneurs in the context of improving the organization.

Intrapreneurs want to constantly outperform themselves. They do things at a level others marvel at, but this doesn't satisfy them. Instead, they continue to push the boundaries of what's possible. My own mentor once told me, 'You define your upper limits, and it doesn't matter what others think is possible.' In his opinion, the highest-performing employees evaluate themselves by their own metrics, not those of anyone else. Every employee, regardless of hierarchical level within the organization or span of control, can become an intrapreneur.

Intrapreneurs are often the troublemakers or the radicals within an organization. They question the status quo and are likely to get into trouble with their supervisors and peers. Seldom do these employees ask for permission when pursuing their ideas. Many will attest that they would rather ask for forgiveness if they're caught than be tangled in the organizational red tape of asking for permission. Successful intrapreneurs, through years of practice and experience, will know how to take risks and how to pick the right problems to play with.

Intrapreneurs are extremely resourceful and self-sufficient when pursuing ideas. These employees know how to bootleg resources, work on ideas when no one is looking, and even work on ideas outside the confines of the organization. At one software engineering firm I studied in early 2000, a group of employees religiously came into the office every weekend over a three-month period to work on their ideas. They were convinced that the innovation they were working on was valuable and needed extra time and attention. Two employees in the team told me, 'the organization was [expletive] for not believing in us!' Since these employees lived at great distances from each other, the office functioned as a central meeting location where they could collaborate. In addition, the team needed resources they couldn't procure on their own (three team members were close to bankruptcy after investing in ideas that were supposedly dot-com stars). One weekend, a manager went into the office and ran into the renegade team by chance. Luckily for the organization, this manager recognized the idea's potential. Ultimately, the intrapreneurs built an application that was instantly adopted by over 90 percent of the organization's customers.

Intrapreneurs are often lone knowledge seekers and researchers. The unfortunate reality is that they normally learn and work in isolation, leaving their teams or organizations out of the loop. For example, consider a prominent engineer at a major U.S. defense contractor. For over a year, the engineer was working independently on a device that could redefine the nature of a whole product line. During this year, the engineer kept diligent notes on his discoveries, failures, and lessons learned. Since he was working under the radar, he never shared any of these findings with his peers. As his manager remarked to me, 'we could have saved millions . . . he had already tried twelve prototypes that we were still designing . . . someone should have asked Johnny [the engineer] what he was playing with.' Individual learning, no matter how valuable, can only prove of value to the organization if the lessons learned are also shared.

Intrapreneurs care deeply about their organizations and are seldom motivated by traditional rewards like gifts or bonuses. This loyalty is one of the main reasons they try to fight the odds and innovate within their organization. They want to see the organization achieve new heights and break new boundaries. Consider Apple, whose employees aim to create products and services that change the lives of people around the world. This is their motivation to work long hours, far beyond what they are compensated to do. As such, the rewards that motivate them are not simply the potential to earn more money but the potential to share in the glory of the organization if their ideas succeed. At 3M it was once common for employees to lead efforts and build new businesses within the company. Similarly, in academia it's common for professors who are successful at being intrapreneurial to run their own research institutes and centers within the university. Increases in stature within the organization are important for intrapreneurs.

Like any superhero, intrapreneurs have their shortcomings. For one, they're often too stubborn to give up on their ideas. To a certain extent, their persistence is a good thing as it gives them courage in the face of negative feedback or even direct orders to abandon a line of work. However, this same persistence can prove to be a weakness if the individual doesn't learn to stop committing to a failed course of action. It's quite common for intrapreneurs to take things personally when their ideas fail ('If my ideas die, so do I . . . if my ideas do not work, I have failed'). The successful intrapreneur will know how to detach him or herself from the idea and work on it in an objective manner. Immature intrapreneurs may be too emotionally attached to the idea to process relevant negative feedback. Too often, they work on an idea well beyond a point that is reasonable. For example, it's common for engineers to keep perfecting a prototype and not be satisfied with just getting a 'workable' solution. This perfectionism may cause them to lose the window of opportunity for which the idea is relevant.

Not surprisingly, intrapreneurs set high standards for their work and are often their own harshest critics. At Engaged Enterprise, I once had an employee who had brilliant ideas but was reluctant to share them unless they were 'perfect.' To overcome her perfectionist tendencies and get her ideas into the organization, where they could be used to full advantage, we forbade her to evaluate her own ideas and instead encouraged her to share them 'raw' with an independent evaluator. The ideas that emerged from this arrangement helped us land our first major Japanese government client and thus secure several more projects in the Pacific Rim. Good mentors are essential, as they can nudge the intrapreneur to stop refining the idea and move it into the organizational domain.

Finally, intrapreneurs often miss 'the big picture.' They are too involved with their ideas to ask broad questions like 'How does the idea contribute to the bottom line of the business?' Or, 'How should the idea be priced and promoted in the marketplace?' As such, they need help from good mentors and advocates to help them see the forest beyond the trees. In addition, it's quite conceivable that the 'inventor' of an idea may not be the person who sees its value and works to create an opportunity for it within the organization. In my experience, inventors of good ideas are rarely the most skilled intrapreneurs. Indeed, one of the reasons I am writing this book is to help the inventors learn the art and science of intrapreneurship. Inventors seldom like to get involved in the nitty-gritty of how the idea is commercialized (e.g., how it's priced, what legal issues are involved, etc.), nor do they care much about the later stages of idea diffusion and implementation, which they view as someone else's headache. These are opportunities where rookie intrapreneurs can gain from the counsel of an experienced mentor and advocate who can help them push the idea from concept to implementation.

The Manager

Managers of employees who are innovative and entrepreneurial have a difficult job. Yet if these managers are able to get out of the way and allow employees to develop their ideas, they may share in the glory and the rewards when an idea is successful. Both internal and external audiences will view this manager as the person who, either directly or indirectly, helped move the idea from concept to fruition. In the organization, this person will gain a reputation as the manager who supports and develops the talents and creativity of employees.

Managing ideas is central to building the intrapreneurial organization. Yet managers must learn not to take the traditional approach of *controlling* the idea. Too often, we get comfortable with the concept of control that we learned in business school. Control is needed to ensure that projects are on time or that products are properly managed. However, for *ideas* the role of the manager is to facilitate, empower, and orchestrate. Facilitation calls for building an environment where employees can optimally generate and enact ideas. Empowering ensures that rewards and incentives are in place for all players in the intrapreneurship process. And finally, orchestrating involves stepping back and considering how to provide direction rather than micromanaging the ideation process. Good orchestrators resist the temptation to judge ideas and control them. You will be a better manager if you give ideas the freedom to grow.

The ideal manager can serve as an alter ego to the employee. The manager's role is to support the entrepreneurial spirit in employees while at the same time assisting them to overcome the shortcomings of intrapreneurs described earlier. Equally important is the crucial role managers can play in instilling a sense of belief in employees that their ideas do matter. Most employees are not natural intrapreneurs. On the contrary, most employees just want to do their job, take their check, and go home. Employees need to be reminded and encouraged to share their ideas, even if they don't think they're valuable. As we'll see in chapter 3, managers who can get employees to share their ideas, allowing others to discuss them in a collegial manner, will go a long way toward encouraging the spirit of intrapreneurship.

Managers are instantiations of the 'organization' to employees. Their behavior, actions, and communications are signals to the employees about what the organization values. Therefore it is vital for managers to serve as good conduits for building the intrapreneurial environment. Consider the case of a medical instrumentation company based in the U.S. Midwest. This organization grew out of a group of physicists who were trying to build better radiation technologies that could be used for administering cancer therapy. One of their employees, a brilliant innovator, combined his knowledge of physics with his love of software programming and prototyped a valuable application that could help capture test data, synthesize it, and then outline latent trends. This application was estimated to save the physicists a large amount of time in terms of their ability to test equipment, refine their system, and run experiments. The employee's manager realized his potential and worked with him to develop a revised career plan. The manager worked with senior leadership to secure resources for the employee to attend an MBA program and gain business knowledge. In addition, the manager ran interference for the employee during the early days of building the prototype by changing the work assignments of the employee so he would have time and energy to flesh out the application. The employee is now on the verge of completing his MBA program and is in line to run an entire division of the organization around building better software applications for testing medical instruments. The manager was not only able to retain this employee and see him blossom but showed by example that the organization is serious about leveraging the human potential in each employee. As we explore the stages of the *intrapreneurship process*, the role of the manager will be represented in the *organizational perspective* section of each stage.

The Observers

An observer may choose to get involved or watch from the sidelines. This book will, I hope, entice you to get up and engage with intrapreneurship. Chances are high that you may be asked to take on the role of a mentor or sponsor. Mentors play a special role in the intrapreneurship process. They help channel the energy of the intra-preneur, counsel the intrapreneur about how to negotiate organiza-tional obstacles, and act as a sounding board for the intrapreneur. Quite often, mentors have already had experience with intrapreneur-ship within the organization. They understand how to get ideas acted on, and many of them have built their careers in the organization by being intrepreneurial. Mentors have strong social networks and track records for leveraging ideas. Hence, they can be strong advocates for intrapreneurs who may not yet have credibility within their organiza-tion. Not only intrapreneurs but also their managers can benefit from the guidance of a mentor. Troubled managers often call me with stor-ies of one or more employees who have the potential to be great intra-preneurs but who are difficult to manage. As a result these managers often make the common mistake of interfering with the idea-genera-tion process, being too critical rather than allowing ideas to bloom, or even trying to manage the intrapreneurship process the same way they would a traditional project.

While a mentor may be an intrapreneur's coach, a sponsor must be the agent. Sponsors provide the necessary resources to help intrapre-neurs develop their ideas. For example, sponsors can provide portions of their discretionary budgets, or can help intrapreneurs plan for and engage in political battles that might emerge in the development pro-cess. Sponsors are essential to helping employees prepare a sound business case for their ideas.

Even if you can't be a mentor or a sponsor, it will serve you well to lend a listening ear to the employee who is struggling with an idea. You will learn a lot from the experience. In many instances, your peer may just need a person to take a look at the idea, allow him or her to vent about a challenge or an opportunity that is ripe for new solutions, or even just encourage the entrepreneurial spirit. At best it may require a few hours of your time (a lunchtime discussion, an online survey, or testing out a prototype), and at worst, even if you think the idea is doomed to failure, you are now aware that someone is working on a solution. There's a valuable academic analogy here. One reason researchers spend time and effort reviewing scientific papers for jour-nals they want to publish in is not only to ensure that scientific ideals are instantiated through the peer review process but also for the chance to read cutting-edge research that hasn't yet made it to print! What better way could there be to learn about what their peers are thinking and working on?

The Owner and/or Organization

As an owner (or, to take a global view, an organization), you have deep responsibility for facilitating intrapreneurship. You have to ensure that people feel comfortable developing their ideas. Rewards need to be in place to support not only those who develop ideas but also those who stick their necks out to advocate for ideas. Ensuring that members of the organization understand, appreciate, and positively engage with the intrapreneurship process is also essential. To this end, you will need to provide adequate training that addresses the roles and responsibilities of all parties involved in the process. Training is essential for a number of reasons, from ensuring that people understand the nature of intrapreneurship in the organization to knowing the specifics of how to navigate any particular stage of the intrapreneurship process (for example, writing a business case or engaging in idea experimentation). Finally, you will need to be a role model who shows by example that intrapreneurship is a valued and essential aspect of growing the business.

A critical role played by the organization is to foster a teamwork approach to intrapreneurship. Why do we need to focus on the team approach to intrapreneurship rather than the isolated individual? Individuals very rarely have all the skills, experience, or networks needed to push an idea through from conception to implementation. Seldom does the lone intrapreneur make any significant change in the organization. Most intrapreneurs who are successful have huge supporting casts that help them achieve their objectives: everyone from their colleagues who appreciate them, to their manager who might provide them with resources or training, to the advocates and sponsors who provide feedback on the experimentation process, and, finally, to the team of experts who help diffuse and implement the ideas. Most intrapreneurs get excited about one or two parts of the overall process but need others to help them in areas there they lack interest or expertise. The organization plays a vital role in empowering the employee, and the manager, by providing them with access to complementary skills and resources that can help them be successful at intrapreneurship. The absence of an organizational culture that believes and invests in intrapreneurship will lead to a steep uphill battle for employees who are seeking to contribute and commercialize ideas.[4] Conversely, an enabling organization can turn even the most skeptical of employees into believers in the power of ideas and innovation.

Organizations take many approaches to intrapreneurship. Wolcott and Lippitz uncovered four major approaches, based on resource authority, ranging from ad hoc to dedicated, and organizational ownership that goes from diffused to focused.[5] Resources for funding can be managed through dedicated funds (i.e., pots of money), or can be handled in a more casual manner (i.e., through ad-hoc support from departmental or divisional budgets). The organizational ownership dimension relates to who in the organization owns or has responsibility for the creation of new businesses. In the case of diffused ownership, responsibility is spread across multiple units, while in the case of focused ownership responsibility is housed in dedicated units.

The first, most relaxed and least focused approach is the *opportunistic model*. No formal approach or strategy for intrapreneurship exists here! Unfortunately, this approach is not uncommon, and most organizations begin their intrapreneurship journey as opportunists. In these organizations, idea selection and development are left to the discretion of individual departments and managers.

With the second approach, the *enabler model*, resource authority is dedicated to support intrapreneurship while being diffused throughout the organization. Organizations such as Google, 3M, and Johnson & Johnson, among others, subscribe to this approach. In these organizations the paramount goal is to facilitate entrepreneurship by individuals and teams. The organization dedicates resources to support the incubation and development of new ideas, while not overly restricting their focus, thereby casting a wide net. In these organizations, the critical challenge is to develop robust processes to advocate and screen for ideas (a topic addressed in chapter 4).

The third approach, the *advocate model*, takes a more ad-hoc approach to resource authority, although ownership is focused. In this model, the organization restricts the range of ideas to those that have the potential to fundamentally transform the business in predefined spaces as agreed upon by senior leadership. In this model, the CEO and an elite group of corporate veterans focus on supporting and advancing ideas that have the potential to advance the current organization by opening up new businesses closely related to its core. Employees are engaged in the process of intrapreneurship through their ability to submit ideas for consideration. Radically transformative ideas that pass muster are then advocated for, and supported by, the senior team through the provision of resources, time, and personnel.

The fourth approach, the *producer model*, features a dedicated re-source authority and focused organizational ownership. This is the most focused model. Organizations such as Cargill, Motorola, and IBM, among others, have systems in place for identifying, funding, and harnessing ideas with the potential to exploit capabilities and re-sources that cut across business lines and that can lead to disruptive innovation. Within this setup, resources to support intrapreneurship are vested in dedicated departments, which have a fair degree of autonomy and their own staff. The role of these departments is to serve as incubators for ideas with the potential to disrupt the industry and lead to new business opportunities for the organization. One of the downsides of this model is that ideas that do not have disruptive potential but are nonetheless valuable, say for internal business pro-cess improvement, are not looked upon favorably and are most often given low priority.

It is critical to have a dedicated process in place to leverage ideas. The process that is described in the pages that follow can be used in the *advocate*, *enabler*, and *producer* models. However, it's best used in the *enabler* context, as it has the greatest potential to engage employ-ees at all levels of the organization in intrapreneurship. Resources are distributed in the organization to support intrapreneurship, albeit not in an ad-hoc manner, and the ownership for intrapreneurship is also spread across the organization: everyone is responsible for and can support the effort.

The Process

The intrapreneurship process is circular and has several discrete stages: generating and mobilizing ideas, advocating for and screening ideas, experimenting with ideas, commercializing ideas, and finally diffusing and implementing ideas. Information gathered from the final stage is fed back into the first step of the process (the idea-generation and mobilization stage), thus creating the cyclical movement of the process. A map of the intrapreneurship process (figure 2.3) reveals how information artifacts are moved out of the minds of individuals to become concrete, explicit documents such as business plans, and then converted into artifacts of commercial value – products, services, or business practices that can be leveraged by customers.

The first stage of the process is the fuzzy front end, called *idea gener-ation and mobilization*. In this stage, we are concerned with the ideas

Figure 2.3: The intrapreneurship process

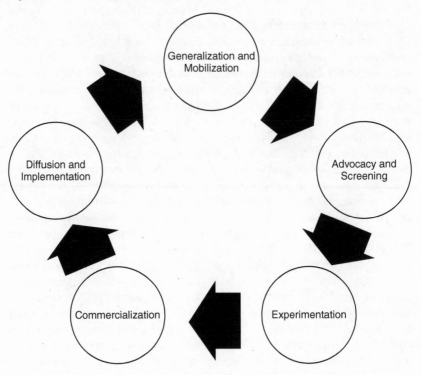

that lie in the minds of employees and the entities that members of the organization come into contact with. During the fuzzy front end, we focus on generating and mobilizing a large number of ideas, each of which may have varying levels of impact, focus, risk, and cost. Think of this stage as the opening to a funnel. As we continue through the intrapreneurship process, we move into the funnel and begin narrowing down to the best ideas. Those ideas we choose to advance will receive some of the limited resources of the organization. Ideas generated and mobilized may be of interest to internal or external customers, but all ideas must have a customer in mind. Having a customer in mind is important, as organizations must be able to consider the value of the idea in the context of the end users who will gain from it.

The next stage of the intrapreneurship process is *idea advocacy and screening*. Here, the focus is on (1) supporting good ideas through effective advocacy, and (2) evaluating the potential of ideas through effective screening. Advocacy and screening procedures need to be efficient; they shouldn't be cost, resource, or time intensive. It's not uncommon to find idea screening processes that take about three to five times longer than actually writing a proposal, a large waste of energy by all parties concerned at the organizational level. In this stage of the intrapreneurship process, we take a focused look at the idea from the perspective of its intended customer. Questions such as the following are asked: Why would a customer pay attention to the idea? What are the barriers and challenges a customer may face to adopt the idea? Or, how might the value proposition be sold to the customer? Attempting to answer these questions helps build an initial business case.

The business case is then used to screen for ideas that will move to the next stage of the process, *idea experimentation*. As discussed in chapter 4, at the screening stage, the organization decides which ideas it will invest resources in for experimentation. Naturally, some ideas will be abandoned at this stage – at least for the time being. These ideas don't have to be discarded completely, however. Sometimes even good ideas are not followed up because of limited resources. However, an employee may continue to work on the idea, making it even better, and resubmit it for consideration at a later date. In other cases, employees may choose to invest their own resources to continue experimenting with the idea. Screening processes allow an opportunity for the organization and the individual idea creators to receive feedback on their ideas. This feedback is critical not only for the growth of the particular idea but to provide impetus and energy for intrapreneurship. Simply collecting ideas, rather than providing adequate feedback, is one sure way of killing the intrapreneurial spirit in the organization.

It's important to note that, once an idea enters the *experimentation* stage of the process, the idea is no longer the sole possession of the employee. It's now receiving a serious amount of organizational resources and attention, and hence the developmental role and influence of the organization increase. The employee will still be spearheading the development of the idea, but by accepting organizational resources for experimentation, the employee also consents to work within organizational parameters. During the experimentation process, the organization tests the elasticity of the idea under varying business conditions and also seeks to refine and improve the idea. Prototypes and models of the idea are constructed, tested, and analyzed during this stage.

Unlike the traditional idea experimentation described in most books on innovation, intrapreneurial experimentation should involve a wide spectrum of employees, and not be confined to research and development labs.[6] Employees should appreciate and develop competencies in conducting experiments. The organization should develop a culture whereby employees can test their ideas and intuitions through cost-effective experimentation. This stage of the intrapreneurship process represents another opportunity to collect feedback and use it effectively. Feedback not only improves the ideas and the capabilities of the experimenters but also refines the experimentation process itself by determining which ideas should be selected in the future.

The hope is that experimentation will yield ideas that pass muster as appropriate candidates for *commercialization*. The commercialization stage calls for a renewed external perspective: how to price, package, and promote ideas – all common activities when organizations create goods and services for their customers, but less common when they consider ideas for improving internal business processes. We must remember that the external perspective is important, even for ideas that are going to manifest as process improvements, new business practices, or solutions to internal organizational problems. If an idea is generated in the accounting department, this does not necessarily mean that the idea will automatically be appreciated and embraced by the operations unit or even by all members within the accounting department. The idea needs to be appropriately priced, packaged, and promoted if it is to be willingly adopted. In the discussion of commercialization, it's important to pay attention to how the organization will seek to earn rents (value) from the ideas. Ultimately, it is through earning value, whether from creating a new revenue source or lowering the cost of operations, that the organization will be able to sustain its intrapreneurship program. For every idea that makes it to the commercialization process, there are hundreds – perhaps thousands – of ideas that will not. Hence, it is important to recover value from the ideas that do get commercialized, so that this revenue can be used to foster a culture of intrapreneurship by covering the costs and sustaining the development of ideas that don't. In the commercialization stage, the original idea creator commonly takes a back seat while the organization puts together a commercialization team to help guide the idea to market. The ideal organization will do so in a manner that is acceptable to and in keeping with the goals of the original idea creator.

Once a commercialization strategy is identified, the last stage of *diffusing and implementing* the idea takes place. This stage calls for transferring the idea to the customer (diffusing) and enabling the customer to utilize it to its full potential (implementing). The diffusion process is closely related to the marketing efforts required to launch a product. Rarely is a product ever launched without proper marketing to build hype, gauge demand, obtain feedback from initial impressions, and prepare the customer for transition to the new product. For ideas to be diffused successfully, we must be able to leverage the power of new communication modes, especially those that exploit social networks, to spread the word about the idea. Diffusing ensures that customers understand the value of the idea and can try out, relate to, and ultimately adopt it. Once the idea is diffused, the organization must support the implementation process, which includes providing post-launch support and preparing for unforeseen consequences. It's only natural that customers will face challenges as they begin to implement the solutions in their daily work practices or social environments.

For example, the release of Apple's iPhone 4 was an incredible success, with more than 1.7 million units sold after just three days, making it the most successful product launch in Apple's history.[7] Apple is notorious for being secretive and using the absence of information to its advantage for free marketing and hype build-up as the community speculates about what Apple is going to do next. Apple masterfully diffused their idea – despite a prototype's 'leak' to Gizmodo prior to the launch – but failed at implementing it. When users discovered that the iPhone 4's signal could easily be disrupted by placing a single finger over the antenna (a problem that ballooned into 'Antenna-Gate'), Steve Jobs, Apple's CEO and co-founder, responded inadequately by telling customers to hold the phone differently. Overwhelmed by the negative press for this simple yet profound problem, Apple eventually announced that it would provide customers with free bumper cases. The company also gave the public an inside look at its testing facilities to show that Apple products do indeed go through rigorous testing before launch.

Apple missed an opportunity to learn quickly from early feedback. During the implementation process, the organization has a very important opportunity to learn from their customers. This feedback can arise from traditional mechanisms such as product reviews or calls to the customer help desk, but also from non-traditional mechanisms such as users' modifications or add-ons. It can be used to improve the initial idea as well as to generate new ideas and solutions.

Finally, feedback during implementation can even improve the other stages of the intrapreneurship process – for example, through the design of a more robust commercialization strategy or a better experimentation process.

Again, the process is like a funnel that is widest at the *idea generation and mobilization* stage, but narrows incrementally with each stage. Thus, many ideas enter the funnel, but few are advocated or selected for experimentation. Some organizations have called this process the 'valley of death.' In many organizations, fewer than 5 percent of all ideas make it through all stages of the intrapreneurship process. No one said this was going to be easy, either from the organization's or an employee's perspective. As Thomas Edison said, 'If you want to have a great idea, have many of them.' No organization or employee can have great ideas without having to toil with many 'not so great' ideas first. At every stage of the intrapreneurship process, ideas will be put on hold and denied passage to the next stage. Yet it is critical not to 'discard' any ideas from the outset. Some ideas may not be relevant or able to compete with all the other ideas on the table, but this doesn't necessarily mean that they'll never be useful. As I describe in later chapters, organizations with mature processes build idea libraries to house ideas that have been suggested, advocated for, and experimented with, but that have not made it to commercialization. Some organizations even store customer feedback about products and services. These libraries serve as nice repositories for inventors to do their 'homework.' They can see how the idea that they are developing fits with other ideas in the repository. The feedback can help the inventor, the idea advocate, and the sponsors to plan for organizational reactions to the idea (for example, by identifying key decision makers who need to be involved in the process, or determining why an earlier idea failed to be promoted).

As can be deduced from the preceding discussion, the intrapreneurship process is a set of very closely intertwined stages with some overarching trends. (1) Ideas move from being information elements in the minds of employees to become concrete artifacts that can be used by customers to advance their missions. (2) The number of ideas decreases but the level of organizational investment per idea increases. (3) Ideas move from being the private property of the employee to become organizational assets. And (4) feedback collected at each stage of the process can be used to develop individual ideas and idea creators, and can also be used to improve the overall process of intrapreneurship.

This book is biased toward a process view of intrapreneurship. What are the advantages of this perspective? As noted above, process-based models and frameworks abound in the management literature. When we think of how new products are developed in organizations, how data are collected, information is generated, and knowledge is acted upon in the organization, and how decisions are made, we have an abundance of process models. For intrapreneurship in particular, a process-based view is appealing for several reasons.

First, taking a process view allows us to open up the black box of idea development and to pinpoint the discrete activities and stages that go into leveraging ideas. Management interventions can be developed to support and enhance these activities (as we will see in greater detail in the chapters that follow). Second, a process view allows us to measure the intrapreneurship quotient of the organization at each individual stage of the process. For example, in the experimentation stage we can measure statistics such as the number of experiments conducted or the cost per experiment. These measurements enable us to track more precisely how well each part of the intrapreneurship process is performing. Third, the process view enables us to identify with some accuracy the role played by various human actors (i.e., employees and managers) at each stage of the process, and also to identify the role that can be played by technological solutions. As will become apparent in the pages that follow, the front end of the process is dominated by the employees who take a leadership role in the development of ideas, while in the latter stages the organization comes into the foreground. The accurate identification of roles for each process helps in assigning clear responsibilities and accountability for intrapreneurship. Fourth, the process view allows us to use the same baseline framework, albeit with some customization, to manage a wide range of ideas, from those that are incremental in nature to those that are radical and those that have internal and external customers. Finally, the process view allows us to track how the practice of intrapreneurship is maturing in the organization and what results we might expect. As an organization increases its experience with intrapreneurship and invests in building and refining a robust process for intrapreneurship, one might expect to witness superior outcomes. As was noted earlier, managing *energy* is critical within organizations, especially when dealing with ideas and innovation. As organizations increase in maturity, they become more intelligent in how they leverage their limited energy toward productive outcomes. This point is explored in greater detail in chapter 8.

While this book embraces the *process* approach to managing ideas, I must caution against taking the approach too far. Too often, organizations focus so narrowly on optimizing the process that it becomes very brittle. Engineering processes are a vital aspect of building not only organizations but systems in general. In the world of theory, we can develop processes that are highly efficient and optimized. In the world of experience, our focus should be on building processes that are robust. Sacrificing optimums may be desirable in order to build processes that withstand internal and external pressures, can be adapted to accommodate varying conditions, and can be deployed across a wide range of users. Idea management is fundamentally a human endeavor. Therefore, viewing things as basic input-output processes is simplistic. This is where the *art* of managing ideas comes in. Managers and employees must recognize that processes are meant to *guide* the overall process of intrapreneurship and not *stifle or restrict* it. When the sanctioned process does not fit the peculiarities of an idea or a particular opportunity for intrapreneurship, it would be more astute to modify the process than to discard the idea.

These caveats notwithstanding, there are manifold benefits to viewing intrapreneurship as a process – as a cycle of continuous feedback and refinement. This view recognizes the creative energy that drives intrapreneurship, which is never in a perfect or static state. As the environment changes, processes need to evolve. As we have seen, if an intrapreneurship process is continuously evolving, it is being 'mindfully' managed rather than just left to 'exist.' Managers and employees must avoid complacency and instead assert themselves in the energetic pursuit of improvement, refinement, feedback, and new ideas. Further, as Lord Kelvin noted, 'If you can't measure it, you can't improve it,' and, 'To measure is to know.' By focusing on continuous improvement, you are forced not only to measure but also to balance the art of intrapreneurship with science. Science allows us to use measurements to make disciplined improvements, while art reminds us that we need to constantly modify the process, customizing it to meet the various contexts of the organization and the people who engage with it.

Conclusion

This chapter outlined the three main ingredients of intrapreneurship. (1) We began by identifying different types of ideas. As is evident from the discussion, ideas come in many shapes and forms. Organizations need to help employees understand and visualize the idea space of the organization. (2) We then explored the range of roles that are brought to bear on intrapreneurship. Intrapreneurship does not just happen. Organizations need to have a framework, a process to guide how ideas are leveraged within the organization. Moving forward, we will focus on how the two perspectives – of the employee (i.e., the *intrapreneur*) and the organization (comprising *managers* and *observers*) – play out across the stages of the intrapreneurship process. An appreciation of the roles played by each party to the intrapreneurship process is critical in order to build a culture that can harness and develop ideas. (3) Finally, we outlined the intrapreneurship process.

The chapters that follow will explore each stage of the intrapreneurship process in detail. The intrapreneurship process provides a solution to the problem of sustaining innovation in large organizations, sometimes in surprising ways. In the next chapter, we'll focus on the first step of the process – the generation and mobilization of new ideas.

3 Idea Generation and Mobilization

This chapter is about idea creation and mobilization, the important first stage of the intrapreneurship process; without this there would be no input for the remaining stages. Yet it can be a stage fraught with frustration.

> I have a million ideas in my drawer . . . ideas are a dime a dozen and cheap . . . everyone has an idea of what I should do and how to do it . . . what I need are good and workable, ideas . . . and employees who do more than just blurt out random ideas, but are willing to commit to them. (A Frustrated Manager)

> My boss did not get it and I lost patience . . . they say they want ideas and are open to taking everyone's input, but it is a black hole . . . ideas go in and no one knows what happens . . . I have contributed well over a dozen ideas over the past two years and have nothing to show for it . . . this innovation mantra is rubbish. (A Disheartened Employee)

These comments epitomize the challenges faced by organizations when managing ideas. On one hand, employees are routinely surveyed for ideas only to find that the ideas they create and submit are given lip service, or no service at all. On the other hand, managers are inundated with ideas that are seldom presented in a useful or workable state. Managers also complain that it's easy for employees to spit out ideas but that it can be difficult to get employees to take responsibility for their ideas, pursue them, and invest in them. In the end, both parties are frustrated, the organization loses, and the process of intrapreneurship is dead in the water.

In most organizations, ideas are not generated on a regular basis. Organizations commonly focus on ideas during their annual budgeting processes, so that they can invest in new projects. If you want to build a culture of intrapreneurship, you will need to take a different approach. Ideas need to be generated on a continuing basis. Waiting for budget cycles to generate and submit ideas is not the best way to stay afloat in today's fiercely competitive and dynamic environment. Organizations need to have the capacity to capitalize on ideas in an expeditious manner.

One of the main goals of intrapreneurship is to enable employees across all divisions and hierarchical layers to engage with ideas. To this end, the organization needs to build mechanisms for generating and mobilizing ideas that can be integrated into the work practices and daily lives of employees. Too often, idea generation remains the privilege (or burden) of a few souls in the organization. As Tom Davenport noted in the foreword, even in firms that are considered highly innovative, such as Google, resources for idea generation (e.g., time) are not evenly distributed throughout the organization.

In my experience, organizations seldom lack ideas – but ideas that represent relevant opportunities or solutions are hard to come by. Even rarer are ideas that can truly engage people in the discovery and innovation processes. It is important to focus on the quality of ideas rather than the quantity. High-quality ideas have a clear focus on customers. All ideas should have a customer in mind, since ultimately they must meet the needs of stakeholders, either internal or external.

As well, ideas are only as valuable as the will and perseverance of the individual who implements them. To quote Siddhartha Buddha, 'an idea that is developed and put into action is more important than an idea that exists only as an idea.' Many of us have ideas that we don't follow up on. Others may not have a lot of ideas, but they pursue the ideas they have to implementation. We must remind ourselves that ideas are just ideas until they are tested in the real world. As many executives have told me, ideas are cheap, but individuals who can implement their ideas to the benefit of the organization are pure gold.

Often, people encounter ideas through conversations with colleagues and friends.[1] In the context of mobilizing ideas, the real challenge faced by organizations is to see the whole forest rather than just the trees – that is, to take locally generated ideas and fit them within the larger context of the organization. Ideas are generated locally, and this is natural, given the nature of work and the individual perspectives of employees. The assimilation and synthesis of locally generated ideas needs to take place at a higher level. Some of the most valuable ideas are those that cut across multiple units of the organization – ideas that, when combined with other insights, might lead to interdisciplinary opportunities. Ideas need transport mechanisms to move from one sector or layer of an organization to another. In most organizations that have immature processes for intrapreneurship, you will find executives who think that just because employees have an e-mail address, a telephone, and access to the corporate directory, they have adequate tools for idea mobilization. This could not be farther from the truth. These very technologies have allowed us to avoid face-to-face dialogue and have reduced opportunities for the reflective conversations needed to mobilize ideas. Consider the case of Pixar, arguably one of the most innovative firms in the movie business, the company that launched the first computer-animated feature film (*Toy Story*) and followed it up with other blockbusters such as *The Incredibles, Ratatouille*, and *A Bug's Life*. Steve Jobs played a crucial role in the design of the Pixar office building.[2] To increase the likelihood (or, more accurately, to guarantee) that employees would run into each other, he built a big atrium in the center of the building. This atrium housed several key elements of an office facility, such as mailboxes, conference rooms, and, most importantly, the restrooms! This simple design strategy made it impossible for employees to go through their working day without running into their co-workers. To flow smoothly and travel distances, ideas need fluid, human-centered communication pathways.

This chapter explores the role played by the organization and the employee in the first stage of the process of bringing ideas to market – the generating and mobilizing phase. Each party involved in the process has a distinct and key role to play. The organization has two primary responsibilities: (1) to design environments that are 'friendly' to idea generation, and (2) to shape a creative space or culture for the organization by encouraging customer-centered thinking, publishing problems, and setting up competitions for ideas. For their part, employees must learn how to (1) recognize and respect their ideas, (2) effectively manage the process of pursuing ideas, and (3) build and maintain viable social networks to support idea mobilization.

Organizational Perspective

The ability to create an environment in which employees believe in the transformative power of their ideas is central to intrapreneurship.

The environment at 3M provides a good example. As Lew Lehr has commented,

> For many years the corporate structure [at 3M] has been designed specifically to encourage young entrepreneurs to take an idea and run with it. If they succeed, they can and do find themselves funding their own business under the 3M umbrella. The entrepreneurial approach is not a sideline at 3M. It is the heart of our design for growth.[3]

Only passionate employees create ideas that will transform the organization. To enable them to do so, organizations need to build an environment where employees can create and mobilize their ideas with ease. The organization that is able to encourage the generation and mobilization of ideas in an optimal manner has taken the first steps toward creating a highly intrapreneurial organization.

Idea generation and mobilization are central to the intrapreneurship process. Approaches to managing idea generation and mobilization can vary widely. Some organizations have strict controls governing the process. For example, Boeing, the aerospace and defense giant, which employs well over 140,000 people across the globe, maintains strict controls over how information is shared among individuals, teams, departments, and even business partners. Some of these controls are a natural outcome of being involved in contracts of a sensitive nature (e.g., building military aircraft). As a result, employees interface with different technical systems and follow strict protocols for talking, collaborating, and sharing information with employees in other departments. However, other controls are *artificially* created by managers who see their peers in other departments as their competitors and prefer a strong hierarchical, command-and-control style of operation. As a result, ideas are kept within units, and the 'rule-book' is often thrown at employees who deviate from this practice.

Other organizations take a laissez-faire approach, relying on the creative spirit of passionate employees for idea generation and mobilization. In these organizations, while employees are not subject to strict controls and rules, they are also not provided with a supportive structure or framework. Being successful with an idea in these organizations, or even just generating an 'appropriate' idea from the organization's viewpoint, takes place serendipitously. The organization is betting on the fact that it has hired the best and the brightest employees and that they have enough zeal to take on the organization if they have a good idea. Unfortunately, in most cases, this is wishful thinking! As Sir Martin Sorrell, CEO of WPP, a global marketing and communications giant, noted, 'One of the biggest challenges is that there are diseconomies of scale in creative industries. If you double the number of creative people, it doesn't mean you will be twice as creative.'[4] Creative people, while they do not want to be led or ordered around, do need some structure.[5] They expect an organization to take advantage of their ideas and enthusiasm. They need time to focus on what is of most value to the organization, rather than being overloaded with less significant work.[6] And, finally, they need the protection of the organization when they fail in their pursuits.

Striking the right balance between these two extremes is vital. This chapter explores the role of the organization in setting up the right environmental conditions and mechanisms to promote optimal idea generation and mobilization, while resisting the temptation to micromanage or overly structure this stage of the process.

Idea Generation

As we all know, generating ideas isn't something you have much direct control over.[7] You can't simply tell people to generate ideas. In the worst case, people will generate ideas out of fear of repercussions, and quality will be low. You need to build an environment in which employees feel comfortable generating ideas as they conduct work, as they interact with internal and external stakeholders, and even when they take a break. Creating an environment where people feel comfortable generating ideas is the first and most important goal. Responsibility for doing this rests with the organization – and with both managers and employees. Alcatel-Lucent runs an entrepreneurial boot camp program in which 'senior managers act as coaches, help with planning, put teams into contact with people inside and outside the organization, and help find needed data.'[8] The employees' responsibility is to communicate their ideas, listen to ideas from their peers, give constructive feedback, and even serve as a channel or a router that might help move ideas from one domain to another.

ENVIRONMENTS OF NEED AND ENVIRONMENTS OF PLAY

Organizations can be considered as a collection of zones, each of which has its own environment. In terms of idea generation, organizations

Table 3.1
Types of environments

Type	Characteristics / Description
Environments of need	• Problem-driven
	• Solutions relate to existing products or service
	• Time-sensitive
Environments of play	• Blue-sky thinking
	• Focus on the process of discovery
	• Seldom produce ideas that can be implemented immediately

may find themselves operating in environments of 'need' or 'playfulness' (see table 3.1).[9]

Environments of need are those with a focus on problems for which solutions must be found. Perhaps the organization is engaged in resolving troubles with products and services – for example, a customer service center or a maintenance depot. The primary goal here is basically to find quick fixes using incremental ideas. Usually staff members are under pressure to come up with solutions at short notice. But sometimes time pressure is not as severe – for example, in an information technology organization that finds bugs in the software code that need to be fixed. In environments of need, ideas are mainly incremental and can be implemented quickly. These ideas are valuable. A large percentage of the ideas generated in the organization originate in environments of need – for the simple reason that most employees spend a large percentage of their working life in these environments. Within these environments, as we will see, organizations need to find ways to publish problems of interest to employees and pull solutions from them in an effective and efficient manner.

Consider the case of Samsung, an organization that has been successful in generating ideas within environments of need. As described by P. Lewis in *Fortune* magazine, Samsung's research and development take place not in a playful, relaxed environment but under pressure of tight deadlines. Employees may live on site in research areas like the VIP (Value Innovation Program) center, where they work until problems are resolved (the VIP center's demanding schedule requires dormitories and occasional apologies to families for long-absent spouses).[10]

Employees have individual work stations, but teamwork and collaboration, as well as a sense of crisis, are key: one employee likens the VIP center to a 'smaller version of NASA,' noting that the center is 'designed for smooth communication and fast decision-making.'[11] The VIP center focuses on market-driven products, and engineers are bombarded with information not only about technological abilities but also about consumer desires and purchasing habits, as well as competitors' products. Engineers are also required to match their designs to available parts from supplier catalogues.[12] The expertise of each employee is logged by the administration, so that if a project needs a consultant, residents of the VIP center can be tapped for aid. Further, there are no distractions in the VIP center: desired goals are posted on the walls, and deadlines are everywhere, but there are no telephones and no regular administrative tasks. Lewis's observations revealed a massive schedule undertaken behind the scenes; but for residents of the VIP center, only the problem is present, and they are surrounded by experts who collaborate incessantly. Lewis reports that 'since the VIP Center was created in the late 1990's, Samsung's growth in good ideas, measured in patents, has risen faster than any of its competitors – 1,600 [patents] last year.'

Environments of play are more likely to engage employees in brainstorming and blue-sky thinking. The goal is to get employees to come up with radical, game-changing ideas. Retreats, off-site meetings, and brainstorming sessions are all environments of play. Unstructured environments facilitate thinking that's not possible within the everyday confines of the organization. For example, removing employees from the office may help them think without subjecting themselves to the same constraints that they are used to in their everyday work. Employees may experiment, sketch out ideas, enact skits about how an idea might impact a business process, and even construct quick prototypes, akin to putting a LEGO set together. Environments of play are also interesting spaces in which to include customers and even business partners; they can enrich the dialogue and bring valuable new perspectives to a topic. In environments of need, the goal is the output, but in environments of play, the goal is the *process*: dialogue, discovery, and sharing of experiences. Seldom do these events generate ideas that can be pursued immediately. The goal of these environments is to generate as many ideas as possible, even if they seem farfetched and wild. Ideas will later go through a process of more serious debate and discussion (especially in the circles and units on which they might have an impact) as they are refined to provide a basis for action.

Many companies that work on building successful teams or developing innovative products are known to facilitate playful environments. Larry Page says of Google's work environment, 'We like to innovate in our physical space.'[13] Google's offices feature playful elements such as a slide and a fireman's pole.[14] They also feature functional elements that free employees from technology concerns so that they can focus on ideas; for example, they provide enclosed, noise-free projectors that can be left on at all times and give employees the means to automatically e-mail meeting notes to attendees.[15] IDEO is another company that generates ideas in playful environments. Tim Brown, CEO of IDEO, points to IDEO's minibus conference room and Pixar's wooden huts and caves as examples of creative spaces.[16] IDEO's studios are designed to help people feel relaxed and familiar with their surroundings. This builds trust, an essential prerequisite to play, and supports essential activities such as exploration, building prototypes, and role playing. IDEO's founder, David Kelley, especially encourages ideation with found objects, which he calls 'thinking with your hands.'[17] Tim Brown notes that a designer used a roll-on deodorant as an inspiration for the design of the first computer mouse. Brown calls the typical office environment 'barren' and notes that IDEO also has artistic materials such as glue and construction paper on hand to facilitate the building of models and prototypes. He is quick to emphasize that, although these may appear to be childish or emblematic of a schoolroom, they serve the useful purpose of 'quickly [getting] something into the real world and letting that shape ideas.'[18] IDEO also maintains a more formal collection of materials for building called the Tech Box, a 'library that catalogues some 200 weird physical materials and odd objects, ranging from rubber balls to pieces of space shuttle tile, for inspiration-seeking engineers to play with.'[19]

In sharp contrast to environments of need, playful environments are well suited to the development of strategic, radical, 'there is no box' ideas. Playful environments welcome external individuals to act as consultants, advisors, or facilitators. Hence, the ideas are likely to be externally oriented. In a playful environment, there is a higher chance that you will not arrive at any useful ideas, because the process purposefully omits specifics about the type of idea needed. The process and its interactions matter most.

In providing a space for playful thinking, it's important to consider whether the environment will be permanent or transient. Permanent environments are fixed and require infrastructure. You may wish to dedicate a room for generating ideas – but be careful how you design the room. The best designs are characterized by 'ordered chaos.' The atmosphere should be informal and foster playfulness. Often these rooms feature things like foozeball tables, dart boards, and even pillows that invite employees to rest on the ground instead of sitting in a chair. Yet they also have highly sophsticated audio and visual equipment. Refreshments are often stocked in fridges to promote energetic dicussions. In most cases, these rooms can hold at most twenty people. The important thing is to make sure employees know the main purpose of the room, the type of meetings it should be used for, and the protocol for using the room. There might also be open hours when the room can't be booked but instead can be used for informal conversations among the staff.

Not every organization will choose to create a permanent room to promote an environment of play. Some organizations choose transient environments, most often in the form of off-site meetings, brainstorming sessions, or retreats. The advantage of off-site setups is that you can select them as needed without committing capital to building infrastructure up front. In addition, you can change settings as needed. Some disadvantages of off-site environments are lack of control of the location (think about hosting a meeting in a hotel) and lack of privacy for sensitive discussions about the organization. At off-site locations, you always run the risk of 'leaking' information. It's also important to remember that environments of play can be done on the cheap, for instance at a nearby park or the neighboring coffee shop. In the Pacific Northwest of the United States, a manager of a small consulting outfit would organize 'walking meetings' with his employees and encourage them to do the same. The idea was simple – if there was no need for use of a whiteboard, instead of sitting down for a meeting he'd take employees for a walk around the office. When he began this effort it was to get employees to take exercise seriously, and he wanted to set an example of how it could be integrated into work. After the first three months, he realized that most employees preferred the walking meetings, which gave them a chance to discuss ideas in a fresh, novel context.

Virtual spaces, with their rich content and collaboration tools, are a growing source of innovation and can be ideal spaces to promote idea generation. Philip Rosedale, creator of Second Life, states that the motivation for Second Life is to provide a space where things can be created and shared in a social manner. He notes that the 'ultimate thing . . . would be to use computers and the Internet to simulate a world so that you could get in there and make stuff.'[20] Virtual worlds and multiplayer online role-playing games (MMORPGs) are viewed as tools to create new thinking, where companies once looked to skunkworks and greenfield sites.[21] Michael Schrage, author of *Serious Play: How the Best Companies Simulate to Innovate,* writes about them as a 'third place' where co-creative activity leads to innovation. John Seely Brown 'suggests that MMORPGs may hold some keys to self-directed learning.' Seely Brown notes that people who engage in MMORPGs 'marinate on the "edge." Gamers look for new insights and approaches . . . they are consummate innovators.'[22]

One of the critical questions that organizations face is how much structure to bring into these playful environments. If you have too little structure, people may go off on tangents, leading to unfocused discussion. On the other hand, too much structure makes the discussion narrow. Tim Brown of IDEO notes that 'play is not anarchy, it has rules which lead to productivity'[23] Brown notes that children follow agreed-upon rules in their play and that their play shows valid or broken interactions. At IDEO, 'Brainstorming rules are written on the wall' including 'edicts like defer judgment, go for quantity.'[24] Brown emphasizes that rules are needed to break old norms and patterns of thinking and that you get 'better outcomes when everybody plays by the rules.'[25] The frameworks are designed to discourage self-editing and to build trust. Important best practices call for the a semi-structured approach in which the big picture is in focus and drives the discussion for the day. Characteristics of the semi-structured approach are outlined in table 3.2.

FACILITATING IDEA GENERATION
The organization must take responsibility for facilitating idea generation. To this end, it becomes vital for the organization to help employees take a customer-centered view of ideas. Ideas without customers in mind are difficult, though not impossible, to manage. Publishing problems of interest to employees and seeking their ideas on them is also important. Problems are highly specific requests that call for solutions (ideas) that are of immediate interest and value. Finally, an organization might consider setting up competitions to promote the

Table 3.2
A semi-structured approach to idea generation

Technique	Description
Offer a mix of communication formats	Have a mix of structured presentations and communications along with providing enough time for peer-to-peer discussions and report-outs.
Provide a variety of interactions	Provide enough opportunities for networking and socialization so that the individuals working together have a chance to bond and connect.
Include non-work activities	Engage in social and team-building activities that have nothing to do with work so as to add elements of fun.
Support a variety of work and engagement styles	Be flexible as to how individuals network and collaborate with their peers – for instance some might want to use pen and paper, others might prefer to take a walk and talk, while others might find the use of whiteboards and easels of interest.
Allow sufficient time to let brainstorming discussions play out	Provide enough time for people to throw out ideas and discuss random thoughts. The agenda in an environment of play needs to allow plenty of time for randomness and creative thinking to emerge; people should have enough time to share wild and far-fetched ideas.
Capture discussions	It's important to capture the discussions that take place; this can be done by designated personnel working as reporters, audio and video recordings, photographing whiteboards, and even providing simple sticky boards where people can make notes and jot down ideas.
Enforce the rule that there is no such thing as a bad idea	Encourage open discussions and discourage self-censorship. Even if an idea isn't going to be discussed during the event, there should be a parking lot where ideas can be captured. Parking lots enable ideas to be revisited at a later date, especially ideas that are connected or integrated with ideas that are being considered.

generation of ideas that are radical in nature. Competitions can also be used as a mechanism to send the message that ideas and the individuals who generate them are valued in the organization.

Customer-Centered Idea Generation. Ideas need to have a focus. Ideas that are too broad and don't have a clearly identified focus, and those that don't meet the goals of customers, are difficult to process. Thus, it's vital that the organization identify *customers* or *areas of focus* for ideas. Customers can come from various places within the organization, such as other functional areas like engineering, sales, or accounting. They can also be centers of excellence or cross-domain collaboration teams that are focused on specific initiatives, such as new business development groups focused on specific geographic locations. In addition, customers can also be employees working on specific problems, technologies, or processes that the organization has identified as current or future challenges and opportunities – for example, the market identification and targeting process within a sales department (see the next section, on publishing problems). Customers can also be the actual clients and business partners of the organization. Another option is to identify the future areas that an organization would like to enter. For example, if the organization is thinking of entering a foreign market, it should solicit ideas about entry strategies, clients to work with, and markets that are ripe for investment. The ideal organization will update its focus areas on a regular basis as internal and external conditions in its environments change.

Clearly identifying customers or areas of focus and turning employees' attention to generating ideas about them are the first vital steps to reducing *noise* in the intrapreneurship process. Too often organizations are laden with noisy innovation processes that make it hard to identify ideas and equally challenging to identify the audiences for those ideas. In addition, the organization should appoint key personnel to manage the idea-generation process in each area. These individuals can serve as contact points for employees who would like to submit ideas. They can also champion their focus areas, develop specific guidelines about how ideas should be submitted, specify what kinds of ideas are needed, and determine how ideas will be evaluated. Contact personnel are also important for transferring ideas between domains. An idea submitted to one focus area may be more suitable for another. In addition, opportunities submitted in one domain can sometimes be pursued as cross-domain collaborations. For example, CEMEX, the highly innovative cement manufacturer, has an 'Innovation Committee' composed of three directors, three vice-presidents, and one outside consultant. The team is responsible for defining broad themes for innovation and structure for the innovation process. Often, the committee considers strategic areas that are outside CEMEX's core business; recent focus areas included 'integrated construction solutions for affordable housing, ways to support regional development, and making it easier for customers to do business with CEMEX.'[26]

The contact person for each focus area must be accessible to employees. These individuals should not only be knowledgeable about their area but should also have time and resources available to evangelize for idea generation. They should be given explicit resources – such as travel or release time – to dedicate to the cause of idea generation. If these individuals are too busy or uninterested, they appear unapproachable and spoil their focus area's reputation. Hence, the contact person's performance evaluation should be tied to his or her ability to develop the focus area into an environment that generates ideas. These individuals should also be able to work collaboratively to share ideas that originate within one focus area that might be better leveraged across other areas.

Once focus areas are defined, it's equally important to communicate them to employees and inform employees across hierarchical levels and functional divisions that they should contribute to these focus areas. It should be clear to employees that the work they do on a daily basis is related to at least one of the focus areas. As was noted in chapter 2, a useful strategy is to build archetypes that resonate with employees of what an idea contribution might look like in each of the focus areas. As an example, in engineering firms like Fujitsu and Sony, employees can review ideas within categories and see how these ideas have contributed to the overall goal of the organization. For example, an idea that advances work on plasma screens ultimately helps Sony to be a leader in digital technology.

While a customer-centered approach to focusing ideas has much value, every organization needs to be flexible and open to ideas that may not fall neatly into clear categories. It's impossible for an organization to identify all areas that might possibly be of interest. Hence, it's always wise to keep room for 'other ideas,' ideas that don't fall neatly in one of the focus areas. Having a defined process for submitting ideas outside the areas of focus has several benefits: (1) it will help keep the spirit of intrapreneurship alive in the organization by continuously encouraging people to submit ideas – even ideas that may not be in a current area of focus; (2) the ideas submitted may be related in some useful way to ideas in the focus areas, increasing the chance of capturing ideas rather than losing them; and (3) occasionally the ideas submitted in general categories may actually be game-changing ideas that create new focus areas and change the competitive posture of the organization.

Problem-Centered Idea Generation. Publishing problems is a useful strategy for generating ideas in areas of focus. Yet this method is often an underappreciated part of the idea-generation process. *Problems* may be defined as any impediments that make it difficult for an organization to move from its current state to a desired future state – such as lack of existing solutions or an inability to implement existing solutions in a cost-effective manner. Publishing problems encourages the generation of ideas in a focused manner. A problem is quite difficult to define because most of us are asked to 'solve' problems on the job rather than come up with new ones. As such, many of us haven't the expertise needed to define what a good problem is, or the time to reflect on problems that might yield to creative solutions. In addition, generating problem statements requires one to argue the merits of investing time in creating a solution for the issue. Too often, we are accustomed to arguing about the merits of potential solutions and then choosing the right solution. Deciding which problem might be the most promising to solve among a collection of problems is quite a different challenge.

The characteristics of good problem statements that encourage creative solutions and idea generation are outlined in table 3.3.

Good problem statements can be publicized to members of the organization on a regular basis, but don't overdo it. Publicizing too many problems at too-frequent intervals will result in people being bombarded by opportunities, and no single opportunity will get the attention it needs. You may also choose to be selective about the audience for particular problems, or decide to rank problems in terms of defined criteria if they are going to be published to everyone in the organization.

One approach to targeting communications effectively is to graph the potential audiences, starting with the people who are the most likely to solve the problem (think of a dart board, with the most relevant people as the bull's-eye); you then draw circles around the domain that is the

Table 3.3
Developing good problem statements

Technique	Description
Provide a clear and concise definition of the problem (*what*)	Be clear and concise as to *what* the problem is. This calls for stating the problem, the elements that are within the boundaries of the problem, and how the various components within the problem interact with each other.
Establish the stakeholders (*who*)	Define *who* the problem impacts and how. Problem statements need to be clear in terms of the stakeholders they impact, how the various stakeholders are impacted, and how solving the problem will improve stakeholders' performance.
State the significance of the problem (*why*)	Provide a clear statement about *why* a solution is needed. The statement should describe why this problem may be more important than others, why one should spend the time and energy to address it, and why it should be addressed now rather than at some time in the future.
Provide guidelines to evaluate possible solutions (*how*)	Provide guidelines as to *how* a solution to the problem might be evaluated: what are the metrics that you will use to decide whether a solution is good or bad? This is one of the most challenging and vital elements to be clarified. Think about what primary and secondary criteria you will use to evaluate ideas. People who submit ideas must know the objective of a potential solution. For instance, if your goal is to reduce costs by 10 percent for a given process and this is the most important criterion, people who generate ideas need to know this up front so that they don't spend unnecessary effort coming up with a solution that doesn't meet the goal.
Articulate the benefits to the idea creator (the *'so what'*)	Provide a clear statement regarding the '*so what*' – the rewards that will be conferred on the idea creator who solves the problem – for example, whether the idea creator would gain increased visibility and power in the organization, or resources to develop the solution further with the team/individual that is proposing the problem.

best fit and domains that are closely related. You can continue to draw circles and eventually map all units within the organization. The risk in this approach is that sometimes the best answers might come from unexpected sources within the organization. An engineering problem might be solved by an employee working in customer service; hence, by limiting the distribution of the idea you may lose potentially valuable ideas. Another approach is to 'tag' problems to help in their categorization. With the growth in Web 2.0 technologies, the concept of user-generated tagging of documents has become quite popular. This allows you to tag a problem based on categories that are both predefined (e.g., the names of departments or teams within the organization) and user-created. Using this system, employees can search for problems based on their specific interests. Moreover, under this approach you don't have to push problems to all employees; instead you can communicate at a summary level via routine updates or through e-mail. The locus of activity for employees will be a website (Intranet) where they can search through the problems of interest to them. But be warned, if users generate too many categories, there is a point of diminishing returns at which the system becomes unwieldy. On the other hand, predetermined categories that are too specific may overly restrict the system. To avoid such pitfalls, you can (1) ensure that people who post problems use at least one tag to identify where the problem is coming from, such as its domain, or who the stakeholders might be, and (2) prompt users who want to generate their own categories to choose first from categories that might be similar to theirs and create a new one only if no similar category exists. Periodic maintenance is required to clean up unused categories so that the system filters and search capabilities will be useful.

Prize-Centered Idea Generation. Today, organizations are stimulating idea creation by experimenting with prizes and competitions. Offering prizes is a nice way in which to involve customers in problem-focused idea creation. In October 2006, Netflix created an ongoing prize to foster innovation in computer algorithms capable of predicting how much customers would love a movie based on their previous movie ratings. Anyone can compete for the Netflix Prize. Entrants can go to the Netflix website, work with the test data set provided, develop their algorithm, and then submit it. Netflix then tests the algorithm against a data set, records its performance, and posts the algorithm's name to a public list of ranked submissions.

Table 3.4
Types of prize-centered competitions

Prize Type	Advantage(s)
Exposition prize	• Minimal prize purse
	• Create a wide range of ideas
Participation prize	• Encourage employee participation
	• Everyone wins
Market-stimulation prize	• Create a radically new market
	• Collective research investment often exceeds actual purse prize amount
Point-solution prize	• Narrow focus
	• Pre-established evaluation criteria
Exemplar prizes	• Reward behavior that inspires others
	• Celebrate discovery process

Netflix has offered up to $10 million for the first person to beat their algorithm by 10 percent, and annual awards of $50,000 (known as Progress Prizes) are given out for the best incremental improvement of at least 1 percent over the previous year.

Competitions to promote idea creation are not a recent phenomenon. The oldest prizes can be traced back several centuries, to prizes such as the Longitude Prize, won by an English peasant, John Harrison, in the eighteenth century.[27] Rejecting conventional thinking that sought to estimate longitude at sea using astronomical references, Harrison constructed a clock that used time and distance calculations. The British Parliament offered Harrison a prize of £20,000 in 1714 as a reward for his contribution to reducing shipwrecks resulting from poor navigation capabilities.

Ideas can be solicited through several types of prize-centered competitions (see table 3.4).[28] *Exposition prizes* seek to highlight promising ideas around a complex problem or opportunity. Organizations use these competitions to engage employees in the solving of specific organizational challenges. In these competitions, the prize purse is normally minimal, because the goal is not to choose a winner but to highlight a range of promising ideas that are then candidates for investment.

Participation prizes are very common in organizations. They have a very humble goal, which is getting employees to engage more closely with organizational challenges. Exposition prizes can be considered a subset of participation prizes in that their goal is to highlight a collection of good ideas on a problem, and hence to engage a large number of individuals. Participation prizes seek to change behavior and mindsets by engaging employees in the competition in such a way that everyone wins. For example, team-building exercises at corporate retreats seek to get individuals to work together to solve challenges. Of course, one team will be deemed a victor and get the bottle of champagne, but from the organizational perspective all individuals and teams have won, since they've gained valuable teamwork and collaborative decision-making skills. Participation prizes can be found in abundance in the popular media. For example, NBC's show *The Biggest Loser* awards $250,000 to the contestant who loses the most weight. The goal is for all who enter the competition to lose a significant amount of body weight, change their eating and exercising habits, and improve their health.

Market stimulation prizes, as the name implies, seek ideas that have the potential to create a radically new market. This kind of prize requires the organization to create enough of an incentive (prize) that individuals invest a serious amount of resources (often much more than the eventual prize purse) to win the competition. Examples of these include the Ansari X-Prize competition for the first private spaceflight, where twenty-six teams spent well over $100 million to win the $10 million prize. The winning of this prize led to the creation of a new market: the private spaceflight industry.

Next, there are *point-solution prizes*, with a narrower focus on specific, complex problems. Here, ideas are evaluated as either 'best of breed' (i.e., the best of all submissions at a given date) or the first to cross the line (i.e., the first to reach a minimally acceptable solution that addresses the major design constraints). These competitions are similar to the act of publishing problems, with the added dimension of setting up competition guidelines and criteria for evaluating submissions.

Finally, we have *recognition* or *exemplar prizes* that seek to reward advances and good behavior. The classic examples of these are the Nobel Prizes that recognize individuals for achievements that benefit society. These prizes set the bar for what is desired behavior in the field, and what others should aspire to. Recognition prizes celebrate the discovery process and home in on the concepts of risk seeking, intrapreneurship, and good behavior. Almost all organizations award such prizes (e.g., 'Employee of the Month!'), and are often tied to idea generation (e.g., 'the Employee Who Saved the Organization,' or 'Most Innovative Idea of the Month').

Prize-centered competitions offer some interesting benefits. First, prize-centered competitions reward outcomes and hence do not require large cash outlays up front. The payout is made only if someone wins. Only the administration costs (i.e., the costs associated with running the competition, vetting and screening entries, etc.) need to be covered. Second, if no one wins the prize, the prize remains open and can be redesigned or abandoned. Third, prize-centered competitions have the ability to stimulate markets and organizations and to mobilize individuals. Consider the case of the Orteig Prize, won by Charles Lindbergh for the first flight across the Atlantic Ocean between New York and Paris. If it had not been for Lindbergh's successful endeavor, we might not have witnessed the development of transatlantic (and long-haul) aviation. The aircraft Lindbergh flew, *The Spirit of St Louis*, was viewed by a quarter of all Americans, and the achievement had an astonishing economic impact, including a 300 percent increase in applications for commercial flying licenses in 1927, the doubling of the number of U.S. airports within three years of the flight, and an increase in airline passengers in the United States from 5,287 in 1927 to more than 173,000 in 1929.[29] A comparable impact would have been hard to achieve by other means. Think of the publicity that surrounds the announcement of the Nobel Prizes or the Man Booker prize to celebrate the best of fiction writing. Fourth, and perhaps most importantly, prize-centered competitions open up the solicitation of ideas to a diverse community and are ideal mechanisms for engaging external constituents in idea generation. In the case of the Longitude Prize, Harrison was not a seaman or an expert in the navigational sciences; he made his breakthrough by thinking differently from the experts at the time. The NASA Centennial Challenges, announced during the hundredth anniversary of the birth of aviation, focus on small-to medium-scale prizes.[30] The prize purses range from about $50,000 to $2 million and seek solutions that are of interest to NASA, such as a design for new astronaut gloves or a lunar lander. Peter Homer won the competition for new glove design. He was not a NASA employee nor did he work for any of the major contractors in the defense and space industries. He was an unemployed engineer from Maine who worked on the solution at his home sewing machine! He successfully built a glove that passed dexterity and finger-torque tests to evaluate its performance in a zero-gravity environment and won $200,000.[31] Bringing in external constituents is a good idea when there is dearth of good ideas or problem-solving capabilities internally. They can also be attractive when you want to bring customers, business partners, and other external entities closer to the organization.

Idea Mobilization

Most ideas aren't created from scratch; often, they've existed for a long time in one domain but have yet to be applied in another. For example, at CEMEX, managers 'travel around the world to find ideas,' which they not only transfer to their own environment but retool to fit it: 'they take pieces of practice or technology that they find and recombine them in novel ways to solve customer problems.'[32] In this case, an intrapreneur may not necessarily be the inventor of the idea but one who brings the idea into the organization. A focus on idea mobilization is important for promoting the infusion of ideas from the external environment. The concept of *internal* or *external* depends on your perspective. From the viewpoint of a department, ideas that come from other departments or geographic locations of the organization might be viewed as external. If you take a broader view of the organization, ideas that come from business partners, academia, suppliers, or governments may be viewed as external.

Beware of the not-invented-here syndrome that regards outside ideas with suspicion – sometimes, great ideas come from customers, competitors, or outside experimenters. Another unhelpful myth is that best practices generally move from the 'developed' or 'headquarters' locations to the 'emerging' or 'underdeveloped' areas – a version of the imperialistic mindset. In reality, good ideas may move in the other direction just as easily, and organizations always benefit from local knowledge, especially as they expand into emerging markets. As Ray Johnson, Lockheed Martin's CTO, says of the relationships that Lockheed has developed with the Indian Institute of Technology Delhi (IIT) and Delhi Technical in the areas of biotechnology and nanotechnology, 'Our Indian Innovation Growth program is in its third year and has been very enlightening . . . It's tough for us to think differently, and innovation comes when people with different perspectives look at problems.'[33] The knowledge generated in local markets may have transformative potential for the larger organization.

DESIGNING ORGANIZATIONAL NETWORKS

To adequately mobilize ideas you need to know the sources and destination of ideas. Imagine a knowledge map that identifies who has certain expertise within your organization, who is working on what, and who might be in need of a certain kind of knowledge. This mapping could be accomplished on a corporate Facebook-like site, which system employees could use to manage their own knowledge networks. They can use their profiles to share information about their expertise, connect to other employees, and even provide updates on the tasks and projects they are working on. Employees can then use the system to search for other employees with whom to share ideas. Moreover, they can post interesting ideas and concepts to an employee's page, and even connect him or her with other employees with similar or complementary goals and skills. One of the big advantages of these sites is that there is social pressure for employees to keep their profiles updated and current. This reduces the burden on the organization to manage employees' expertise and current efforts. In addition, these sites allow a large amount of flexibility whereby employees can enter as much information as they want and update their status as regularly as they choose. These kinds of sites are subject to network effects, where the site is only valuable when there is a critical mass of people on it. Hence, you may have to provide incentives to get early adopters to kick-start employee participation. In addition, you may want to target key people who have deep social networks to join the site first. This will attract others to join as well.

To bring ideas from the external world into the organization, individuals must maintain and develop rich personal networks that encompass industry, academia, and other professional affiliations. The Department of Homeland Security (DHS) recognizes this in its process of reaching out to 'academia, [and] think tanks . . . to test emerging technologies and create prototypes . . . This new strategy explicitly recognizes that it's a big world out there. Most solutions already exist – somewhere – and most problems are eminently solvable if you ask the right person.'[34] The most capable intrapreneurs are well connected; they attend lectures at universities and know individuals working in similar domains in other organizations. These individuals feel deeply connected to their work and are not primarily focused on external rewards. Many of these individuals participate in discussion forums online and in open-source communities. They want to be known as experts within their domain, beyond the confines of the organization.

Communities of practice or technical communities – in other words, spaces where people can share ideas within specific domains – are another means of mobilizing ideas. These spaces provide valuable social checks and balances for good ideas. Parsons Brinckerhoff uses Practice Area Networks (PANs) to facilitate the movement of ideas by creating communities around topics/expertise areas/practice domains. PAN members post problems, share ideas, and facilitate learning in these environments. They share problems as they arise in their work settings and either (1) find other people who have the same problem – meaning that the problem is recurring and needs a lot of attention – or (2) discover existing solutions that may be fully developed and ready to use or under experimentation – temporary fixes that still need enhancement. These enhancement requests can then be developed into proposals that flow into the next stage of the intrapreneurship process.

An organization should monitor and frequently evaluate its knowledge networks. For example, through the use of social networking software, the organization can identify the volume of traffic and exchanges between various employees. In addition, they can use the data gathered to identify which employees serve as integrators between multiple domains or departments of the organization. For example, if most of the traffic that involves moving ideas between two departments goes through only one or two employees, the organization must invest more resources to train and hire individuals who can strengthen the links between these departments. In addition, if the organization finds no movement of ideas between people in two different domains, this might signal the need to connect employees or find out why there is no interaction. True 'idea transporters' – also known as 'boundary spanners' or 'gatekeepers' – should be rewarded with resources and incentives to share knowledge across organizational domains.[35] Not every employee can act as an 'idea transporter.' Most individuals simply don't have the deep expertise and know-how. Use of mapping and networking tools can be of great value here.[36]

The organization should draw a social network analysis (SNA) map and keep it active. One good example of an SNA is the Central Intelligence Agency's (CIA) Analytic-Space (A-Space). It functions as an internal Facebook site that can be used to get answers to queries and also to facilitate work and promote sharing of intelligence between analysts. One initiative of the U.S. government is to encourage agents of the Central Intelligence Agency, the Federal Bureau of Investigation

(FBI), and the National Security Agency (NSA) to connect through their own social media network. A-Space is a Facebook-type platform that allows individuals from the three agencies to share intelligence information on subjects that usually wouldn't leave one agency's boundaries. For example, each agency can contribute its knowledge to the section tracking al-Qaeda movements in the Middle East, creating one central and complete knowledge base of the intelligence focused on that subject. New ideas, theories, and information are shared in a collaborative workspace where analysts come together to create new meaning and knowledge out of many smaller pieces of knowledge.

PROMOTING THE FLOW OF IDEAS

We typically classify idea mobilization mechanisms into two broad categories – push systems and pull systems.[37] A push system is one in which ideas are routinely pushed from a central source to employees in the organization. A pull system is one in which the employees get to see the ideas that are being submitted – for example, in a database – and then decide if they want to contribute and use (i.e., pull) them and engage with them. For example, at MicroArts, a brand-design and marketing communications company, the innovation process is democratized and distributed with the help of information communication technologies (ICTs). Design teams' ideas are posted three times daily on computer monitors around the office to receive feedback from all employees.[38] The company promotes a sharing culture and encourages creativity; ideas are discussed and developed from the earliest stages.

The advantage of the push system is that it can be standardized. Employees can choose their idea preference domains and receive updates as ideas are submitted. This eliminates the problem of employees' forgetting to check the idea repositories and removes some of the responsibility from the employee. The disadvantage of this approach is that it is hard to customize the pushing of ideas to suit every employee's work style. Moreover, some employees may occasionally be too busy to consider ideas, and sending them frequent e-mails may cause information overload and alienate them instead of engaging them in the process.

The rules for promoting the transfer of ideas (summarized in table 3.5) are the same as those for promoting the optimal flow of most information elements in the organization. Rule one is: *Ensure that there are reliable channels to connect the various entities of the organization*, in this case the employees. Any employee might at any given time be either a source of or a destination for an idea. Channels may be fixed or dynamic, human or electronic (e.g., e-mail), or direct or indirect (through intermediaries or middle managers), as long as they promote the optimal flow of ideas. Optimal flow has two dimensions: effectiveness and efficiency. Effectiveness measures whether the right ideas move from a source to a destination, and if the ideas are held intact during the transmission process. Efficiency measures whether the transport was conducted with the least possible amount of time and cost.

Rule two is: *Establish clear-cut protocols for identifying sources and destinations for ideas.* The organization should have a knowledge map that lists the expertise of individuals along with details of their interests, the projects they are working on, and other relevant information. This type of knowledge map can be as basic as a detailed corporate directory that has more information than simple phone numbers and e-mails. Employees can use it to identify colleagues to contact should there be a need to pull in ideas for problems or opportunities. It may also help employees to route ideas and publish problems that are ripe for idea generation. Simple strategies can help mobilize ideas; for example, at Motorola employees can use prediction markets (a topic covered in the next chapter) to trade ideas, and can send ideas to their peers by clicking the 'Tell a Friend' link. If you're the friend receiving the idea, you're more likely to act on it because it has come through a trusted intermediary. Furthermore, your friend knows you and already has a good sense of your interests. With this simple approach you can also easily entice others to engage in idea mobilization. For example, if your friend sent you an idea, you are more likely to reciprocate and send him or her an idea as well. Hence, by creating dyadic ties, you may actually be able to scale the system to a point where employees are mobilizing ideas through person-to-person connections.

Rule three is: *Maximize channel efficiency and effectiveness.* Ideas should take as few intermediary hops as possible on their way to a destination. In a fully connected network, where every node is connected to every other node, there is no need for intermediaries between any two nodes. But in reality, fully connected networks are rare; they are very expensive and not feasible to maintain. In a less-than-fully-connected network, middle managers usually serve as intermediaries. The organization should identify intermediaries and remind them that delaying ideas is costly, asking them either to allow others direct access to the nodes that they are connected to or to deal with ideas that come to them efficiently to avoid bottlenecks. Think of the network as an air-travel system for moving passengers from one location, or hub, to another. The hubs are the airports that the aircraft fly into, where passengers board or change planes to get to other destinations. The ideas are the passengers. Ideally, you want to limit the number of transfers passengers have to make to get to their destination. Similarly, organizations need to think systematically about the 'hubs' in their networks and how they might be managed so as to promote the most optimal flows of ideas.

Rule four is: *Find ways to preserve the integrity of the idea as it moves across contexts.* Ideas, like other information elements, are subject to distortion due to noise in the channels, and may get corrupted en route. To ensure the integrity of the ideas being transported, your communication channels must be able to carry rich information. Channels that promote transport of rich information curb the level of distortion. In face-to-face video conferencing, for example, oral and visual cues add to meaning, whereas a text message is less suitable for transmitting rich information. An effective channel will preserve the intent and meaning of the idea during the transfer, so direct access is ideal. When this is not possible, it is important to build processes for the idea sources and destinations to communicate directly upon the receipt of ideas. Good boundary spanners help in this regard, as they connect different functional areas of the organization, understand the diverse occupational languages and cultures, and know how to navigate them. Boundary spanners who can navigate different geographical spaces of the organization in order to move ideas across physical locations are also vital.

Rule five is: *Remember that great ideas may work in one context but be irrelevant in others.* Hence, simply transporting ideas is not enough; the environmental information around the idea must also be communicated. This can be done through various mechanisms, from adding explanatory notes on a document that explains its boundary conditions to adding an 'expiration date' for an idea, since most ideas are not only domain specific but also time sensitive. Today, organizations are using creative electronic platforms to promote the sharing of ideas. In these spaces, ideas can be tagged by the creator, and metadata describing details of the idea can be entered. Users can then search for ideas and understand the context within which the idea creator conceived them.

Rule six is: *Manage the network of links from a global perspective.* For example, if one of the nodes is unavailable because an employee is on holiday or gets transferred, a backup must be prepared to take on

Table 3.5
'Rules' for promoting the transfer of ideas

Rule	Description
Ensure that there are reliable channels to connect the various entities of the organization.	Channels may be fixed or dynamic, human or electronic (e.g., e-mail), or direct or indirect (through intermediaries or middle managers), as long as they promote the optimal flow of ideas.
Establish clear-cut protocols for identifying sources and destinations for ideas.	Have a knowledge map that lists the expertise of individuals along with details of their interests, the projects they are working on, and other relevant information. Employees can use it to identify colleagues to contact should there be a need to pull in ideas for problems or opportunities.
Maximize channel efficiency and effectiveness.	Ensure that ideas take as few intermediary hops as possible on their way to a destination. Organizations need to think systematically about the 'hubs' in their networks and how they might be managed so as to promote the most optimal flows of ideas.
Find ways to preserve the integrity of the idea as it moves across contexts.	To ensure the integrity of the ideas being transported, your communication channels must be able to carry rich information. An effective channel will preserve the intent and meaning of the idea during the transfer. Direct access is ideal; when this is not possible, you need to build processes that allow the idea sources and destinations to communicate directly about ideas. Good boundary spanners can facilitate such communication.
Remember that great ideas may work in one context but be irrelevant in others.	Not only the idea itself but also the environmental information around the idea must be communicated. This can be done through various mechanisms, from adding explanatory notes on a document that explains its boundary conditions to adding an 'expiration date' for an idea.
Manage the network of links from a global perspective.	If one of the channels breaks down or seems to be clogged with ideas, alternative channels need to be available to help manage the load. The organization needs to invest time and energy in maintaining the network's ability to meet requirements – for example, by collecting metrics on the number of ideas flowing or the load on each of the channels.

ideas that would normally be routed to the absent employee. Similarly, if one of the channels breaks down or seems to be clogged up with ideas, alternative channels need to be deployed to manage the load. The organization needs to invest time and energy in maintaining the network's ability to meet requirements. To this end, it's important to be able to collect metrics on the number of ideas flowing or the load on each of the channels. Learning can take place and interventions can be deployed as needed to address problems. Through simple deployment of social networking technologies, along with routine surveying of employees on their idea mobilization patterns, an organization should be able to collect enough information to facilitate the management of knowledge networks from a global perspective.

KEEPING IDEA MOBILIZATION SIMPLE

Idea mobilization should be kept simple and infused into the daily work practices of employees as much as possible. Employees shouldn't have to abandon their work in order to mobilize an idea. The lower the barriers for idea mobilization, the greater the chance that employees will actually move ideas.

One method of encouraging the exchange of ideas among employees is to establish a simple mechanism for encouraging employees to spend time talking with their peers about ideas. In 2006, I spoke with Jaime Green, then managing director of NPower, a non-profit organization that helps other non-profits leverage technology. NPower encouraged employees to take time to talk in pairs to exchange ideas. This worked superbly well; most employees didn't recognize the value of their own ideas until they had communicated them to their peers. The peers, in turn, reported the shared ideas to a broader group. The solution to virtual adaptation of this idea is to get employees to meet on corporate networking sites to comment on the ideas that are posted by their peers. Commenting on ideas from a peer will encourage idea mobilization and lower inhibitions about idea sharing. At CEMEX, they use a technique called 'Ping-pong' to help stimulate idea sharing. Teams are split into two groups. One group proposes an idea that targets a specific objective, and the other group works to improve the idea. The teams pass the idea back and forth until they are unable to improve on it further.[39] These techniques not only help in mobilizing ideas but also build a culture that invites talking about ideas in general.

Another simple strategy is the debriefing session. In a fifteen-minute session, a manager might ask the following questions: What new challenges are you facing? What problems are troubling you, and what might the ideal solution looks like? These debriefing sessions can be organized around a working lunch or an informal meeting over coffee. Think of them as matchmaking sessions to facilitate idea sharing. Each session should be followed by a report to the group. The results of the impromptu interactions are often amazing, especially in terms of building trust in the idea-sharing process at the local level within the organization.

At Texas Instruments, idea generators are called 'lunatics,'[40] and with good reason. Idea generators often think outside the box and are often people who have difficulty accepting reality. They see past constraints and difficulties and straight into possibilities and potentials. The type of person who thinks up radical innovations all day long is likely to be a dreamer, someone who may not excel at day-to-day tasks but who becomes obsessed with a problem for long periods of time. Allowing members of an organization to take on these roles and to dedicate part of their work time to pursuing projects with no specific goal in sight can seem risky and unintuitive, but it does help to create a culture of idea generation. At Texas Instruments, when engineers get excited about a technological problem, they are often given free rein to pursue it.[41] The marketing department doesn't vet the ideas first, so the avenue for innovation is wide open. Idea creators often pursue ideas for their own sake, not for economic reasons,[42] so the strategy at Texas Instruments won't work for everyone. Idea creators are often focused on value creation, not on methods of using and benefiting from ideas, so appropriate managers or 'stewards' are crucial to supporting idea creators.[43]

There are useful techniques for helping employees to mobilize ideas from outside the organization. One organization I know has a policy whereby employees are free to attend whatever conference or training they want, so long as they come back and brief their peers on what they learned. They are encouraged to share not only material that is directly related to their job but also any unrelated ideas they find interesting. The unexpected, but significant, benefit of this policy is that employees learn about the diverse practices of their peer organizations, network with their peers, become alert to mistakes that other organizations have made, and begin threaded discussions around conferences within their organization. They also learn who in their own organization might be interested in similar topics. Rewards are given out after conference reviews. And the exchanges help shape the organization's training and education budget for the next year, thereby rewarding those who contributed to mobilizing ideas.

Design Considerations for Idea Generation and Mobilization

QUANTITY VERSUS QUALITY OF IDEAS

In the first stage of idea creation the emphasis is on quantity more than quality. To this end, an organization must make the cost of submitting ideas low enough that people won't hesitate to submit them. For example, there should be multiple avenues to capture ideas, both electronically and physically. There should be a means for an employee who is working on a task, say, using particular software, to easily connect to the online idea repository and submit ideas – that is, using the fewest possible number of clicks to lower barriers to follow-through. Similarly, in the physical world – for example, on the factory floor – there should be multiple drop boxes where employees can fill out 'comments' or 'idea cards' and submit them for consideration.

Nevertheless, the cost of submitting ideas shouldn't be absolutely zero: you want employees to think about their submissions before making them. Think of this as analogous to going to a meeting where you are seeking feedback from employees on a proposal. If you set no criteria for the feedback, chances are high that you will get all sorts of opinions, debates, and even criticisms, many of which may be useless, knee-jerk reactions. To gather thoughtful comments and ideas, you need to provide employees with a framework that requires them to give their idea some thought before submitting it. The very act of writing down an idea and describing its merits, its origin, and its areas of impact may give the employee sufficient time to reflect on its value. In addition, a section of an idea submission document may require that employees list three individuals with whom they have shared their idea. This promotes the sharing of ideas and ensures that employees have received some feedback from their peers.

INCENTIVES

An important question arises: what kinds of rewards should a manager provide for idea generation and mobilization, if any? Having seen a wide array of approaches in organizations that have attempted to build intrapreneurial programs, I suggest the following approach.

First, in most cases rewards should not be given for merely generating new ideas. By rewards, I am referring to extrinsic rewards such as bonuses, American Express gift cards, or even recognition such as 'Idea Generator of the Month.' In my experience, extrinsic rewards don't work well because they set an inappropriate precedent. In the first case, employees shouldn't be rewarded for a required activity. Contributing ideas needs to become second nature, part of the fabric of work, and employees shouldn't be additionally rewarded for the same reason that they are not additionally rewarded for simply carrying out their regular job responsibilities. I would even go so far as to suggest that employees who do not contribute ideas receive negative feedback. In an organization focused on building a culture of intrapreneurship, managers who support the generation of ideas by helping their employees and creating positive intrapreneurial work environments should have their efforts recognized – though not through extrinsic rewards; and managers who don't foster employee creativity by building a constructive environment should be coached or moved out of their management positions.

One reason that I think rewards don't work for idea generation is simply that they can be gamed. In the case where a reward is given for the most ideas submitted, employees are motivated to submit a large number of low-quality ideas in order to get a reward. Employees may contribute worthless ideas in order to get gift cards or a leg up on their peers. Moreover, this system may turn the intrapreneurship process into a competitive game among employees, killing true intrapreneurship in its very earliest stages, as Alcatrel-Lucent discovered. The company offered a new car for the best idea as part of a 'Stretch Your Mind' event. As Guido Petit, senior director at Alcatrel-Lucent commented, 'It was a big event, but a bad practice . . . It created more negative energy than positive energy because there was one happy person and 149 unhappy people . . . And although the contest tripled the ideas generated, none of them became products.'[44]

On the other hand, I do believe that recognition and rewards play a vital role in fostering the mobility of ideas. Employees who voluntarily take time out of their schedules to communicate ideas to their peers need to be rewarded. Employees who look beyond their own interests and collaborate with their peers also need to be recognized and rewarded. In some organizations, employees are regularly polled for the names of people from whom they received the most and most valuable ideas, and are asked to describe how they furthered the idea. The employees then write a personal letter of thanks and appreciation. In some cases rewards will be given across departments, where one department will use part of its budget to reward an employee in another unit who has helped them with their ideas.

When Whirlpool convened a research team in the Alps for the sole purpose of creating exciting new products, the team returned with only non-starters.[45] David R. Whitwam, Whirlpool's recently retired CEO, didn't give up. Instead, he decided that innovation could occur along with normal work, with every employee contributing. The first successful step toward his innovative scale-up was convening an Innovation Team to examine every department and ask employees for ideas – and no ideas were rejected outright. (In fact, Whitwam demanded that employees come to him with ideas – any ideas – if their managers wouldn't listen.) The Innovation Team included employees from almost all departments and almost all functional areas. They created a screening process to review every idea, focusing on customer needs rather than existing technology or skills. Every idea was graded and recorded. (The review board, as a crucial component of the innovative effort, is still in place to this day.) The grading scheme focused on customer needs and Whirlpool core competencies to maximize the possibility of finding the very best ideas.

Whirlpool also created an internal course on innovation that focused on two components of creating good ideas: product development skills (such as identifying customer needs) and venture-capital skills (such as identifying marketing and implementation needs). Employees who complete the company's five-and-a-half-day internal course on innovation skills and then oversee the generation and advocacy of a few products can become I-mentors, or Innovation Mentors. These mentors are key figures in the Whirlpool innovation process, because they serve as innovation managers: their role is not to control or oversee, but to support and advocate for those with ideas, and to connect ideas with departments or people who might benefit from them. Mentors nurture the beginning stages of innovation. The role of mentors involves not only seeking ideas but also actively generating them. I-mentors lead team meetings in which employees reflect on customer knowledge and business trends and have their own experiences and insights developed and recorded.

Encouraging innovation at Whirlpool isn't limited to company ventures. The company also supports employees who act like entrepreneurs and funds their ideas, both by providing time and by investing in employees' business notions. For instance, one employee developed an idea for offering in-home cooking classes across the country, using

Whirlpool's KitchenAid® line as well as other Whirlpool products. Whirlpool's generous budget for innovations also has a carrot for managers: managers' pay is linked to revenue derived from new products and services.

ORGANIZATIONAL SUPPORT FOR SPONSORS AND MANAGERS

Sponsors and managers must run interference by protecting employees from ridicule and criticism as they work on their ideas. In addition, managers need to give employees the necessary time and space to develop their ideas. Organizations can provide employees with budgets to charge their time and effort to when working on their ideas. This becomes very important, especially in organizations where there is a pressure to meet targets for billable hours.

Managers can take time to observe how their employees conduct their work and point out areas for idea development. Employees may not know whether the work they are doing represents an idea that deserves more attention. In addition, these employees will appreciate positive attention and feedback from their manager – a sure way to encourage the spirit of creativity and innovation in the organization. Managers can also push problems and remind employees of key focus areas in which ideas are needed. This helps ensure that employees are aware of organizational needs and that managers serve as conduits through which employees can channel their ideas. Another obvious way in which managers can support idea creation is through active engagement with employees to help them turn their random thoughts and musings into prototypes and then refined conceptualizations. In doing so, managers can help employees think through their ideas (and even serve as a 'good-idea advocate,' a role that is explored in detail in the next chapter). Managers can use narratives to shape a culture of intrapreneurship – telling stories of employees who have been successful in generating ideas that have been commercialized. Such a culture instills self-confidence and belief in the process in employees so that they can take the necessary risks to generate and develop their ideas.

Another important role managers can play is occasionally to move employees a bit out of their comfort zone. Employees too often get pigeonholed as having a specific area of expertise, and are asked for ideas with a strictly limited focus. Employees may have ideas outside their domains that they never have a chance to share, or, if they do end up sharing them, may have their credibility challenged: 'Stick to what you know best,' as the saying goes. The ideal manager will know how to give employees exposure and avenues for presenting their ideas in different domains. In one of my very early research projects, I examined some of the reasons why experienced software engineers never shared their knowledge. To my surprise it wasn't because they feared that sharing their knowledge would make them less valuable to the organization but that they might be 'typecast' and be offered fewer opportunities to work on a diverse range of projects, limiting their future career prospects.[46]

Managers have a lot to gain from building nurturing environments that promote idea generation. Besides simply being proud of the things their employees are working on, and even advancing their own careers through the ideas that emerge within their span of control, they benefit in other possibly more important ways. For example, they are able to keep tabs on emerging problems and opportunities that their employees confront on a daily basis – information that can help them decide where best to invest their discretionary resources of money, time, and energy. Employees appreciate a manager who is in touch with their immediate concerns and interests. Second, one of the best ways to identify emerging leaders within an organization is to see how ideas from an employee help motivate or mobilize their colleagues. Do some employees have a knack of bringing people together around ideas? Are some viewed as good collaborators and nice to work with on ideas? As noted earlier, the need to groom intrapreneurial leaders is a serious challenge facing most organizations, and managers have the opportunity to address this by taking an active role in observing how effectively employees generate and mobilize ideas. For example, as one of the managers of a major manufacturing firm remarked, 'Every year, I look and see who are the individuals within my unit that are being talked about in other departments . . . this gives me a good indication of who is making an impact beyond the confines of my unit . . . Obviously, I would like this impact to be positive!' Employees who are natural idea generators and mobilizers have a lot of innate traits that can make them valuable leaders in the organization. They know how to communicate, they have the capacity to bring people together, and they don't mind the risky nature of working on ideas.

Last but not least, managers who engage with idea generation and mobilization can bolster their own social networks within the organization. Consider the following: while you may have eight or ten hours a day to make connections and collaborate within your organization, multiplying this same work by the number of your employees and the number of hours *they* spend on the same task gives you an exponentially greater reach. Learning about the connections being made by your employees, helping them to make new connections, and even getting connected to new spaces of the organization through your employees are all valuable outcomes. The bottom line? Sitting on the sidelines is not advisable when it comes to idea generating and mobilizing.

Employee Perspective

As the first stage of the intrapreneurship process, it is critical for all employees to try to engage with idea generation and mobilization. Employees who don't generate ideas can still contribute by helping to mobilize ideas. Employees create ideas as a normal part of their work. The challenge is to get these ideas fed into the intrapreneurship process rather than ignoring or abandoning them. To this end, it is important for employees both to recognize ideas where they see them and to pursue them strategically. Too often, employees take the easy route of putting forward ideas, sometimes half-baked ones, and then not being able to focus and follow through on them. This leads to the dreaded 'death by opportunity' syndrome. To mobilize ideas, employees need to focus on two very important elements: (1) establishing trusting relationships with their peers (too often, employees believe – usually wrongly – that people will try to steal the credit for their ideas), and (2) developing the professional networks through which ideas can flow, both to them from others and from others to them.

Idea Creation

Employees need to think of idea creation in the context of intrapreneurial 'energy.' Barriers to successful idea creation that I've seen in many organizations include: (1) employees not paying attention to or underestimating their ideas, and (2) employees falling into the trap of 'death by opportunity,' the condition of having too many ideas and not knowing how to focus on one and see it through.

If you think you don't have ideas, you're either being too critical or are not looking hard enough. From having talked to thousands of employees across a wide array of industries, I can unequivocally state that more than 99 percent of employees do have ideas. I have seldom met an employee who had no ideas. In fact, employees are likely to have more ideas than they can manage effectively.

HOW TO RECOGNIZE YOUR IDEAS

If you think you don't have ideas that might be valuable to your organization, consider the following two strategies. First, lower your internal threshold for what qualifies as an idea. Often I find employees disregarding and criticizing their own ideas, killing them without even giving them a chance. Ideas don't have to be path-breaking or Nobel Prize-winning insights. At their core, ideas are simple. An idea could be anything that improves how we do things, gets us to do something new, or even helps us look through a new lens at the things we're presently doing. An idea can be as simple as a new method for printing a document or as complex as how to develop the next chemical sequence for a breakthrough drug. As you can imagine, the variety of ideas between these two extremes is huge. Ideas can simply improve the work practices among your team or department, or can transform the strategic posture of your organization. The bottom line is that the more you lower your threshold for what constitutes an idea, the more likely that you'll realize you have a lot of ideas, the raw material needed to begin the intrapreneurship process.

Another reason you may think you have no ideas is that you aren't looking hard enough, or in the right places. Throughout your workday, you are engaged in numerous tasks; in carrying out these tasks you're likely to have a large number of ideas. What normally happens is that we put these ideas into our subconscious. Or, if we are carrying out our daily tasks in a routine fashion, we may not be paying conscious attention to our ideas. A lot of the blame for this falls on managers who focus on short-term measures of performance (e.g., how many widgets you have produced) rather than on evidence of more lasting contributions (e.g., how you have contributed to the redesign of the widget manufacturing process).

Table 3.6 outlines a few practical suggestions employees can use to recognize and capture their ideas as they occur.

Ask yourself who the ideas are for. In other words, who are the customers you want to influence with your idea? It's best to think about ideas in terms of improving the daily life of the customer. If you have an idea for a new product, ask yourself how the product is going to fit the needs of the customer. Identify whether the idea is meant to address a possible pain the customer is feeling or a hurdle the customer

Table 3.6
Ways of identifying and capturing ideas

Suggestion	Implementation Steps / Benefits
Keep a journal	Buy a small pocket-sized notebook and carry it around with you at all times while you are at work. Take short (10–15 minute) breaks every 2 hours and write down (1) issues or problems you faced during work, and (2) any solutions you think might help address these issues. If you don't know of a solution, spend a few minutes reflecting on what a potential solution might look like. Doing this on a regular basis will help you be mindful about the ideas that surface during the normal conduct of your work.
Schedule regular chat sessions with a colleague	Identify a colleague you work with and meet with him/her on a regular basis (say, once every 2 weeks). Sit across a table and spend 20 minutes describing new problems in a constructive manner. Also, talk about your actions in response to the problems that may or may not be part of your official duties. Listen to what your colleague has to say. Then, exchange thoughts on what you found in the other person's reflection that was of interest and that could be useful in your work.
Do a brainstorming exercise on internal processes	Ask yourself what you would do to increase the performance of your department, team, or organization. Once you capture your ideas, try to rally a group of colleagues and begin a discussion about your ideas. Doing so will give you a chance to reflect on improving the *effectiveness* or *efficiency* of your work environment.

encounters on a daily basis, or to enhance the customer's capabilities. Your thinking about customers shouldn't be limited to those outside the organization. There are plenty of potential customers inside the organization that your ideas can serve as well. Too often, employees only focus on external ideas that might become blockbusters. I urge you to take a broader, all-encompassing view of your ideas. Even ideas you think are small can be hugely valuable to internal customers in terms of redesigning business processes and improving operational performance. Don't undervalue internal ideas; most of the time, these are the ideas you'll run across in the daily conduct of your work.

AVOIDING 'DEATH BY OPPORTUNITY'
Most employees can't decide which among their collection of ideas they want to pursue. Without a disciplined approach, you could be

perceived as generating a lot of noise by proposing ideas but lacking the *focus* or *guts* to see any idea through to completion. Needless to say, this is not how you want to be viewed. Too often, as a manager, I have found employees who are eager to expound their ideas but are less willing to work on them, even when provided with the resources to do so. Over time, I've lost confidence and trust in these employees, and I've heard similar stories from a number of managers.

Employees need to be aware of how much time and energy are required to pursue ideas. For any idea you have, take your initial estimate of the amount of time it might take to develop, then multiply by five; this is how much time it will really take. Then, remember a fundamental law of economics: wants (ideas) are unlimited while resources (time and energy) are limited. So be selective about the ideas you focus on in order to optimize these two most valuable resources.

Not only your personal resources but significant organizational resources will also be required when you pursue an idea. You may need to draw on your personal networks, the time and energy of your idea advocate, and even the financial resources of your organization in order to take an idea from concept to implementation. To do this successfully, you need to be judicious about allocating these resources, both financial and non-financial. The fewer ideas you pursue at any one time, the easier it will be for you to focus the available resources. Consider the simple issue of trying to get your manager to sponsor your idea. If you have one idea, the chances are high that your manager will be able to give it the necessary time and energy. This may even be true if you have two or three ideas; but when you reach ten or twenty ideas, your manager's attention will be divided at best – and at worst, your credibility will be damaged.

One way of avoiding 'death by opportunity' is to manage your ideas as a portfolio (in the next chapter, we will talk more about a portfolio approach to idea screening used by organizations). Think of managing your ideas as akin to managing your retirement portfolio. The ideal retirement portfolio has a balanced composition of assets and is tailored to meet the needs of investors. Investors routinely update the portfolio as conditions in their internal and external environments change. Identify the various dimensions in which your ideas differ. For example, consider their zone of influence. Some may be concerned with local operations, while others have global or organizational implications. Some may be ideas that you can pursue as an individual, and others may need to be developed by a team. Other dimensions of your portfolio may include the resources needed to pursue an idea, or the idea's timeliness and/or expiration date. For ease of analysis, I suggest trying to identify dimensions that are of primary and secondary importance. Then, map your ideas on a two-by-two grid, with the dimensions as the axis, moving from low to high or easy to difficult. Try to achieve a balanced collection of ideas in the four cells, and pursue the ideas that come from the various cells. If, however, you have never pursued an idea before (or have pursued one unsuccessfully), begin with the easiest so you can demonstrate success before moving on to more difficult ones. An initial success will win you credibility and will also give you the experience you need to pursue more challenging ideas.

Remember that you do have a 'day job,' so you need to be conscientious and deliberate about the time and energy that you use to pursue ideas. Don't frustrate yourself by taking on more than you can handle. Remember, pursuing ideas is not easy, nor is it something that will garner you instant accolades. Continue to conduct your assigned duties in a satisfactory manner. Ideal intrapreneurs know how to continue to do their day jobs well; this competence helps them gain trust and space to work on their ideas. Conversely, if you're not doing your assigned job properly, you'll be subject to greater amounts of scrutiny and oversight, which will limit your ability to pursue ideas.

Don't think that having too many ideas is *bad*. Having too many ideas is good, as these ideas can compete with each other in your mind and for your time and energy. However, trying to pursue too many ideas at the same time is not wise. On the other hand, having too few ideas – placing all your eggs in one basket, as the saying is – is also unwise. So, you need to strike the right balance. The only way you're going to recognize the right balance is through experience. My suggestion is to start with a few and then scale up over time as you figure out how to prioritize and focus your attention.

Idea Mobilization

The image of the lone employee who comes up with a billion-dollar idea unaided, while appealing from a Hollywood perspective, doesn't represent reality. Academia might be the only place you find lone-star innovators today (and very few of them, too). The complexity of our society places the solo innovator at a disadvantage – a reality that employees need to recognize. Instead, it's vital for employees to understand the value of social networks and the economics of managing them.

In most organizations there are barriers to the free flow of ideas. Some of these are structural – the result of a work environment that is organized into units – and some of them are cultural – the result of such things as competition, infighting, or mistrust. Despite such barriers, however, creative and dedicated employees can still find ways to circumvent obstacles and mobilize their ideas. For example, superior listening skills are critical to being able to mobilize ideas. Employees are very willing to talk about their ideas but are seldom as willing to listen. One strategy I've used in workshops is to charge employees with the task of keeping a notebook and writing down how many ideas they *hear about* in a given week. As the number of ideas they record flattens out, their focus moves on to (1) the sources of the ideas, (2) the channels through which the ideas are received (e.g., if an employee receives a lot of ideas from electronic communications, trying to balance this out with face-to-face interactions), and (3) the characteristics or dimensions of the ideas (e.g., if most ideas have similar dimensions, moving towards a more balanced portfolio of ideas of varying dimensions).

TRUST

A critical impediment to idea sharing and mobilization is the *perceived* need to mistrust one's co-workers. I highlight the word *perceived* as, to the best of my knowledge, most of the time mistrust is not justified. As most of the research on trust has shown us, trust takes many forms and has varying degrees.[47] You don't need to trust an individual completely (to the extent that you trust your spouse, say) in order to share ideas and know-how. All you really need to do is to have some trust (more accurately, confidence) in your colleague's professionalism. Trust based on mutual respect allows you to rely on the feedback you receive from colleagues. At the next level, you need to trust that a colleague will not try to take the credit for your ideas. This is a common but in my experience largely unjustified fear. Chances are high that most employees are too busy to play with other people's ideas; moreover, it's not that easy to run with someone else's ideas.

Several strategies may help you collaborate to generate and mobilize ideas. First, when encountering a problem at work, try not to frame it negatively; instead consider how you might address the problem positively, through ideation. Second, when you do encounter problems you think are broadly relevant to company goals, share them with trusted peers and work to co-develop ideas for solutions. For example, you might schedule a brown-bag lunch at which you can present the problem, begin a discussion, and hear other points of view. This initial processing will help you begin to refine your idea. It will also start your community thinking of it as a work in progress, and this will help you when you need to make a formal submission and request for resources. Third, find trusted people to help you improve the idea and develop it further. Build a viable team. As noted earlier, the lone inventor is a myth.

Remember, too, that few inventors are able to succeed every time. Consider the case of Lars Rasmussen and Jens Rasmussen, who created the stellar Google application Google Maps. The Rasmussen brothers also created Google Wave, which failed to live up to its promise to be a social collaborative platform to replace e-mail. Being successful once is no guarantee of continuing success, so collaborating with people and getting different perspectives is crucial. Be open to the concept of co-creation, and be prepared to give up some control of your idea's trajectory in order to benefit from the expertise of others. When collaborating, be prepared to argue, debate, build, break down, and strategize about the idea. I urge you to err on the side of sharing more, rather than less, and being more trusting of your colleagues.

MANAGING YOUR NETWORK
The more you share an idea, the greater the chance that you will enrich and develop it. Describe it in a few paragraphs. Then, describe your idea to a friend exactly as you wrote it. Chances are, you've already refined how you communicate the idea. Furthermore, your conversation may help develop it further and provide you with other factors to consider or other people to talk to. Now, imagine how much farther you might be able to develop the idea by sharing it with more people.

Intrapreneurs can learn from entrepreneurs how to manage their social networks and share their ideas. Entrepreneurs recognize the power of networks and spend a lot of time and energy building them. They understand that they need to rely on these networks for everything from financial investment to sources of referrals and contacts to build their organization. As such, they gravitate toward social events where they rub shoulders with people who can advance their cause. In these settings, they share their ideas with intoxicating passion.

They develop 'elevator pitches' for their ideas (a concept that will be discussed in chapter 6) and know how to target their communications to their intended audiences. Intrapreneurs need to do the same within the confines of their organization.

Too often, as employees, we limit our professional relationships to the people we interact with frequently and work with directly. This limits our ability to mobilize our ideas. To be truly intrapreneurial we need to realize that we are more likely to receive new information from people who are *different* from us than from people who are similar to us. Google has a practice of hosting regular 'Tech Talks.' Speakers include distinguished researchers from around the world but also experts in other fields, such as artists, writers, and chefs. Employees love Tech Talks, and Google values them as well. In fact, the number of talks an employee has hosted is noted in the employee's performance reviews.[48] According to social scientist Mark Granovetter, 'whatever is to be diffused can reach a larger number of people, and traverse a greater social distance . . . when passed through weak ties rather than strong.'[49] In short, seeking out opportunities to build ties with people from different perspectives will help you diffuse your ideas.

Even for the introverts or bystanders, I strongly recommend actively engaging with your organization beyond the specifics of your task assignments. You'll find that your peers often just need your ears and are willing to share their ideas. In addition, if you think you don't have ideas, the simple task of participating in the listening process and sharing feedback will lead you to discover your own ideas and thoughts. Moreover, building social connections is much easier when you are not under pressure of time to achieve a specific goal such as getting feedback on your idea. Attending internal and external events in your areas of interest is a sure way to begin to construct these networks. In addition, in most fields there are an abundance of scholarly journals and practitioner magazines that publish material of interest. I strongly urge you to survey the sources on a regular basis for ideas and insights and see how you might use them inside your organization. Sending your feedback on ideas to the authors of articles that interest you is another way to engage in dialogue and expand your professional networks. Having had the pleasure of receiving feedback from readers of my own articles, I can tell you that most authors love to enter into dialogue with their readers. In several instances, I have been able to connect readers to other professionals in their field to help them get better answers to the questions they asked me!

Other ways in which you can build social networks include (1) attending open houses and events hosted by other teams and units, and (2) identifying professors at your local university who have similar interests to your own and volunteering to mentor students, speak to classes, and/or attend research talks that take place on campus. These are excellent venues in which to learn and get feedback from young minds and free thinkers who might be working on cutting-edge solutions to your problems.

Conclusion

We need not feel overwhelmed by the seeming unruliness of the world of ideas. We have seen that there are ways to create a nurturing environment for idea generation and to develop systems within an organization for capturing ideas. This chapter has explored some ways in which ideas can be harnessed, defined, categorized and presented in a form that an organization can use. By understanding the type of idea and its potential impact, an organization can determine which route the idea should take from its inception as a raw thought in the mind of its creator to become a processed, public artifact that can be leveraged by the organization.

After idea generation and mobilization comes the next phase of the intrapreneurship process – idea screening and advocacy. A number of factors may trigger the transition to this phase. For example, (1) you have exhausted all personal contacts and resources in the pursuit of the idea and can't bootleg any more resources to develop the idea further; (2) the organization has issued a specific call for ideas in the area that you are working in and is willing to invest in new ideas; and/or (3) the idea is ready for consideration by the organization. In short, there is nothing more the individual employee can do with the idea; it is ready for experimentation and eventual commercialization.

4 Advocating and Screening

Once ideas have been generated and mobilized, they need to be evaluated in more detail. Making decisions without good information is a risky proposition; hence, an organization must have robust processes to collect and synthesize information on ideas and use this information in decision making. Through the process of advocacy, we find champions for ideas. During the screening process, the organization evaluates the ideas that the advocate has championed, including how well the ideas meet current and future needs.

Evaluating ideas calls for *acting* on ideas; many organizations' Achilles heel isn't generating ideas, but doing something with them. Most organizations make the costly error of collecting ideas with no plan in mind on what to do with them: costly not only because they lose opportunities to advance the organization but also because of the opportunity costs – the time and effort spent on collecting ideas that could have been used for other purposes. Consider the case of a global technology organization that flourished during the Internet boom days. As one senior executive remarked, 'We were not only running on all cylinders, but were actually borrowing cylinders and fuel rods to keep up with demand.' Founded in 1990 by three graduate students, the company grew to almost 200 employees within five years. When its glory days came to a screeching halt with the dot-com bust, the organization had to do some hard thinking to redefine its business strategies. Its solution was to engage employees by soliciting ideas on the company's future. Under the slogan '10 for 10: 10 big ideas for the next 10 years!', they set a goal to think big and to identify ten broad areas for growth.

The company created online 'idea drop boxes' where employees could submit their ideas by filling out a brief online questionnaire.

Within a week, the company received more than 500 ideas, and by the end of four weeks, they had more than 1,200 ideas – a little more than six ideas per employee! As one executive remarked, 'We underestimated the whole [idea solicitation] thing . . . Employees were scared . . . Their friends were losing jobs, companies like ours were closing, venture capitalists were getting tighter with the purse strings . . . All of this contributed to fear . . . Employees wanted to help the company, and themselves, by sharing their best ideas that would not only keep us afloat but secure a better future . . .' Getting ideas was easy, but unfortunately the organization didn't have a process for advocating and screening them. The end result, according to a statement made by the CEO, was an 'absolute disaster . . . We ended up pissing off more staff than those we appeased, lost good employees who felt their ideas were not duly considered, and what hurts me most, employees lost faith in the organization as a place that valued ideas . . . Front-line programmers and system designers who are our most important assets felt ideas got promoted based on one's political network and clout . . . We all lost, I will never do this again . . . We might never recover the trust and camaraderie that we had prior to this undertaking.'

When it comes to screening ideas, we're dealing with unknowns. Most companies haven't learned how to handle ideas, so they try to feed ideas into established processes like gate reviews, which they normally use to screen project proposals. Project Management Offices (PMOs) ensure that projects meet operational and strategic objectives, but screening for projects fundamentally differs from sifting through ideas. Most of the time a project already has a well-developed logical plan that just needs to be put into an implementation schedule. Even somewhat exploratory projects, such as market research, still have distinct beginnings and endings that make them predictable. As such, well-structured processes and historic data are useful in the project evaluation process. Ideas, however, are more nebulous. Trying to screen ideas the same way we do project plans results in flawed outcomes. Ideas are best screened as areas of investment or thoughts to bet on, not as artifacts that can be planned to the last detail with all contingencies and risks accounted for.

Organizations need advocates to move truly innovative ideas through the organization and secure resources to implement them. Without advocates, great ideas wither and die on the vine, damaging the intrapreneurial spirit of the organization. Yet idea advocacy is seldom appreciated in most organizations. Too often, only those who create or commercialize ideas are rewarded, while those who exert themselves to promote the ideas of their peers are neglected. Idea advocates are needed to communicate the value of an idea across both hierarchical layers and vertical silos.

Consider the process followed by the IT organization at British Petroleum (BP). Under the leadership of P.P. Darukhanavala (Daru), CTO of BP, the organization adopted a rigorous process for evaluating technology innovations. The process starts with surveying BP's business units and asking the question, 'What do you wish you could do in your business if technology could be found or created to enable it?'[1] The ideas that come in are passed on to BP's network of suppliers and partners, who propose solutions, which are then screened based on the following three criteria derived from the venture capitalist model: (1) relevance (i.e., to BP's business needs), (2) technical readiness (i.e., based on emerging versus established technologies), and (3) economic viability.[2] The ideas that survive the screening process are presented to BP's leadership, and a percentage of those are selected to move on to the experimentation and pilot phases. Because of the rigorous nature of the screening process and the requirement to communicate the results of each phase to BP's decision makers, the organization is able to cull ideas that are valuable to the organization. 'Some of the innovative programs – called "game changer initiatives" within BP – have generated business impacts up to $100 million.'[3]

The discussion in the following pages starts with an examination of the organization's responsibility for facilitating idea advocacy and screening. The organization needs to formalize the role of the idea advocate, design communication mechanisms to connect employees to idea advocates and idea advocates to one another, build platforms to support idea advocacy, and reward idea advocates for sticking their necks out. The organization also needs to put in place a variety of mechanisms to screen ideas – democratic mechanisms to support the evaluation of ideas (e.g., by leveraging the wisdom of crowds), mechanisms to bring external stakeholders into the process, and mechanisms for choosing the ideas that will move into the experimentation stage of the process. The employees' role in the process is examined next. Employees need to choose and ally themselves with advocates who can help them promote their ideas. They also need to have a realistic view of the idea screening process – realizing that for every idea that survives the screening process there might be a hundred that were passed over. They need to be aware of the pressures on the organization (e.g., resource constraints) and also learn how to refine their ideas through the feedback received during the screening process.

Organizational Perspective

The idea advocacy and screening stage gives employees across the organization, even those who don't have ideas of their own to contribute, a chance to engage with the intrapreneurship process. The intrapreneurial organization will embed idea advocacy principles in its culture, through dedicated resources and formal channels. It will also provide a structured screening process that extends to its network of customers and partners.

Idea Advocacy

An idea advocate is someone who effectively communicates the value of an idea to other people. Most academic treatises on organizational innovation ignore idea advocacy. We have been told to build cultures that tolerate failure, encourage open communication, and encourage diversity, but not to identify potential advocates to promote ideas. In the example below, we'll see how far an idea can go with the right advocate.

In a large manufacturing organization, a twenty-year veteran employee discovered a novel way to increase production by twenty units per 110 minutes. On several occasions the employee tried to get his boss and supervisors to listen to his idea, but failed every time. As he recalled, 'they did not care . . . they did not have any reason to help the factory . . . all they cared about was their own job.' Unbeknownst to the employee, however, the factory management and its union representatives were involved in an initiative to improve productivity and quality on the factory floor. During a visit by members of the corporate engineering team, a curious engineer was trying to figure out why certain materials were left in one part of the factory, disrupting the workflow and risking damage to raw materials that were being moved too often. He commissioned a small meeting with the factory staff, and it was then that he had a chance to hear about the employee's innovative workaround. The engineer took the necessary time and resources to understand the proposed solution and worked with the factory worker to arrive at a new process design that was approved by the union and corporate leaders.

Although he was beloved by his peers, the factory worker in this story didn't have the organizational capital to get anyone to listen to or move his idea. He needed an advocate who believed in his idea and was ready to support it. Had it not been for the engineer, the employee's idea would never have seen the light of day, and the inefficiencies in the factory would have persisted. Innovative organizations such as Tesco, a large supermarket chain in the United Kingdom, recognize that 'frontline employees often have . . . better ideas about how to improve performance,' and instead of relying on chance contributions from employees, the company tells employees the needs of the organization in straightforward language – ideas are valuable if they are 'better for customers, simpler for staff, and cheaper for Tesco.'[4]

FORMALIZING IDEA ADVOCATES

Employees need access to idea advocates in each zone of innovation. Furthermore, since some of the most interesting and radical ideas fall outside these zones, idea advocates should know how to operate in the gray areas, remain open to changes, and recognize stale orthodoxies, or 'the standard industry practices, if you will, that silently strangle radical ideas.'[5] Idea advocates are needed within each of the various functional units of the organization so that ideas within these silos can be promoted. Employees within a functional area should know about and have access to the idea advocates in other units. An organization will also be well served by having a 'general idea advocate,' an individual (or individuals, depending on the size of the organization) who can expedite ideas that (1) don't fit neatly into a functional area, or (2) haven't yet reached an appropriate contact person. Ideas submitted to general advocates can then be routed to functional areas if they are deemed to be applicable to a given unit, or can be shared with multiple units if the idea is applicable across units.

It is also important to identify advocates for externally oriented ideas – ideas that may relate to customers or business partners of the organization. A single 'point person' should be identified to field ideas relevant to 'gold clients' and business partners (also known as global accounts and highly valued customers). This person would normally be the primary manager of the organization's relationship with these clients, and would have deep knowledge of the customers, including their preferences, needs, and challenges. For other clients, advocates could be appointed to field ideas related to the various industries (e.g., health care, education, government) or other logical categories (e.g., geographic areas) of interest to the organization.

Idea advocates for incremental ideas are best chosen from within functional divisions of the organization. These individuals should have achieved a level of expertise that earns them the respect and trust of their peers, and should ideally have the time and resources to encourage idea generation, meet with idea creators, push problems of interest, and continuously draw attention to areas that need new ideas. Idea advocates for radical ideas must have a broad expertise across departments. These individuals should ideally have a good understanding of the strategy of the organization, its current and future environments, its external networks, and the research and development efforts within the organization. Advocates for radical ideas should have senior roles and the power to act on these kinds of ideas, and should be given a mandate to take on projects with a higher risk profile. The resources to fund these ideas shouldn't come from departmental (or unit) budgets, but directly from corporate budgets, so as not to disadvantage or favor any unit relative to the others.

One company that has successfully implemented an advocacy program is Air Products and Chemicals, Inc., a Fortune 500 company whose main focus is the supply of gases and chemicals to industrial and medical customers. I visited Air Products in 2006 to learn how they managed ideas and was impressed by the processes they had developed for identifying idea advocates across the entire organization. The company was organized into four main domains and met the challenges of idea advocacy by forming the Corporate Development Office (CDO). The role of the CDO is to (1) ensure that the company has a healthy business portfolio, (2) ensure that the portfolio meets and exceeds investors' profitability and growth expectations, (3) ensure that the company is well positioned to generate solid, sustainable returns for the foreseeable future, and (4) critically examine performance using internal and external criteria. The CDO does not get involved in the day-to-day running of the business units. Instead, it studies new ideas that have high risks and a potentially high payoff. One of the major functions of the CDO is to engage the senior leaders of the organization with risky or radical ideas that don't neatly fall within an established business group. Each business group has idea advocates and screening procedures designed to meet the nuances of the divisions' cultures, work practices, and knowledge domains. The business units are responsible for ideas that fall neatly within their areas of expertise, while ideas in the gray spaces (between two zones) are managed by cross-functional teams with guidance from the CDO, and ideas in the white space (outside any of the individual business units) are advocated for and screened by the CDO. The structure helps ensure that no idea can roam aimlessly around the organization without finding a home.

PROMOTING COMMUNICATION

Good communication is central to the process of advocating for and screening ideas. It is obvious that idea advocates need to communicate freely and fully with idea creators. Less obviously but equally importantly, idea advocates must also communicate with one another to share ideas and best practices.

The process for advocating ideas should be transparent. Transparency will encourage employees to have confidence in the process. An employee should know where to submit an idea, how long will it take for an idea advocate to review it, and when the idea will receive feedback. Leading organizations have built idea advocacy maps that work in the following way. The minute an idea is submitted, it's given a unique ID number that can be used to track its progress as it's reviewed and considered by the idea advocate. An employee can ensure that the idea is electronically submitted to the right idea advocate, or the system can route it to the appropriate person. The idea advocate then sends comments back to the idea creator via the system, or sets up a meeting. In this way, the idea creator is kept abreast of what's going on – a key component in reducing any anxiety the employee may feel about the prospects for success. This electronic system also ensures that the organization has a record of all ideas submitted and the feedback received. At Washington Mutual (before it was acquired by Chase), I spent time studying how innovation processes worked within their IT unit. They created an online repository where ideas could be submitted, allowing peer-to-peer feedback to support the screening process. Through collaboration with their mentors, idea creators were able to refine their ideas, understand their business value, and learn how best to communicate their ideas to the executive team. Another way to provide transparency is to occasionally host 'town hall' meetings where employees can speak directly to idea advocates. The goal is to show that the process is inclusive and participatory, thereby giving it credibility.

Idea advocates should regularly exchange advocacy strategies with and cross-pollinate ideas from different units. If an idea advocate in marketing based in Spain gets an idea that is better suited for engineering based in China, the movement of the idea is facilitated by frequent communication. Moreover, as a matter of routine, idea advocates should be able to take inventory of all incoming ideas to try to identify trends and patterns. If a large percentage of the ideas received globally happen to relate to a single client or business line, the organization should attend carefully to this space. Each individual idea advocate will only have a *local* view of the organization, so it is through dialogue that a *global* view will be constructed. Otherwise, the 'right hand won't know what the left is doing' or, worse yet, the 'right hand may wash away what the left did.' Idea advocates should also have opportunities to talk regularly with leaders across the organization so as to keep management abreast of the kinds of ideas they're hearing about. They also need to hear from management both about the various challenges within organizational units (in order to be aware of areas and problems that need ideas) and about strategies and plans for future growth.

PLATFORMS FOR ADVOCACY

Organizations should also leave room for serendipity in idea advocacy. Identifying formal idea advocates is important, but the organization should also encourage all employees to advocate for ideas. The organization needs to design forums and platforms where employees can showcase their ideas and interact with interested parties. When idea creators have opportunities to present their ideas, advocates may emerge from among the employees to whom the ideas are presented. Organizations such as Microsoft, Hewlett Packard, Google, Intel, and Johnson & Johnson, have sponsored 'idea fests,' fairs where employees display posters or give demonstrations of ideas to internal and external stakeholders. By calling company-wide attention to employees' ideas and giving them visibility, this forum gives employees a chance to practice presenting the merits of the idea, hear direct feedback on it, and refine their thinking. And the events produce results for organizations. For example, in a recent 'Innovation Days' event at Cemex, 'ten stars emerged from 250 submissions, including a new way to cast cement that allows contractors to double the returns they get on their investments in casting molds.'[6] Most employees who participate in these events are extremely pleased by the feedback and interactions they have. As one employee at Microsoft told me after an idea fest, 'I never knew so many people cared about my work and the small idea I had . . . apparently, I hit the jackpot . . . [I need to] go now and revise it to make it better.' Employees enjoy the chance to show-case their work, interact with peers on a creative level, and recruit new advocates for their ideas. In several cases, executives have told me that the most beneficial outcomes of such events are that employ-ees extend their social networks, appreciate the ideas and work of their colleagues across departments, and become advocates for their own units.

Some organizations have gone a step farther and begun to invite their major clients, customers, and business partners to these events, providing external validation for ideas and initiatives. In some cases, organizations have found that external stakeholders are willing to assume the risk of developing ideas, to participate in experiments, to be test-beds for concepts, and even to partially fund the experimenta-tion process. (However, while inviting external stakeholders can be beneficial, the organization needs to ensure that intellectual property protection agreements are in place, and that the infrastructure is in place to capture stakeholders' ideas and provide adequate feedback. If mishandled, involving stakeholders can be damaging to an organiza-tion's credibility.)

When organizations invite customers to participate in idea fests, they use these opportunities to help them judge the value of ideas. For example, through soliciting customers' feedback, they get a sense of which ideas are immediately interesting to the marketplace. Some-times customers take an active role in supporting ideas. For such col-laboration to be successful, organizations need to know (1) why they are inviting their customers, (2) which customers will provide useful feedback, (3) how they are going to use the feedback provided, and (4) how customers will be informed about how their feedback may be used. In most cases, companies report great success with idea fests that include external stakeholders. For example, a chief innovation officer once remarked to me that, 'best case we get them excited about ideas that may change their business in the next three years . . . worst case we energize their thinking and solidify the fact that we take inno-vation seriously.' Survey data also support this view: 'A recent McKinsey survey found that 20% of companies have opened up their innovation processes to employees and customers and they report a 20% rise in the number of innovations, on average.'[7] Some companies have taken this strategy a step farther and have begun to co-host idea fests. For example, companies such as Boeing and Northrup Grumman invite their business partners to events where they discuss and advocate for ideas collaboratively. These ideas are then worked on by both parties jointly.

Idea fests should tackle ideas ranging from incremental to radical and internal to external. Having a wide range of ideas will be the best use of your resources. You might create categories such as 'wild and crazy' or 'low-cost hits' within which people can submit their ideas – and give out awards based on feedback. In addition, idea fests can be organized *within* each unit of the organization. These efforts don't need to be as resource and time intensive as the ones described above, but can be as simple as having an extended department meeting every two months at which employees can showcase and talk about ideas. These forums are an especially effective way to promote incremental ideas for improving the processes of the unit, addressing customer challenges, or even signaling areas for further exploration and conversation with allied units.

REWARDING IDEA ADVOCACY

If an organization really wants to cultivate strong idea advocates, it needs to recognize their efforts. One way to do this is to create a 'Giraffe Award' for advocates who 'stick their necks out to support risky ideas.' Since not all ideas are equal, advocates who stick their necks out for radical ideas should be rewarded more than those who take the easier path of advocating for incremental ideas – although not in a manner that makes it harder to move incremental ideas ahead. (Perhaps all idea advocates could be asked to support a certain number of radical ideas per year, or per quarter.) Idea advocates who have developed ideas from sectors of the organization not traditionally interested in intrapreneurship, or sectors where it is more difficult to come up with ideas, should also receive special consideration when rewards are assigned.

Even if idea advocates fail to implement ideas of any significance, an organization should still reward their efforts. In the beginning, failure will be the norm and successes the exception. If you reward only successful efforts, you can kill the process before it develops roots and takes shape. When running the Engaged Enterprise, I had a simple rule when it came to advocacy of ideas: *Activity doesn't necessarily translate into accomplishment, but without activity there would be no accomplishment.* Employees were urged to advocate for ideas, and spend the necessary time and resources engaging in activities such as working with idea creators and developing idea concepts and proposals. Even though few of these initial ideas were successful, getting idea advocates to make time for this role while carrying out their so-called day jobs was essential for building an innovative enterprise. Idea advocacy must be a top priority in promoting an enterprise-wide culture of intrapreneurship.

The practices outlined in this section should serve as a good foundation for a culture that values advocacy. The following questions will help you gauge your progress:

- Are employees talking about ideas developed by their peers or are they still touting their own?
- Are employees taking the time to listen to their peers' ideas or are they too busy to be bothered?
- Are employees seeking out ways to champion ideas not directly tied to their day jobs?
- Are there ideas coming from advocates in sectors of the organization that were previously silent?
- Are the idea advocates overworked and starting to complain?

If possible, you should manage the workload – the inventory of ideas – allocated to each advocate, as well as the resources designated for advocacy. Doing so can be difficult, however, because, as we found at the Engaged Enterprise, our busiest individuals were also the most popular idea advocates. These advocates would take time from their busy schedules and even make time outside of work to help employees develop ideas. Simple market economics dictate that good idea advocates will be chosen more often and hence be in greater demand. The organization needs to find ways to manage the demands on their time to prevent overwork and burnout.

Idea Screening

There's little point in collecting ideas without a process for screening them. Simply collecting ideas will lead to frustration. When employees invest time and energy in documenting ideas and submitting them for evaluation, their efforts should be acknowledged.

Idea screening can be a difficult and uncomfortable process for both the idea submitters and the screeners. If an idea isn't selected, the submitter will want to know why, and may question the judgment of the screeners. For screeners, the most difficult task is identifying and selecting a few of the most promising ideas from a vast collection. Inevitably, good ideas will be turned down because of limited resources for idea development. In addition, screeners face the possibility that their decision about a given idea will be viewed as political.

However difficult it may be, idea screening must happen. No organization can fund all ideas (not even great places for innovation with piles of cash, such as Google!). Even when firms commit millions or billions of dollars toward funding ideas, not every idea will make the cut. Given this reality, successfully intrapreneurial organizations make sure that both idea submitters and screeners understand how difficult the task of idea screening is.

LEVERAGING THE WISDOM OF CROWDS

'Prediction markets' are a popular mechanism that has worked well for screening incremental and radical ideas. Motorola successfully capitalized on this technique in 2003 when it built ThinkTank, a system for collecting ideas. Thousands of suggestions poured in, and the teams that were supposed to weed through them were overwhelmed. To solve this problem, Motorola brought its employees into the selection process. Using prediction market technology, employees voted for the ideas they thought had the most business potential. Ideas that received at least five votes were eligible for the ThinkTank Idea eXchange (TIX), an internal prediction market in which each idea was initially valued at $10 per share.[8] Any employee who wanted to participate received $100,000 with which to start buying stock in the ideas he or she liked best. As employees bought or sold shares, the value of the various ideas rose – or fell. After thirty days, an idea review team determined which of the top-valued ideas to pursue. Winners were judged based on their stock performance, and participants who held stock in the winning ideas got a bonus.

Hollywood Stock Exchange (HSX; www.hsx.com) is a prediction market that allows online users to 'buy' shares of actors, actresses, and movies. Players use their purchases to predict which movies will be blockbusters and which will bomb. Buying inexpensive shares in an up-and-coming actor whose next movie becomes a blockbuster creates 'wealth.' Buying more expensive shares in an established actor and seeing the actor's movie flop results in loss of 'wealth.' Other prediction markets that have sprung up include Intrade (www.intrade.com), a market where people trade stock in political figures and current events. Prediction markets such as HSX and Intrade have proved to be uncannily accurate. For instance, in 2006, HSX correctly predicted thirty-two of the thirty-nine big-category Oscar nominees, and seven out of the eight top category winners. The idea selection process of intrapreneurial businesses could benefit from setting up internal prediction markets. New software tools allow just about anyone to build a prediction market. The trick to developing a successful one is engaging enough people. The more people you involve, the more of a 'crowd' you have. Building internal prediction markets for idea screening is increasing in popularity. Organizations of all sorts are trying to set up these markets to facilitate a democratic and participatory idea screening process. The following points should be considered when setting up these markets.

Establishing the rules: All markets have rules. Rules determine the behavior of the buyers and sellers, the governance of the exchange and trading mechanisms, and the market environment. Clear rules prevent confusion about roles and responsibilities and describe what constitutes acceptable behavior in the market. If adequately described, market rules promote good behavior – such as fair trading and efficient exchanges – and curb tendencies to 'game' the procedure.

When setting up a prediction market, the first thing to establish is who can participate. Is the market open to all employees or only a subset? Does the market involve participants outside the organization (e.g., customers, business partners)? The rules should also specify what participants can do. Can every participant be a buyer and a seller, or are some individuals limited to posting their ideas while others are able to evaluate them? As we'll see in later sections, some companies stipulate that players must rate or comment on a certain number of ideas before submitting their own idea. Penalties prevent people from abusing the market, sometimes by specifying what happens when they break the rules. These penalties range from fines to more serious and permanent consequences, such as being banned from the market. The rules should also clarify the role played by the organization that runs the market: how the organization will conduct daily settlement, provide information about buyers and sellers, or resolve conflicts. For simple internal markets, rules need not be elaborate, but establishing them up front prevents surprises later on.

Creating idea-capturing mechanisms: Once the rules of the market are in place, an organization should devise a semi-structured approach to capturing ideas in the market. A too-structured approach might hinder the capture of more complex ideas, but a completely unstructured format may prevent fruitful comparisons of ideas. Idea submissions need to have a common set of structured data, and the key information should include (1) the name or title of the idea; (2) an abstract or executive summary; (3) the expected benefit from implementing the idea; (4) the organizational impacts of the idea; (5) the external impacts of the idea on customers, business partners, and other external stakeholders; (6) the costs and level of investment (both real costs and opportunity costs); (7) the risks of implementing the idea, and how to manage those risks; (8) thoughts on next steps to develop the idea further; (9) clarification of assumptions; and (10) the names of supporters or advocates, along with their feedback. These fields will help a reviewer get a good sense of the idea, its impact, and how the idea might be developed from concept to implementation.

In addition to these structured fields, the idea creator should be given some space to include additional material. For example, some idea creators may be better at describing their idea orally or visually than in a text format. Currently available information technologies make it easy to create and append audio files, illustrations, PowerPoint slides, or even video recordings. The goal is to capture and document the idea in the best way possible.

Ideas should also be submitted in appropriate categories that are relevant to the organization: related products or service lines, management practices, information technology, and so on. As well, idea creators should categorize the idea as either 'incremental' or 'radical' and identify which units within the organization might be most appropriate to implement or review their idea. Another option is to use tagging, which allows individuals to use their own terms to define their ideas. This bottom-up method for identifying information artifacts is gaining wider usage: many people already tag their photos, blog posts, and the material they read online. Tagging ideas may evoke some categories and keywords that may not have been conceived a priori. Moreover, using tags allows you to search and gather ideas that are similar or related through the building of tag clouds and maps.

Seeking feedback on ideas: Once ideas are submitted and categorized, the next step is to tap into the wisdom of the crowds. Your first design decision is what form of feedback mechanisms would work best, and there are hundreds to choose from. The most basic is the 'thumbs up' or 'thumbs down' rating system. This choice is attractive because it's easy for a reviewer to use and requires minimal effort; however, its simplicity is also a drawback since it can't capture nuanced feedback. An alternative is to have individuals rank the idea in terms of the various dimensions discussed above. This approach requires a clear explanation of the evaluation criteria so that the reviewer doesn't misinterpret them. Examples of the two extremes and the middle should be included. An additional option is to allow reviewers to add comments and reactions to the ideas using simple text boxes. While this task is more complex than simply choosing a thumbs-up or assigning a number of stars, it begins a richer dialogue between the idea creator and the organization at large. A reviewer's comments may trigger feedback from the idea creator or from other reviewers. For example, it's common for reviewers to ask questions about details or to clarify assumptions. These posts trigger further dialogue, thus helping to refine the ideas. For example, Swarovski's 'Design a Watch Challenge' (http://www.enlightened-watch-design-contest.com/) directly targeted designers. Participants could use a watch configuration tool or upload a freely created design. Using the former, they could design a watch using 24 components and 108 different Swarovski gemstones. Thirteen hundred configured designs and 700 freely created designs were submitted. In a follow-up contest, users could design jewelry. This contest yielded 3,000 designs.

Choosing parameters: Identity or anonymity? Volunteerism or required participation? Should the identity of the idea creator be provided to the reviewers or kept anonymous? When people review anonymously posted ideas, the idea creator's personality and influence are taken out of the equation, with the intent of promoting more frank feedback. However, anonymity is no panacea.[9] Anonymity can neutralize credibility. Some ideas are intimately tied to their creators. Some creators have enough credibility and expertise in the organization to justify giving them resources to try an idea, while other, less credible creators would have a more difficult time attempting the same idea. In addition, comments and feedback may have to be evaluated in the context of who submitted them. Some comments might get more traction if given by a senior, more experienced researcher rather than an employee who has limited knowledge of a given process or the intricacies of a product line. Anonymity hides this difference. As well, there are always some individuals who abuse the protection of anonymity to defame ideas and provide unproductive comments.

Explore the dynamics in your organization and choose what works best in your environment. If you're dealing with ideas that are within a given community or domain (say engineering or IT), and you're seeking feedback from people within these communities, it might be fine to have ideas reviewed anonymously. Most people submitting and reviewing ideas will have the same level of knowledge and expertise. In addition, it might be helpful to require people to review ideas as part of the idea submission process, as this will encourage members to learn from each other and increase their collegiality and sense of community. On the other hand, anonymity might not be ideal on an organization-wide level. Here, people would need to know who submitted an idea and what department it came from. Also, to enhance the viability of an idea, you might want to study not only the comments but also where the comments originated. Suppose one idea drew only twenty comments but the comments came from six different departments, and another idea drew thirty comments but all from one department; what could you read into this? I would suggest that the first idea has a broader impact across the organization and might be signaling a deeper need, while the second one is a local idea that affects only one area of the organization.

You also need to determine whether submitting feedback should be voluntary or mandatory.[10] Some organizations have witnessed tremendous results with volunteerism. In other organizations with no requirement to comment on ideas, feedback has been limited, completely absent, or inadequate. Consider the case of the IT department at Washington Mutual. As part of their innovation program, employees could only submit ideas if they agreed to rate and comment on three other ideas. This effectively engaged the community in the intrapreneurship process. To build a culture that values intrapreneurship, I would recommend making the submission of feedback mandatory. The reason for this is simple: it drives home the point that if you expect the organization to review and consider your idea, you should take the time to consider ideas from others in the organization. This builds a sense of community and highlights the fact that it takes the entire organization to move ideas from conception to implementation.

Setting up the trading unit: It's common to use shares as the unit of trading. People can buy, or be allotted, a number of shares to get started. An idea creator can decide how many shares are needed to implement the idea – for example, an idea creator who thinks $100,000 is needed to develop the idea into a product or service could sell

10,000 shares at $10. In one organization, the company used a formula based on a simple menu of items and their cost. Everything needed to develop an idea was assigned a price, and the idea creator could then do the rough math and come up with a cost. In another case, a management consulting firm decided to use broad categories to decide on the cost of the ideas based on analysis of the historical data. For example, marketing ideas that were of an incremental nature would cost $20,000 to $30,000; marketing ideas that were more radical, where there might be a greater need for research and analysis, would cost $100,000 to $200,000; engineering ideas that were incremental (e.g., small product modifications) would cost anywhere from $200,000 to $400,000; and so on. An idea creator could use these as guidelines for valuing the idea.

Engaging the crowd: Rating, for the most part, involves only passive engagement with the idea. Anyone can rate an idea and share comments on it. However, when participants decide to commit resources to an idea by investing virtual money in it, they become actively engaged with the idea. When employees become active players in the organization's internal prediction market, they have a vested interest in seeing the idea develop further. They have an interest in advocating on behalf of the idea, and they will want to support the idea creator. In addition, while there are no limits on the number of ratings an employee can provide, they should be given a limited amount of virtual money to spend. This helps the employees focus their attention on the ideas that they value and has the added benefit of reinforcing awareness that there are many ideas competing for limited resources.

Designing the trading dynamics: You should aim for simplicity when you set up the trading mechanisms for an internal idea market.[11] In external markets such as the stock market, the trading and monitoring mechanisms are geared to capture value for the individual. The goal is for people to make money on the stocks they trade by buying low and selling high. However, in private internal markets the goals are different. The goal is to make sure that the best ideas bubble up, and to provide criteria for choosing which ones to invest in and implement. In this type of market, trading mechanisms should be kept as simple as possible. The first priority is to ensure that people can buy shares in an idea through a simple application interface or website.

Once you develop an efficient market, you can make things a bit more complex by adding nuances to the trading mechanisms. For example, you can remove the fixed limit on an idea so that players can buy as many shares as they want – a small way to tweak the trading rules. Thus, if an idea is really good, it may attract a lot more 'buyers' than the idea creator had originally anticipated. This would be a good sign, signaling that people believe in the idea and concept, moving the idea to the top of the list for possible funding.

You could consider experimenting with a staged approach to trading, offering three or more time periods within which people can bid on ideas. At the end of each time period, trading is halted to see which ideas are getting the most attention in terms of various measures – such as the number of shares purchased or the number of positive ratings. The ideas are then sorted into three categories: raise, hold, and lower. Ideas that have received a lot of attention will have their values increased. Ideas in the middle keep their value unchanged. Ideas at the lower end may have their value lowered to see if this encourages more people to purchase them. The procedure simulates a financial market. The original idea creators may have either overvalued or undervalued their ideas, and this type of adjustment mechanism allows you to see if a price change stimulates purchases. In addition, having a set procedure for periodically evaluating and adjusting the market motivates people to invest in the ideas they care about quickly before the price changes.

You can continue to complicate the market dynamics with further tweaks, but in my experience, the adjustments outlined above are sufficient. While it's important to tailor the prediction market to the specific requirements of your organization, the more complex the trading rules, the greater the chance people will get confused and lose interest in participating. In addition, complexity may overburden the people who build and manage the system.

Determining the duration of the market: How long should you leave the market open? The best answer is long enough to collect useful information about the ideas and to engage employees in the intrapreneurship process. There are normally two kinds of markets: transient and permanent. Transient markets are created and closed down as needed. The market is open for a fixed period, during which trading is permitted, and then the market is closed. Permanent markets, like your neighborhood grocery store, remain open in perpetuity. These markets have a longer life and allow for trading at all times. An organization should decide which form of market fits its needs.

If you are just starting to use prediction markets in your organization, I suggest opening one for a fixed duration (a transient market).

This gives you an opportunity to learn from the experience, see how the market works, make the requisite design changes to any features of the market, and choose if or when to reopen it. Opening up a market for a short time also adds an element of suspense, and the time constraints will entice users to get into the market quickly in order to see how things work. The excitement of a first-time idea market energizes organizations.

If you've already experimented with transient idea markets, try a permanent market. Keep it running ad infinitum so employees can continuously contribute ideas and invest in them. Using the market as a mechanism for continual idea collection is a useful way to realize more value from the investment of creating the market. You could also set trading periods and calls for ideas of a particular kind. For example, decide that, on an annual basis, the third quarter of the year will be the trading period, and that the purpose of the trading period will be to decide which ideas to fund for the next annual budget cycle. During the beginning of this period, give users their trading currency and open the trading period – as in ringing the opening bell at the stock exchange. At the end of the trading period, the closing bell is rung, and input on the ideas is tallied up. In the ideal scenario, idea creators will use the pre-trading period to get feedback on their ideas, build a good base of community support, refine their ideas, and improve them in the hope that they will fare better in the next trading period.

Another option is to create special calls for ideas and trading. For example, if you're a management consulting firm that has identified a potential project to bid on and for which you need specific ideas, you might create a special call just for that project. You could create a task force to choose ideas for a proposal and ask for feedback from employees in specified departments of the organization. This is like creating a temporary special market for invited guests only.

Providing information within the market: When people enter an actual market, they should quickly be able to find things they want to buy, determine the price of the items, and proceed efficiently to the checkout. These features hold true in a virtual market as well. For example, a ticker bar might show how shares in the ideas are being sold and how many are left, or a bar graph might show the activity in the market for the last few hours. A table might be used to display links to ideas that the user is tracking and their current status – that is, how many shares are sold and any new comments posted. A good notifications tool alerts the user when other users post comments on ideas they have tagged. A good idea market website fosters community building; it should allow users to build profiles easily and quickly in order to share information about themselves and the projects they are working on, and to reach out to their colleagues and communicate with them about particular ideas. For example, let's say that Person A recognizes a potentially valuable idea and is not competent to review it, but knows Person X, who is an expert and can review it. There should be functionality available for Person A to quickly and easily e-mail a link to the idea to Person X, tag the idea in Person X's profile, and even send a note to encourage the idea creator to connect with Person X. Finally, the portal should have excellent information-collection capability. As a manager, you should be able to log on and get all relevant data on the site, including (1) the number of users on the site, (2) the items being traded, (3) the comments posted, and (4) the average number of shares purchased per idea. For example, in some organizations, managers may want to see the top ten most frequently viewed ideas, the top ten most valuable ideas, the top ten most commented on ideas, and so on. This information can be made available at different levels of detail, and the website should have the capability for drilling down to the different levels. Information dashboards enable managers to get a quick sense of how the organization is progressing, so they can get insights on the performance of key projects and make quick decisions. In most project management dashboards, projects are marked in red, yellow, or green on the screen. Similar thinking can be applied to an idea market dashboard. If participation – as determined by a combination of the number of users who have visited the site and the number who have posted comments – dips below a certain threshold, the manager should quickly be able to see this. The manager can then intervene – for example, by sending an e-mail to encourage people to contribute.

These guidelines identify the main design considerations related to building the market. A healthy market also provides a variety of access points, allowing users who are outside the idea creator's network to critique an idea or champion it. Though the particulars of its implementation and usage may vary, the idea market will help in the process of building a community of intrapreneurs.

BRINGING OUTSIDERS IN

Partners and customers from outside the organization bring both objectivity and a variety of perspectives to the idea-screening process.

Organizations can benefit considerably from bringing outsiders in. This is especially true when the ideas under consideration will directly affect the customers and/or current or future product offerings. A common strategy used by product-development organizations is first to create a 'short list' of possible ideas to fund and then engage their customers in the final stage of the selection process. Customers are brought in not only to vote on ideas or identify which ideas they would be willing to co-fund, but also to engage in a rich conversation about how the ideas can be refined, developed, and deployed more effectively. Such feedback has great value during the processes of experimentation, commercialization, diffusion, and implementation in the marketplace. Customers may also offer themselves as guinea pigs during the experimentation phase of the idea.

For radical ideas, it's common practice to bring external experts and thought-leaders into the screening process. These individuals normally have deep domain expertise related to the ideas being considered, or knowledge of the dynamics of commercializing ideas. In a situation where the idea under consideration leads to entry into new markets and geographies, access to external expertise will be critical. It's also not uncommon for firms to invite retired employees (normally seasoned managers and innovators) with knowledge of the industry and the organization to help in screening radical ideas. Academia can also provide valuable feedback. In many cases, academic researchers will be thinking of innovations that will affect their fields in ten to fifteen years' time. They may also have valuable insights about how to experiment with ideas (and could potentially be good partners in the experimentation process).

Several key issues need to be attended to when bringing outsiders into the screening process. First, the individuals need to have a certain distance from the ideas being considered. At the very least, they shouldn't stand to gain anything significant from having a particular idea funded – that is, they should be vetted to exclude the possibility of a conflict of interest. Second, traditional non-disclosure agreements should be in place to protect the ideas. Third, there should be a structured process for reviewing the ideas. This can take the form of a one- or two-day meeting where the short list of ideas is presented by the creators, evidence for supporting them is reviewed, and a rich discussion takes place about key objectives (such as moving into a new market or reducing customer churn). At the end of the day, a report is prepared, and then recommendations are made to the organization.

Finally, it's important to ensure that the external audience makes *re-commendations* for funding only, not the *actual decision*. The authority over which ideas to fund and how much to fund them should ulti-mately be vested with the organization and not outsourced. The key reason for this is that at times, regardless of the recommendations made by the external body, there might be external factors and/or internal information that make it difficult to follow through on the recommendations.

SELECTING IDEAS FOR EXPERIMENTATION
The next step after screening and advocacy is to decide which ideas should advance to the next stage – the stage of experimentation. While there are no hard and fast rules, certain guidelines apply. First, it's a good idea to build an idea map. Next, narrow down the ideas to a manageable set by applying threshold conditions (for example, the ideas that were most favorably commented on, or the top twenty ideas that received the most investment dollars).

Idea Maps. These can help you visually organize your ideas on a series of decision-making dimensions or criteria. For example, you can map ideas based on the departments they have originated from, the areas of the organization they are going to affect, the riskiness of the idea, or the level of investment required. Ideas can be segmented across multiple dimensions. In figure 4.1, the X axis indicates the riskiness of the ideas, from the least to the greatest amount of risk; the Y axis indicates the type of market for the ideas, in this case an existing market or a new one. The size of the circles represents the number of votes the idea has received (the bigger the better).

Visualizing the idea space will help you see the diversity in your ideas. Usually, a good rule of thumb is to fund a balanced portfolio of ideas – which will differ slightly for each organization. One interpreta-tion might be to represent ideas from across several departments, while another might be to fund an equal number of low-risk and high-risk ideas, or short-term and long-term ideas. Just as you would not invest all your money in one company or in one investment fund, it's never a good idea to bet everything on one idea. To create a balanced portfolio, you need to consider four key questions: (1) the riskiness of the idea, (2) the level of investment required, (3) the potential impact of the idea, and (4) the origin of the idea. In making decisions based on level of risk, it's a good practice to balance low-risk ideas with

Figure 4.1: Visualizing the idea portfolio

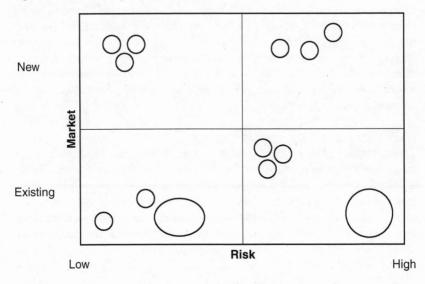

high-risk ones. Levels of investment can range from low to high. Simple economics dictate that you fund several ideas that require a low level of investment, to get a quick bang for your buck, as well as a few ideas that require higher levels of investment, to capture greater returns. Ideas that require high levels of investment are obviously subjected to closer scrutiny, and may be funded in phases.

The costs of developing an idea go beyond financial capital to include the cost of the human resources needed to work on the idea, the impact on the organization's infrastructure (setting up a lab or moving people around to create space to work on the idea), and the opportunity costs and tradeoffs involved in moving the idea ahead. For example, focusing on one idea may lead to abandoning projects that are underway, making these projects obsolete. This illustrates the traditional economic problem of trying to satisfy unlimited wants with limited resources.

The third question concerns the potential impact of the idea. The first consideration is temporal: Will the idea have a short-term or long-term impact? If an idea is successful, when would it require implementation and deployment? This is important to know so you don't create a choke point in the system by funding ideas with overlapping timelines for implementation. From a spatial point of view you can think about the zones the idea will impact: will it impact a specific part of the organization, the entire organization, a select group of business partners or customers, or your entire external constituency? You may find that you have business reasons to spread the impacts around. For example, if you are thinking about funding five ideas, all of which affect a single set of customers, you might not want to fund them at the same time, as customers might grow impatient with too many new ideas and changes – a reaction that could backfire on you.

The fourth question relates to the origin of the ideas. From a management perspective, it is advisable to select ideas from diverse areas within the organization. One sure way of discouraging intrapreneurship is to fund ideas that come from the same sources all the time. Other parts of the company may think that no matter how hard they work, their ideas will not be selected. Over time, this frustration damages the process of intrapreneurship. Historical analysis will reveal how the sources of short-listed ideas change over time and will identify which sources received funding in previous years (see figure 4.2). It's important to spread the wealth around. Even if some departments are more successful than others in realizing their ideas, it's a valuable practice to take chances on newcomers in order to promote a spirit of intrapreneurship. It's also quite likely that the sources you funded in the last year or two are still working on implementing their ideas – another reason to focus on new contributors in other areas of the organization.

In choosing ideas, don't neglect internally oriented ideas that may have relevance for interactions with your customers and business partners. Too often, I find that firms find internal ideas less 'sexy' than external ideas. Don't make this mistake. For one thing, internal ideas have a better chance of being experimented with and actually implemented, as the organization has more control over its own resources and structures. Second, internal ideas uncover the challenges that your employees face as they conduct their daily work. Addressing these challenges can boost productivity and increase employee morale. When employees are happy, they're more attuned to the organizational mission and are more likely to serve customers well. Last but not least, a commitment to internal ideas shows that all employees can contribute ideas to make the organization a better place, even if their ideas don't directly affect the customer or lead to creation of a product or service.

Figure 4.2: Historical analysis of ideas submitted versus ideas funded

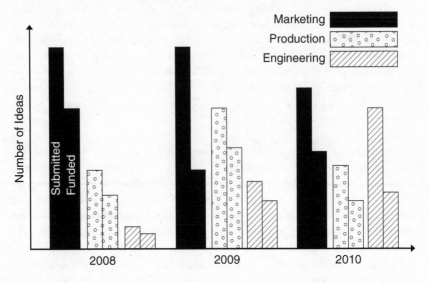

Funding Ideas. How do you assign resources to the chosen ideas? Assigning resources for idea development can range from providing budgets for employees to charge their time to as they work, to buying required technologies and resources, or hiring staff with particular expertise. Depending on the nature of the idea being pursued, funding can be allocated all at once or using a phased approach. For ideas that require a small investment, it might be easier just to fund these outright and move them along. But if the cost of moving the idea along could have a significant impact on the business, it may be better to fund the idea in stages. One method for funding large ideas is to use the 'real options' model.

The following two examples of the use of the real options approach, (1) by universities in hiring professors and (2) by the National Science Foundation (NSF) in awarding grants, illustrate its applicability in a wide range of situations. Most professors enter university employment with a limited contract during which they need to show promise in developing new ideas and knowledge. Untenured professors may start out with a three-year contract, which the university will extend for another three years if performance is satisfactory. When the candidate successfully demonstrates innovative capabilities and productivity, the university grants tenure (i.e., makes a longer-term investment in the individual). In the second example, the NSF gives out grants for exploratory projects. They may choose to continue their investment if the project's initial results are productive, or they may refuse further investments if the project fails to show promise. This limits the initial amount of funding for each project but provides the opportunity for work to continue if the project produces good results.

'Real options' is the application of options methodology to business decision making, specifically with respect to investment decisions.[12] The real options approach to decision making is an extension of option-pricing theory, the Nobel Prize-winning work of Fischer Black, Robert Merton, and Myron Scholes.[13] By analogy with financial option contracts, the real options approach becomes attractive when investments are irreversible, have uncertain returns, and allow flexibility in their timing. A real options contract's objective is to limit the commitment of resources to projects with uncertain rewards.[14] It provides the right to make further investments but not an obligation to do so if prospects for future reward look bleak. Should you decide not to invest further, your loss is limited to the initial investment. The upside is that the door to exploration of future opportunities is kept open.[15]

In stage 1 of the approach, a manager chooses to buy the option, and subsequently waits to see the change in the option's value due to changes in market conditions. For example, a firm may invest in a university research project. By investing an initial sum, this firm has the right to commit more resources later if the project progresses well, but it is not obligated to do so if the project seems to lead nowhere. At stage 2, when the option period expires, the manager may choose to make a subsequent investment in the university project or lose the initial investment, based on a better knowledge of market conditions with the passage of time. The real options approach to investments surpasses traditional analytical tools like net present value (NPV) methodology in cases of high uncertainty, high irreversibility of investments, and the possibility of sequential investments.[16] For strategic decisions, outcomes are too uncertain to warrant the organization's committing all resources in the beginning, as happens with a traditional methodology such as NPV. The real options approach provides the flexibility of sequential investments, which in turn give organizations the opportunity to probe while learning to make better decisions over time.

The arcane mathematics of Black-Scholes valuation as expressed in the real options approach can be forbidding, which may explain this analytical method's lack of popularity. However, managers don't need to have deep mathematical expertise to use real options fruitfully. The central idea of flexibility makes real options a valuable strategic tool for managing innovation. And it applies to all kinds of ideas, from the incremental to the radical. Using the options-based approach helps mitigate risk at all levels. Of course, if the risk and the cost of investment in an idea are low, and you are quite convinced that the idea will make it through the next stage of experimentation, you may just want to go ahead and fund it fully to lower management overhead.

Design Considerations for Idea Advocacy and Screening

An organization must avoid politicizing the idea screening process. It's only human nature that we are influenced by biases and allegiances to certain groups, teams, friends, and colleagues. Thus, for a disgruntled employee whose idea was not selected, politics becomes the scapegoat. The potential for discontent intensifies when the screening process lacks transparency, leading to rumors and gossip about how ideas were chosen. Employee support will be weak if idea screening is seen to be politically motivated and based on special interests or behind-the-scenes dealings.

An intrapreneurial organization can neutralize this perception by adopting a democratic approach and making the entire screening process open and transparent. A democratic approach to screening ideas taps into 'the wisdom of crowds,' a belief in the power of the many to outperform the expertise of a few. Of course, there are limits to the wisdom of crowds. Be wary of allowing the crowd to hijack the process and turn it into an endless debate that never moves ahead. Also, you must make sure you have the right 'crowd'. For example, an engineering idea might require a crowd with some basic knowledge of the subject. The wisdom of crowds isn't helpful when evaluating the idea being discussed requires significant expertise, such as a degree in mathematics or chemistry, or is highly technical in nature. As well, ideas that are highly proprietary, sensitive in nature, and vulnerable to leaks should not be widely circulated.

ENCOURAGING ENGAGEMENT
Even when employees don't contribute ideas during an idea fest or a call for ideas, they can still engage with the intrapreneurship process

by participating in advocacy and screening activities. Every employee can learn how to be a good advocate for ideas by being a good listener and responding in a constructive manner. Many good idea advocates learned their skills by first being informal and sometimes even hidden (or dark) advocates early on in their careers. So get involved. At worst, you will develop useful skills; at best, you may be the idea advocate who supports the next big idea in your organization.

Getting involved in the screening process also gives employees the opportunity (1) to get a first-hand view of the organization's priorities for ideas and its process for choosing which ideas to move ahead with, and (2) to learn about the spectrum of ideas that are being debated and discussed. This information helps employees remain open to new possibilities and stay abreast of the cutting-edge thinking in the organization. Consider the case of new doctoral students. One of the first things they are often asked to do is review and critique papers that are being submitted to journals and conferences in their disciplines. Even though the students may not yet have developed their own ideas, participation in the review process imparts valuable knowledge about what constitutes a good paper, how to structure an argument, and which ideas are 'hot' in their discipline. In similar ways, every employee can gain from participating in the screening process.

APPRECIATING RISK

Organizations often get hung up on the issue of managing risk. All ideas contain some element of risk, and some involve more risk than others. Risks also differ in type as well as degree – some ideas have a feasibility risk (i.e., can you actually implement or manufacture the solution?), while others may carry a financial risk (i.e., are you going to earn a payoff?). Organizations that cannot appreciate risk (those that are very risk averse) will not have successful intrapreneurship programs. At the same time, organizations that take risks without making the necessary calculations to assess the possible consequences will also not be successful.

Organizations need to take an enterprise-wide perspective on appreciating risk when screening ideas. First, recognize that risk is inevitable and that risks can signal opportunities if they are managed carefully. Second, assess the organization's tolerance or appetite for risk – that is, how much risk the organization is willing to take and in what areas of the organization (e.g., for what products or with what customer engagements). Third, determine how the portfolio of ideas can be managed to offset potential risks. The appetite or tolerance for risk will differ from one organization to another. Moreover, depending on where an organization is in terms of its growth cycle, risk tolerance may evolve (i.e., startup organizations are likely to take more risks than incumbents). An organization may be willing to take higher risks in emerging markets than in mature ones; or an organization may be willing to pursue riskier ideas with clients with whom they have a long history. At any given time, if one or more units are taking on a greater amount of risk than the organization is comfortable with, other units should aim to fund projects that are 'sure bets' so as to cover potential losses. Organizations should also delegate risk taking to all levels of the organization. Too often, organizations place decisions about risk taking in the hands of a few. This leads to bottlenecks in the process of evaluating ideas, especially radical ideas, as only a few people have the authority to act on them. Intrapreneurship requires that those closest to the idea be involved in decisions related to accepting risk. Idea advocates need to be able to support risky propositions, and the screening processes need to be sufficiently elastic to appreciate and make allowances for the risks associated with radical ideas. Finally, at regular intervals the organization needs to evaluate how well it is performing in terms of the bets it is making, and make any changes needed to improve its chances of success without going overboard and shying away from risks altogether.

Employee Perspective

As an employee with an idea you want to pursue, the first and most important thing to keep in mind is that you need allies to help your ideas gain acceptance within the organization. Romantic stories of a lone employee battling the forces of the organization and being successful are just that: stories. It takes a community of believers within the organization to see an idea through the process of development.

Idea Advocacy

Employees should find an idea advocate who recognizes the value of their ideas and who will provide good feedback. For example, at W.L. Gore (makers of Gore-Tex), 'When an idea emerges, it's up to the innovator to recruit colleagues to support its development.'[17] There are many intangible qualities that make the employee-advocate relationship fruitful. Finding idea advocates is akin to finding a life partner – it's about knowing what you want and finding someone who fits. You must provide your partner with value and meet his or her needs. You may well have to endure a few bad relationships before you find someone you click with.

SELECTING AN 'IDEAL' IDEA ADVOCATE

Based on conversations with several dozen individuals who have found good idea advocates, and in many cases their long-term mentors in the business of intrapreneurship, I have identified several criteria for finding the 'ideal' idea advocate (see table 4.1).

First and more important, you must feel able to trust this person. Trust allows people to take chances in order to help others. In terms of intrapreneurship, trust boils down to two things. First, do you have confidence in your idea advocate's abilities to execute his or her job with diligence and integrity? The best way to find advocates you can trust is to look for people who are good at what they do. Second, do you trust the person outside the context of work? Ideally, you will find someone you trust in both situations, but this might be difficult to be sure of at first. Most of us get to know someone at work and, if things click, the relationship might develop a social dimension. The greater the amount of trust that develops, the greater the chances are that you will feel comfortable discussing ideas, even those that are half-baked or controversial.

Second, it is also important to maintain an appropriate distance. Common sense will tell you that you should minimize the distance between you and the advocate. However, too close proximity can actually be problematic. The closer someone is to you, the greater the chance that he or she will become overly involved. Consider the people you work with day in and day out. They probably can't give you frank feedback, but if they do, their honesty may harm your working relationship. Moreover, people in the same department often have a similar way of viewing things in the organization. Proximity will also limit the amount of time you can give to discussing ideas because you both spend most of your time doing your 'day jobs' and focusing on how to put out current fires rather than engaging in blue-sky thinking on ideas for the future.

But if too close proximity can be problematic, too much distance can also cause problems. Too much distance makes it difficult for you to

Table 4.1
Characteristics of the 'ideal' idea advocate

Characteristic	Description
Trust	You need to have trust in your advocate's abilities and character in order to share your ideas with ease and be receptive to criticism.
Proximity/distance	You need proximity in terms of physical location and job knowledge in order to interact with your advocate and communicate effectively.
Network size	Your advocate's network should be broad and deep within the organization.
Character profile	You will benefit from working with an advocate with different job strengths and temperament.
Tenure	Your advocate should be enough of an 'insider' to know how and where to track ideas.
Risk seeking	You need to identify an advocate who actively seeks risks.
Persuasion	You will benefit from working with an advocate who possesses outstanding persuasion skills.

meet, and face-to-face meetings are important when you want to throw out ideas, debate issues, and have rich discussions. In addition, if the distance is too great, you may have little knowledge in common, and this can hamper the smooth flow of ideas. Shared knowledge serves as a foundation for the discussion of ideas and experiences and the appreciation of viewpoints. With too little shared knowledge you won't be able to understand each other. Consider the case of a chemical engineer trying to discuss a technical idea with an accounting professional. The accountant will not know advanced chemistry or even understand the technical superiority of the idea. Moreover, the two individuals will be coming at the problem from such diverse backgrounds that the chances of a meaningful exchange are minimal. The ideal idea advocate will be somewhere in between (see figure 4.3), sufficiently distant from your daily routine to bring a genuinely fresh perspective, but close enough for effective communication.

Third, you need to look for an idea advocate who is well-connected, both laterally and vertically. Lateral connections span the organization's departments, teams, and units and even extend across other organizations. Vertical connections provide the ability to communicate ideas

Figure 4.3: Ideal distance between idea creator and idea advocate

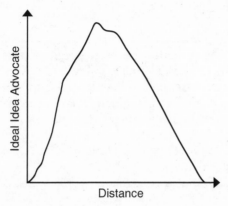

through levels of decision makers in the organization, from the bottom to the top, and vice versa. It's very rare to find one person who has well-developed networks of both types, so you need to consider which type of network is most important to you. Your decision will depend on the nature of the idea. If the idea being proposed is within a vertical structure such as a unit or a product line, then access to a network with strong vertical connections is important. If, on the other hand, the idea is one that impacts various groups within the organization, such as a cost-cutting proposal that spans the entire organization, then you will need to tap into a network that has breadth rather than depth.

You should be aware that the extent of an individual's network affects your access to him or her. The more developed an individual's network, the less time the person will have to spend with you. Well-connected individuals have tremendous demands on their time, so you need to be well prepared when you approach them. If you come to an advocate with an underdeveloped idea, you may not get another chance with that person, even if the idea has great potential value. On the other hand, an individual with a less fully developed network who is nevertheless well placed in the organization might be more willing to take a chance on your ideas and spend time developing them with you. Well-placed individuals have an incentive to support ideas and connect with the people who are going to be the future movers and shakers because they are rewarded for contributions to the organization's strategic goals. They're likely to be willing to take chances on ideas they see as contributing towards strategic objectives, as this can also make them look good and may advance their careers.

Fourth: You need to look for someone with a different character profile from your own – an alter ego, so to speak. If you are an extrovert and enjoy networking and thinking aloud, choose someone who is reserved and measured, and enjoys thinking in isolation. You will gain a lot from the person's complementary experience and approach. If you think logically and enjoy structure, choose someone who breaks the rules and thinks 'big picture' rather than getting into the nitty-gritty. Similarly, if you have a local perspective, work with someone who brings a global viewpoint. Consider the examples of successful partnerships in organizations such as Apple (Jobs/Cook), Starbucks (Shultz/Smith), and Pixar (Bird/Walker) where each person brought a different skill set to the mix.[18] You will learn a lot from trying to explain your idea to someone who is different from you, and who can play 'devil's advocate' to test the depth and clarity of your thinking. The difference in perspective will also help the advocate remain detached enough to probe the merits and features of your idea dispassionately. For incremental ideas and those to be deployed within the organization, try to find advocates among the primary consumers of the idea. For ideas that have an external focus, try to find advocates who work with the specific customers or business partners your idea is intended for.

Fifth: Look for an advocate with tenure or status in the organization who can provide the social or political capital needed to move ideas along. Your advocate should be experienced enough to understand the social and political climate of the organization, acclimated to its culture, and comfortable maneuvering within it to get things done. Veterans of an organization know the informal channels – often more valuable than formal channels – for getting attention. Individuals with tenure have a well-developed map of where expertise and knowledge reside in the organization. As such they can be great connectors. They know how to connect an idea source with an advantageous destination. They can open doors, make introductions, and bring organizational personnel into the conversation to help refine the idea. Of course, a potential advocate may not need to have tenure within the organization if he or she is a newly hired but seasoned manager. This person may not know all the ins and outs of the organization but will have the credibility of a fresh perspective. In most cases, new hires come with organizational resources and a commitment to developing new ideas. They often have the ability to improve their new unit and the organization as a whole. Newly hired managers are often actively looking for good ideas to champion and will be good listeners and springboards.

Sixth: Look for an advocate who is a risk seeker. With their track record of supporting and developing non-traditional ideas, risk seekers are easy to spot. In many cases, they have accelerated through the corporate hierarchy because they have believed in very successful ideas that others ignored. Risk seekers, more often than not, see opportunities where others see only challenges, and are more likely to see an idea's strengths rather than its weaknesses. They normally have a can-do attitude rather than a 'preserve the status quo' attitude. You need someone to motivate you and inspire your creativity but who is not afraid to give you frank and critical opinions. Risk seekers know how to get others to believe in ideas by showing how the positives outweigh the negatives. They are also experimenters who don't immediately dismiss an idea but like to see how it plays out. As such, they frequently take ideas, even quite controversial ones, and experiment with them. Risk seekers seldom view experiments as failures; instead they see them as learning episodes and opportunities to refine knowledge, skills, and expertise.

Seventh: look for an advocate who is persuasive. This quality is vital for helping ideas get traction in an organization. While there are many good communicators, few people have a talent for persuasion, an under-practiced skill in college and university training. While most students out of college are good at delivering presentations, few of them are good at giving *persuasive* presentations. Good persuaders have an arsenal of strategies, including (1) playing to a friendship, (2) playing to their audience's hopes and belief in the future, (3) calling in a favor, (4) connecting an idea to their audience's own agenda, and (5) convincing people that there's no harm in considering the idea. When choosing an idea advocate, look for clues to how they might persuade others to believe in your idea.

ALLYING WITH THE IDEA ADVOCATE

Once you've identified a good idea advocate, you need to get the person interested in your idea. You may feel some nervousness about this step, but appropriate planning and preparation can give you a good chance of success.

First, plan how to make yourself known to the idea advocate. Do some research and identify people in the idea advocate's inner circle. If you know any of these people, ask them to introduce you. If you don't know anyone within the circle, determine whether there are any corporate events (such as company-wide meetings or social gatherings) where you could introduce yourself to the person. If opportunities to meet the advocate in a social setting are very limited, this could be a sign that the two of you may not have enough in common to make the relationship work, and you should probably look for another idea advocate.

Once initial contact has been made, try to arrange a one-on-one meeting in which you can find out what the idea advocate cares about, what strategic initiatives he or she is working on, what his or her challenges are, and what problems are keeping him or her up at night. Understanding where your idea advocate is coming from is very important, so pay attention to details. Once you know something about the advocate's interests and responsibilities, you need to think about and evaluate the information. Does your idea positively contribute a solution to anything that is on the advocate's current agenda? Does the idea help take problems off this agenda by providing a fix? Is your idea good enough to justify the advocate in diverting attention from other concerns to focus on it? Is it important for you to build a relationship with the idea advocate, or is it more important – because the idea is time sensitive – to work on the idea immediately? Answering these questions will help you decide whether to look for another idea advocate or wait for the current one to become available. Of course, if your idea doesn't fit anything the advocate cares about, you should move on to another person.

Assuming that you have found an advocate who has the time and energy to invest in learning about your idea, be very careful how you use this valuable resource. Never go into a meeting with a half-baked idea. Remember, the professionalism and care you show will enhance the advocate's enthusiasm to help you. Prepare before every meeting. Normally, the first few meetings are used for a discussion of the merits, risks, costs, and resources needed to develop or act on the idea. The idea advocate will probe into the business relevance and the direct and indirect impacts of the idea, asking what problem the idea proposes to solve and whether it has enough potential to warrant an investment of resources. The idea advocate will also ask for more clarity and give feedback for revisions. It's important to agree on a clear articulation of the idea so the advocate will be able to practice how to pitch it to others.

Over several iterations, (1) the idea will be refined to the point where it is ready for formal submission and consideration through the organizational screening process (to be discussed in the next section), or (2) it may be put on hold pending further improvements or a more opportune time, or (3) it may be abandoned. If the idea is put on hold or abandoned, it is important not to feel frustrated but to continue to work toward building a lasting partnership. The last thing you want to do is waste the effort you and the advocate have spent on building up the relationship. Moreover, gaining a friend and confidant who can help you with future ideas and connect you with others is not a bad outcome.

Idea Screening

Just as organizations should consider the employee's perspective when developing a process for screening ideas, so too must the employee try to see things from the company's perspective. The key here is to learn about the idea-screening process and to accept the feedback you receive. Don't take it personally when your ideas are rejected. The fact that your idea was rejected doesn't mean that *you* are being rejected. Limited resources or an abundance of better ideas may have caused yours to be rejected. If you received feedback on your idea, you're lucky. In many organizations, unfortunately, employees never get any feedback. Carefully consider the possible reasons why the idea didn't fly. Where is there room for improvement? What did you do or not do? What should you be doing? From whom should you seek advice? If there is consensus that the idea will not work, you have to understand why. Is your organization not seeing something that you are? Perseverance is critical. Ideas are only as good as the people behind them who support them through thick and thin.

Although it's difficult to have an objective view of your own idea, distancing yourself from the screening process is critical for several reasons. First, it allows you to see the idea from another vantage point. Second, it gives you a chance to get feedback for refining the idea. Third, it allows you time to step away and consider other alternatives while someone else is trying to understand your idea. Having someone else review the feedback with you – possibly your idea advocate or even other members of the organization – will help you understand what is really being said. Bringing in others will also help to ensure that you don't take the feedback personally and can view the information in a detached manner with the goal of refining the idea.

DOING YOUR HOMEWORK

Getting comfortable with the screening process takes time. It's only through repeated cycles of participation that you truly understand how to respond constructively to feedback, use it to improve your idea, re-submit the idea, and, you hope, get the idea funded. Let go of your apprehension about submitting ideas for screening; if you can't share your idea with others, you're not ready to move it ahead. In most cases, good ideas receive a positive response in an organization when others are thinking about the same problem or opportunity. An idea about a problem no one is thinking about may be radical and significant, or it may be insignificant and underdeveloped. If others are reluctant to embrace your idea, it may be because they know something that you don't or because they have tried something similar and discovered drawbacks you may not have thought of. Trusting the process, no matter how difficult it is to take criticism, is very important.

Do your homework when preparing an idea for submission to a screening process. Find a good advocate, and get comfortable discussing your idea informally among your peers. The objective is to use cues and signals from other employees to refine and improve the idea. Once this is achieved, you must seek feedback about how you are doing in terms of communicating the value of the idea. Why should someone take the idea seriously? Why is now the right time to consider the idea rather than some time in the future? What are the organizational impacts? Most screening procedures call for you to put the idea in writing, so the ability to write clearly and summarize the idea's key merits and impacts effectively is very important. Your screeners should never be the first people to read your proposal. Get feedback on your write-up so you can revise it to give the screeners the sharpest possible description of your idea. In general, most screeners recommend that idea creators get at least three people to review and provide feedback on their written submission, and that they practice communicating the idea in forums such as internal team meetings to polish their presentations.

Construct the 'elevator pitch' for your idea. The elevator pitch should be a brief summary of your idea, its promising attributes, and its anticipated benefit to the organization. Good elevator pitches are engaging, avoid jargon, and clearly outline the proposal's expected impact. In preparing the elevator pitch, remember to practice delivering it to an audience, in order to check that it can be easily understood. It's also good practice to develop several versions of the elevator pitch tailored to the different audiences you are trying to reach.

You also need to demonstrate to your audience that you have done your homework and considered a number of alternative viewpoints and solutions. Too often, employees submit their ideas as the next big thing but don't provide enough information about how they got there. Idea screeners need to know that you have thoroughly considered a wide range of options before choosing the idea you have proposed. Be sure to share information about other solutions you have considered and explain why they were weeded out. Doing so will strengthen the business case for supporting the idea.

If yours is an incremental idea, it's advisable to do some research into what other, similar ideas have been proposed. Ideally, your organization keeps a record of such proposals, but if not, you should ask advocates and other appropriate people to help you unearth this information. Showing how your idea improves upon previous submissions can strengthen your proposal. Remember, you want to show your audience that you've thought through your proposal and considered its implications carefully. If ideas like yours have been rejected or not funded, you need to give clear reasons why your idea is different and requires consideration. One way to do this is to look at the comments on and rationale for previous rejections and show either that you've addressed these or that they do not apply in the case of your proposal. Learn as much as you can from previous reviews; ignoring them is a sure-fire way to get your idea rejected.

Conclusion

The CEO described at the beginning of this chapter wanted to fund ten ideas that would fall into ten different spaces to help the intrapreneurial spirit blossom. Unfortunately, he didn't have the proper mechanisms in place to identify and screen the ideas; nor did he have anyone to effectively advocate for the best ones. The result was chaos and a lot of hurt feelings among people who felt that their ideas were ignored. The organization not only lost the opportunity to revitalize its business but ended up damaging the organizational culture.

An important step in becoming an intrapreneurial organization is ensuring that there is an effective framework in place to advocate and screen ideas before you ask for them. Once ideas have passed through the screening process, you can begin to experiment with them.

The next chapter focuses on how to move ideas into the experimentation stage. Experimentation is where organizations begin to take an active role in the development of ideas and start the process of transforming them into products or business practices.

5 Idea Experimentation

Up to this point in the intrapreneurship process, the organization has spent time and energy generating and screening ideas that are informed guesses about things that *might* work or *might* pay off. The next step, experimentation – applying scientific methods to generate knowledge we can act on – allows us to test out, refine, and evaluate the potential of an idea and to observe the interplay between causes and effects under various environmental conditions. To put it another way, the experimentation phase comprises all the activities we engage in to test the feasibility and elasticity of an idea. To determine an idea's feasibility, we look at the costs, benefits, effort, resources, and risks involved in transforming the idea into a viable product and/or service. To determine its elasticity, we look at the potential reach of the product or service (either internal or external) that will grow from the idea – including the number of domains in which the product or service can be deployed.

More specifically, through the process of experimentation we seek to uncover: (1) the limits of the idea, (2) the settings in which the idea can be deployed, (3) the refinements and modifications required to improve the idea so as to make it deployable, and (4) the artifact through which the idea will be commercialized (product, service, or business practice). The outputs of the experimentation process are as follows: (1) in increase in the knowledge base of the employee and the organization; (2) new ideas that might be developed further; (3) a product, service, or internal business practice that can be commercialized; and (4) an experimentation process that is refined through the lessons learned while conducting the experiment. Skipping the experimentation process to proceed to commercialization will lead to costly

errors. Investments in commercialization not only cost the organization in real dollars but also have an opportunity cost (investing in the
wrong idea means you are taking resources away from other promising ideas). Finally, experimentation is an opportunity to put ideas on
hold, or even discard ideas that are not ready. We have all seen brilliant products fall by the wayside as a result of being introduced
ahead of their time.

Experimentation shouldn't be restricted to ideas that have made
their way through the screening process. Sometimes good ideas aren't
chosen during the screening process. But even without organizational
resources for experimentation, individuals can proceed with discreet
'bootleg' experiments on their own. As part of the previous stage of
the intrapreneurship process, even ideas that have not been chosen for
organizational commitment receive feedback. This feedback should
not be wasted or ignored; you can engage with the feedback by developing the idea further, testing out the various suggestions received,
and even finding ways to compensate for shortcomings of the idea
that were pointed out in the feedback. The results from the experimentation process can help refine the idea and present further evidence
that the idea works. The results may also serve as an opportunity to
get feedback from potential stakeholders – all of which will help the
intrapreneur move the idea through the advocacy and screening processes in the future.

Developing the capacity to experiment with ideas productively is
the focus of this chapter. The role of the organization is to create a process whereby anyone can experiment, and can do so effectively and
efficiently. Jeff Bezos, founder of Amazon, believes that experimentation is so critical to innovation that he has institutionalized it at Amazon: 'If we can get processes decentralized so that we can do a lot of
experiments without it being very costly, we'll get a lot more innovation.'[1] The role of employees involves learning the basics of conducting experiments, sharing results from experiments, collaborating, and
adapting the organization's process of experimentation to their specific needs.

Organizational Perspective

To test out a wide range of ideas as effectively as possible, the
organization needs to do two things. First, it needs to democratize
experimentation – that is, make it integral to how work is done across

the organization rather than confining it to the R&D lab. Second, the organization needs to build a culture where experimentation is valued as an integral component of decision making. Unless these two conditions are met, supporting intrapreneurship becomes very difficult.

Looking beyond R&D Labs for Experimentation

Organizations are used to isolating experimentation in their research and development labs. Most product development, technology, manufacturing, and even management consulting firms (for example Accenture's Institute for High Performance) have labs. These units are responsible for developing new ideas that might be of interest to the business. Normally, R&D labs are given a fair amount of autonomy and are tasked with working on problems that might be of interest to the organization in the medium to long term. The labs are usually staffed by PhDs looking to make the next breakthrough that will revolutionize their discipline. However, while R&D labs perform an essential function, they should not be the only places where experimentation happens.

Experimentation needs to be a part of every employee's work, because R&D labs have natural constraints that limit their effectiveness. For example, most R&D personnel are detached from the day-to-day running of the business and hence are not the best people to experiment on the problems and solutions of interest for *today*. In addition, these labs are often physically separate from the operational centers of the business, so transporting ideas from the lab to where they are needed on the ground can prove challenging. Finally, R&D lab staff, no matter how brilliant, are relatively few in number compared to the number of employees who run the business day to day. To make the most of all your company's human resources, you need to find ways to tap into the 85 to 90 percent of your workforce who don't work on R&D.

At the Engaged Enterprise, we had an R&D lab called the Institute for Engaged Business Research (IEBR). The IEBR focused on studying applied management problems that had potential value to our clients. In most cases, these problems weren't things we could readily consult on or provide products for, as the problems were ill-defined and solutions weren't immediately obvious. Moreover, we specifically chose to study problems that were not unique to a single organization. Studying problems that were not specific to a given organization provided us with the opportunity to tackle challenges related to advancing organizational agility and performance, and to design solutions that could be implemented in a wide range of contexts.

We determined up front that limiting experimentation and innovation to the R&D lab wasn't optimal. We needed to find à way to capitalize on the experience of those working on the consulting side and transport their knowledge into the R&D lab. Experiments were conducted 'live' while projects unfolded. As we tried to install a new service or strategize with a client, we were in essence engaging in experimentation. We integrated the two sides by having people share their time between consulting and R&D. We had our R&D folks develop a handbook for non-R&D employees explaining the basics of experimentation and how to capture and store results. We also encouraged the sharing of results from experimentation efforts so that others might use the results and/or provide feedback on the experiments.

Intrapreneurial experimentation usually focuses on internal and near-term opportunities within the organization – such as refining business processes – and these kinds of experiments are not well suited to R&D labs. R&D labs are usually tasked with working on longer-term or externally oriented challenges (for example, the next big market blockbuster or innovation for customers). If R&D centers are the only agents of experimentation in your organization, they can become bottlenecks in the intrapreneurship process and are not optimally effective for finding solutions to immediate problems. For this reason, it's important to decentralize your experimentation processes.

A key requirement for decentralizing experimentation is full organizational understanding of the value of data and evidence in moving ideas from basic conceptions to commercialized products. In addition, employees should be encouraged to utilize experimentation not only to refine their ideas and involve their audience (i.e., users) in testing prototypes and simulations but also as a tool for determining when to abandon ideas. (Often, experimentation is the best way to learn that an idea isn't going to pan out as hoped.) Finally, it's also important to encourage a culture of healthy skepticism, making sure that, when employees interact with ideas, they ask the difficult questions, seek out information based on reliable experiments, and don't take things for granted.

The effort to move experimentation beyond the R&D lab needs to be a conscious one. Interventions at both the organizational and employee levels will be needed to promote democratization. Managers should not only encourage their employees to experiment with their ideas but should require experimentation when ideas are being developed and proposed. Employees, too, should take responsibility for engaging with the experimentation process and should work to develop an understanding of appropriate methods and practices for conducting experiments.

Valuing an Experimentation Culture

Only a handful of organizations (Amazon, Google, and Apple, among others) have made experimentation an integral part of their culture. Any idea can be framed as a hypothesis – if you do X it will lead to an increase of Y, or if you invest more in P you will see increased sales of Q – but experimentation is essential to test out such hypotheses.

By conducting experiments and collecting data we find *support* for ideas. Data collected during experimentation also help us gather the necessary *evidence* to support decision making. There's currently a big movement in medicine, called evidence-based medicine (EBM), toward decision making driven less by instinct and more by scientific evidence and data. According to Dr Dave Sackett, a pioneer in the field, 'EBM is saying rather than just rely on tradition, expert opinion, wishful thinking, let's try and find the evidence and apply it.'[2] To build a culture of experimentation one must focus on the following principles: (1) do not discard ideas without adequate evidence; (2) do not support or move ideas ahead without adequate evidence; and (3) always take careful note of data from experiments.

While he was at Amazon, from 1997 to 2002, Greg Linden proto-typed a system that would make personal recommendations to custo-mers as they checked out. A senior vice-president (SVP) of marketing did not like the idea, as he thought it would distract customers from checking out, and insisted the project be scrapped. As Linden com-mented, 'I heard the SVP was angry when he discovered I was push-ing out a test. But, even for top executives, it was hard to block a test. Measurement is good. The only good argument against testing would be that the negative impact might be so severe that Amazon couldn't afford it, a difficult claim to make.'[3] Linden's experiment showed how much customers liked the feature. Now a signature design feature for Amazon, the recommendation concept has been adopted by most online web marketers. This example illustrates the value of testing incremental ideas and achieving innovation through 'continual tiny experiments in such areas as business processes and customer rela-tionships rather than a single, company-transforming idea.'[4]

At IKEA, employees are encouraged to consistently innovate in small ways, and those innovations are tracked on an Internet portal to which all employees contribute.[5] The goal is to experiment with ideas and make self-corrections as projects unfold, reacting to the potentials and possibilities that each innovation reveals through gradual experimentation.[6] From small beginnings, ideas can steadily build momentum; or they can be discarded without a big investment of energy, time, or money. This experimental approach has been embedded in the very fabric of management. IKEA's management approach has been called 'logical incrementalism' because there's no all-encompassing strategy at the outset.[7] Instead, demonstrating an agile approach to implementation, management builds on many small innovations to move each project forward.[8]

Experimentation requires time and energy. If an organization skimps on experimentation or fails to study unexpected results that are deemed 'failures,' the outcome may be dangerously misleading. An example of a program in which an organization lost its objectivity and ignored the results of its research is Crystal Pepsi. Pepsi's innovation team 'ignored focus group participants who hated the taste of this clear cola. It was forced through the Pepsi distribution system on its journey to failure.'[9] The importance of sharing failed research cannot be underestimated as it represents 'a vast body of squandered knowledge that represents a waste of resources and a drag on scientific progress. This information – call it dark data – must be set free.'[10]

Building a culture where experimentation is valued and instilled into work practices promotes the development of ideas and solutions based on hard data. Intuitions and gut feelings bring ideas to the surface and even move them through the advocacy and screening process. However, if the idea is to move farther along in the intrapreneurship process, rigorous analysis must be done. This analysis should not only uncover the strengths and weaknesses of the idea being considered but also examine how well suited the idea is to the context in which it is going to be deployed. To do a thorough job with experimentation, one must begin with the premise that most ideas fail during this process, and that the burden of proof for an idea's viability rests on evidence and data. This thinking sets out the expectation that there is a low chance that an idea will make it through the experimentation process (in most organizations, the odds are that one in every 1,000 ideas will get to the stage of commercialization), and also focuses attention on the fact that much can be learnt during the experimentation process whether the results point to success or failure for the idea being tested. Additional important benefits of experimentation that should be recorded when results are documented are the experience gained and the lessons learned from the process at the individual, team, and organizational levels.

VALUING FAILURE

If an organization evaluates experiments solely in terms of their costs and potential returns, it will treat every idea that fails to yield the expected results as a failure to be abandoned. Yet often experiments that yield unexpected results have great potential to generate new knowledge by offering the opportunity to learn and reflect. Google has integrated the experimentation process and the potential for failure or abandonment into its corporate identity. By launching its products in beta testing mode, Google acknowledges that no product is perfect even though millions of customers might be using it every day. For example, as one analyst noted, with Gmail, they 'could have pulled the plug at any time . . . That focus, and the acknowledgement that nothing is ever perfect, could be a model that Microsoft, and even Apple, are likely to find an increasingly conspicuous challenge in the coming years.'[11]

To quote Tom Kelley of IDEO, 'Fail often to succeed sooner.'[12] The basic economics of experimentation dictate that you are going to spend a lot of effort without producing the intended results: 'Experimenters construct interactive experiences and try to provoke unorthodox responses to see what insights emerge.' The process of setting up and conducting experiments is time-intensive; as Thomas Edison said, 'I haven't failed. I've simply found 10,000 ways that don't work.'[13] These efforts should be viewed as learning episodes, not as failures.

You will fail more often than you will succeed in the experimentation stage of the intrapreneurship process. While it's imperative to review and improve the screening process so that ideas with a low probability of success are filtered out before expensive experimentation begins, you should not be reactive and lock down idea screening and advocacy into a rigid process incompatible with the intangible and fuzzy nature of ideas. In fact, failure to achieve the expected goal may mean there's a flaw in the success criteria for an idea! Take, for example, the case of the U.S. Navy's search for an agent to keep barnacles from growing on the hulls of ships. The solution was defined as one that produced 'a "squeaky clean" surface.' Based on this criterion,

Table 5.1
Stages in the experimentation process

Behavior	Description
Questioning and theory building	Identifying assumptions, asking questions, and constructing theories.
Observing, associating, and contrasting	Observing relationships and patterns, making inferences, and imagining opposites.
Exploring and testing	Engaging in active exploration and hands-on testing.
Analyzing and synthesizing	Interpreting the test results and developing explanations and conclusions.
Communicating and networking	Communicating results and seeking inputs, feedback, and criticism.

a coating that created a slimy surface was abandoned as a mistake. However, a scientist-experimenter continued to experiment on a 'naturally occurring slime' (similar to that on fish), and the idea has now been commercialized as a 'breakthrough non-toxic anti-fouling coating that is environmentally friendly and has the potential to last for many years.'[14]

A successful experimentation process is designed to absorb mistakes and setbacks, recognize biases, and prioritize learning over results. The various stages in an experimentation process are outlined in table 5.1.[15]

Scott Cook of Intuit 'stresses the importance of creating a culture that fosters experimentation, stating that "our culture opens us to allowing lots of failures while harvesting the learning . . . It's what separates an innovation culture from a normal corporate culture." '[16] It's essential for leaders to develop a culture that is open to sharing mistakes rather than assigning blame. Says Charles Prather, 'fix the learning, not the blame . . . Learning helps everyone avoid the same "mistake" in the future, and over time increases organizational capability.' Prather gives the example of 'Thomas Watson, IBM's first chairman. Reportedly, one of his executives tendered his letter of resignation, saying that one of his ideas just cost the company $14 million. Watson took the letter and threw it into the wastebasket, exclaiming, "I just paid $ 14 million for your education, why should I let that walk out the door?" Enough said.'[17]

VALUING LEARNING

The process of experimentation, even when the outcome is unsatisfactory, increases learning at all levels of the organization (see table 5.2). Individuals will acquire new knowledge and skills. Teams have an opportunity for peer learning and knowledge transfer. And through the development of new products and services, the organization can learn as well, even extending learning to external partners of the organization. One example of cross-organizational learning is Thomas Edison's work. His 'products often reflected a blend of existing but previously unconnected ideas that his engineers picked up as they worked in [these] disparate industries . . . as well as ideas developed by others that they had learned about while working in those industries.'[18]

It's vital for an organization to promote learning through the experimentation process, regardless of outcome.[19] Even when experiments don't generate expected results, people still learn. At the individual level, learning is an outcome of working through the experimentation process, testing hypotheses, refining prototypes, and going back to the proverbial drawing board. Learning needs to be promoted on the community level, through collaborative discussions and deliberations during the experimentation process. In most organizations, single individuals seldom experiment in isolation; experimentation normally requires a team. The synthesis of diverse perspectives during the experimentation process is vital, especially during the analysis of information and results and the calibration of revisions. Learning should not only center on the artifact being experimented with but should help team members deepen their expertise around the concept of experimentation. For example, the team can determine whether collaborative experimentation should be sequential (feeding the outputs from one experiment into the next) or parallel (conducting different tests simultaneously) based on what worked and did not work for the team during the experimentation process. When conducting experiments, an organization should strive to build a culture of learning, one that encourages behaviors such as asking questions and observing. A learning culture also encourages 'active experimentation' through 'intellectual exploration . . . physical tinkering . . . and engagement in new surroundings.'[20] These behaviors are sometimes viewed as both a threat to the status quo and a challenge to employees' sense of their own value and expertise within the organization. In 'The Wisdom of Deliberate Mistakes,' Paul J.H. Schoemaker and Robert E. Gunther outline attitudes and behaviors among employees and

Table 5.2
Levels of learning through experimentation

Level of Experimentation	Features
Individual	• Tangible learning
	• Isolated refinement of idea
Community	• Collaborative discussions
	• Deliberation
	• Diverse Perspectives
Organizational	• Development of overall experimentation process

organizations that limit experimentation, including the following: (1) We are overconfident; (2) We are risk-averse; and (3) We seek confirming evidence. Organizations go to 'great lengths to avoid anything that looks like an error . . . because most companies are designed for optimum performance rather than learning.'[21] Individuals are often wired to avoid mistakes and uncertainty because, from childhood onward, they are rewarded for achievement and smarts instead of for their ability to take on challenges and learn from them.[22] Finally, community-level learning needs to extend itself to make an impact at the organizational level. A critical component of organizational learning is the development of the overall process of experimentation. Here, information collected during individual experiments should be used to strengthen, modify, or even abandon (and redesign) the existing experimentation process.

There are four main learning objectives during the experimentation process. First, we need to learn about the idea we are experimenting with. This learning will take a microscopic view of the idea proposed and the learning associated with the experimentation process. We might learn how to improve the idea, or how to refine the original target features of the idea; alternatively, we might learn that the idea is not feasible at a given price point and may need to be abandoned. Second, we need to learn from the idea itself. What can we extrapolate from this particular idea to other ideas that are similar, the domain from which the idea originated, and the screening processes and idea development processes to date? What outcome might be applied to other ideas being considered either now or in the future? Third, we need to learn how to improve the idea creation, mobilization, advocacy, and screening processes based on what we know of the idea experimentation process.

Positive feedback reinforces things that worked well, while negative feedback highlights areas for improvement. Fourth, we need to examine what worked well and what did not work well in the *experimentation* process we used. The process of experimentation needs to undergo constant refinement and improvement as the organization's experience with intrapreneurship increases. To this end, it is essential to reflect on the process of working on the idea.

On Developing an Experimentation Process to Test the Feasibility of Ideas

Because experimentation can be time and resource intensive, it is in the organization's best interest to find ways to use the resources dedicated to the process as economically as possible. One way to do this is to develop a process that is used by everyone – a template for experimentation, so to speak – that provides a mechanism for systematically training employees to experiment with ideas and to share their results with confidence and in a manner that gives them credibility. The template need not be a straitjacket – employees may modify it to suit the particular needs of their project; its purpose is to make it unnecessary for them to reinvent the wheel and help them to avoid common mistakes and to communicate their findings effectively. For example, a more well-defined process might have helped Merck avoid problems related to Vioxx in 2004. In that case, a lack of clear ethical guidelines for experimentation led to the ignoring of evidence that pointed to increased rates of heart attacks and strokes related to use of the drug. According to Calvin Hodock, absent standards for ethics and objectivity, 'unfavorable data or information might be ignored, perhaps even suppressed . . . Successful innovation initiatives are not products of miracles, but simply take a good idea and execute all the basic steps that are part of the discovery process.'[23]

The experimentation process needs to be systematic for several reasons. First, if we are to believe the results of experimentation, we must have some confidence in the methods used to conduct the experiments. Second, when we need to compare results across experiments, we must have the same baseline in terms of the experimentation process in order to do so. Having a prescribed process to follow removes variations in the methods and approach used by different experimenters, so the results are not skewed by the idiosyncrasies of individuals. Third, an unsystematic experimentation process can lead to costly errors and omissions and may allow a flawed idea to be adopted for development.

To summarize: from an organizational point of view standardization of the experimentation process promotes the consistent use of good practices, guards against duplication of effort, and provides a baseline from which to compare and evaluate the results. That is not to say that you should have only one version of the experimentation process. You may need one type of process for testing ideas related to products and services and another for testing ideas related to business processes and practices. Understanding the wide array of ideas you may be dealing with will help you create versions of the experimentation process to suit particular needs. For example, a process for testing radical ideas should allow considerable flexibility, permitting employees to tailor the traditional process to meet particular needs if they can show that the traditional process is too rigid or fails to accommodate the specifics of the idea. However, when experimenters modify the process, they need to clearly document the alternative methods used, to show that they were sufficiently rigorous, that their results are reliable and valid, and that their process may be useful in the future.

Managers need to understand that experimentation is a messy and untidy process. More often than not, experiments won't lead to fruitful results. However, it's not just the outcomes but also the process of experimentation that should be the organization's focus. Through the process of experimentation one can learn and advance domain knowledge. The organization should deploy resources and assets effectively in order to give employees time and space to experiment with their ideas. For example, one organization maintained a policy whereby once a month it encouraged employees to come into the office on the weekend and use the facilities for working on ideas, collaborating, and conducting experiments.

Remember that employees, like all humans, are experimenters by nature. Most experiments are done independently by employees, outside the confines of the organization or outside the normal working day. This prevents the organization from knowing how many experiments are being conducted, by whom, and for what purposes and creates a large amount of waste and inefficiency in the system. Organizations need to find ways to give the experiments of intrapreneurs the same type of welcome as is provided to 'sanctioned' or 'organization focused' experiments. One possibility is to create a platform or bulletin board on which people can share their current experiments, details of their interim results, or challenges they face. Another option is to have working papers and presentation series where both officially designated researchers and 'amateur' practitioners (intrapreneurs) are allowed to share their experimental results and get feedback. These can occur either as informal conversations or as full-blown research talks. Organizations that have R&D labs should consider the possibility of giving intrapreneurs access to these facilities, providing mentors, and supporting visiting positions in the labs. Yet another alternative is to require 'official' researchers to spend time in the functional units of the organization in order to transmit their knowledge of experimentation and technical analysis to intrapreneurs in the general employee population.

Refining the Experimentation Process of the Organization

Experimenters need to be both scientists and artists. The science involves ensuring that experiments are conducted in a systematic manner and that the results are reliable – that is, they can be validated. The artistry involves tailoring each experiment to fit its specific context. Experimentation deals in unknowns. Hence, no experimentation process is going to go like clockwork from start to finish. Continuous refinement and improvement will be required. The experimentation process may need to be tweaked a little or a lot, depending on the circumstances. In a later section, I highlight a process for experimentation that employees can follow. For now, from the organizational perspective it's important to focus on how the organization continuously improves its experimentation process. Refinement of the experimentation process through feedback, both positive and negative, is essential.

It is very important to constantly *capture and share* knowledge about how experimentation is being used in the organization. There will be significant differences between the prescribed and the actual experimentation processes. Capturing the various ways in which the experimentation process is being used will help in developing best practices through the sharing of knowledge. Promoting the sharing of knowledge about what works and what doesn't will also help increase the adoption of the experimentation process. This can be done by identifying unofficial 'experts' – individuals who are frequently consulted for help and guidance. The organization may use these experts to facilitate improvements to the experimentation process.

Written case studies may also help capture the lessons learned during the experimentation process. To generate these studies, organizations engage in a form of postmortem: some use a basic checklist during a single meeting, while others run half-day workshops, or off-site meetings that last several days, or a combination of these. Some organizations prefer to collect information through interviews rather than postmortem meetings. Apple Computers has a multilevel approach that combines a customized project survey, objective project metrics, a debriefing meeting, and finally a 'project history day.' The information accumulated from these sources is published in a final report. Microsoft writes extensive postmortem reports containing details about what worked in the most recent project, what did not work well, and what the group could do better in the next project.

The two most common formats for postmortems are *reports* and *narratives* (stories). Reports are often written using pre-configured templates, making them comparatively easy to put together. In contrast, narratives are loosely structured. Often they open with an introductory 'curtain raiser,' followed by the main storyline about the most important phases of the project, and conclude with lessons learned. The tight structure of reports makes for greater objectivity, whereas narratives tend to be more subjective.

Reports are easier to understand than narratives because they follow an established structure. Moreover, when reports are archived electronically, they are more easily accessible through conventional search and retrieval techniques because they are in a standard format. A narrative's loose structure and direct recounting leave it open to multiple personal interpretations. A reader might even interpret a narrative differently with each rereading. However, postmortem results in reports are harder to remember than results in narratives because narratives are more dramatic. As reports are standardized by nature, it is difficult to recollect the specifics of any one report.

How do you determine whether a postmortem analysis should be written as a report or a narrative? The following guidelines may be helpful in deciding.[24]

The nature of the project: A report is the recommended format for experiments dealing with incremental ideas and/or routine experimentation. When the project is non-routine, and when indisputably distinctive features have emerged in the course of its duration, a narrative is the better format. If an organization has a history of working with ideas of a particular nature it makes good sense to capture lessons learned from all such projects in a report. If the idea being experimented with is radical, a narrative would be better, as it would capture the entire background of the project and could be used to direct behavior in future projects. Reports are more basic, as they lack rich background detail, so they are suitable for capturing knowledge from more cut-and-dried processes. Narratives make a greater impression on the organization than reports because they encourage dialogue and multiple interpretations throughout the organization.

The lesson being conveyed: Reports are better at imparting operational lessons clearly and concisely, while narratives are more effective for communicating ethical lessons. Narratives are an ideal vehicle for transmitting information about organizational standards and core values and for weighing ethical considerations. However, they are not so well suited for outlining regulations or procedures; these are better dealt with in reports. Reports are an ideal medium to build on earlier learning, as they are direct and concise by nature; on the other hand, the 'drama' of a narrative can be useful for promoting far-reaching organizational learning that may require behavioral change.

Early in the development of intrapreneurship, an organization should document a few success stories. These can be used as learning tools for others who will be getting involved with experimentation. Over time, as the process for experimentation with incremental ideas becomes standardized, reports will be a better format for capturing the lessons learned. However, when an organization is experimenting with radical ideas, a narrative may still be the best vehicle, especially for explaining why changes need to be made to the standard experimentation process or a new perspective is needed on a radical idea.

Design Considerations in Experimentation

How much involvement should management have in the experimentation process? At one extreme is the manager who micro-manages the process; at the other is the manager who leaves employees entirely to their own devices. Neither of these extremes is a good choice. Micro-managing the work of an employee during the experimentation process can lead to several undesirable outcomes: (1) the employee does not have enough space and time to be creative; (2) the employee does not have permission to fail; and (3) the employee feels under pressure to doctor results to make them look acceptable to the manager. Falsified results are partly to blame for the Vioxx debacle, where 'in December 2005, the prestigious *New England Journal of Medicine* took the unusual step of publishing an online editorial accusing

Merck of suppressing data that showed a greater risk of heart attack among people taking Vioxx than was already known.'[25] Through a series of court cases, evidence emerged that a number of academic journal articles in support of the drug had been ghostwritten. Principled leadership that focuses on ethics will steer organizations clear of such dishonest practices.

On the other hand, a laissez-faire approach makes it much harder for an organization to get its 'money's worth' from the experimentation process. Experimentation is not cheap, and employees need to know what the organization expects from the experimentation process. Expectations can include the kind of results one is looking for, the nature of the experiments one is expected to run and the reasons for them, and a timeline for when things need to get done.

One of Google's nine innovation principles says 'creativity loves constraints.' Employees need managers to provide 'guardrails' – that is, to set reasonable boundaries within which the employee can be creative and experiment with ideas. The manager should meet with the employee whose idea has been selected to collaborate on an experimentation plan. The plan should be set out at a high level and cover details such as expectations, timeline, and resource commitments. During this meeting, the employee should identify key milestones for the development of the idea to give an expected trajectory of the experimentation process. The manager and the employee must also schedule check-in points where the employee can update the manager on progress (the frequency of meetings will depend on the nature of the project).

The manager's role resembles that of a funding agency such as the National Science Foundation in the United States, the Economic and Social Research Council in the United Kingdom, or the Swiss National Science Foundation. Like project managers in these agencies, managers receive grant submissions in the form of ideas that go through the process of advocacy and screening. They choose ideas they would like to develop further and allocate funds for experimentation. Ideally, resources are provided in phases, but the funding agency doesn't interfere in the experimentation process. The manager's role is to support the employee in such a way as not to hamper creativity. The employee's role is to follow recognized experimentation procedures that will generate results that are valid, credible, and ethical and to report to the manager as identified milestones are reached

At times managers may want to protect employees and allow them to hide during the experimentation process. This was a strategy popularized by Lockheed Martin as part of their Skunk Works initiative, which produced several aircraft, including the SR-71, the U-2, and the F-117 Nighthawk,[26] all designed in record time. Under this approach, the organization removes team members to a different location and frees them from all other work assignments in order to allow them to focus solely on the task at hand: experimenting and moving the concept ahead for development. The experimentation team is kept small on purpose to promote swift collaboration; access and interference by outsiders is restricted, and the team is given free rein to design the experimentation process and complete their assignment. Skunk Works arrangements are good for radical ideas that require significant independence and non-interference from the organization. Separation from the regular workplace and regular duties prevents the culture, history, and politics of the organization from interfering with the process.

Knowing when to pull the plug on failed projects, especially those in experimentation programs, is difficult but vital. Sometimes the results of the experiment are unexpected, and it's clear nothing can be done to change them. Moreover, when experimentation takes several years of effort, either the competitive environment of the organization or the internal composition and priorities within the organization may change, making the experimentation effort obsolete. In this case, it's important not to fall into the 'sunk cost trap' and continue to commit to a futile experimentation program.

An organization must routinely check on the progress of experimentation projects to make decisions about whether to continue to invest in ideas that have yielded disappointing results or have become obsolete due to changes in the environment. An 'innovation committee [should] perform pre-mortems early in the development process, before bad ideas soak up lots of money. There is a rich reservoir of people resources to serve on innovation committees (e.g., academics, retired senior executives, industrial designers, and product and industry specialists).'[27] This must be done with care, so as not to discourage the intrapreneurs or abandon their ideas prematurely. Moreover, employees need to be realistic and inform their managers when they've tried everything possible to make an idea work. A realistic experimenter seeks feedback from trusted colleagues to determine whether there is merit in continuing with the experiment.

If a project is abandoned, it's important to document what has been done to date, the results thus far, and the issues and problems encountered. Sometimes the root cause of a failure may just be bad timing, and it's possible that under different conditions, at a future date, someone will be able to turn that failed experiment into a successful one. Always preserve the knowledge gained from an abandoned project.

Employee Perspective

If you have an idea that has been allocated resources for experimentation, celebrate! Organizational resources are not going to be available for all employee ideas. Employees who proceed on their own will ideally have taken feedback received from the *idea advocacy and screening* stages, worked to refine and develop the idea, and carried out experimentation on their own.

Experimentation needs to become a natural part of your intrapreneurial thinking, enabling you to refine, update, and extend your idea. Sometimes, after the experimentation process, you will realize that the idea, as originally proposed, is flawed and should be abandoned. This represents a valuable outcome as it allows you to bring closure to the idea and consider other options. At other times, the experimentation process will lead to refinements of the idea, enabling you to strengthen the business case for the next time you move it through the advocacy and screening process. Advocates and reviewers love to see that their feedback has been considered before an idea is resubmitted for potential funding. Yet another possibility is that further experimentation will confirm the accuracy of your original forecast and result in a reversal of an earlier decision to reject.

Bootlegging and conducting experimentation even without organizational support and/or under makeshift conditions can also yield interesting results. For example, Len Volin, an associate engineer in the Bonding Systems Division of 3M, was investigating a more efficient way to make adhesive tape. As Volin recalled, 'Traditionally, we started with tape backing, then we applied adhesive and wound the finished tape on a big roll called a "jumbo" . . . The jumbo was stored and later slit into individual rolls of tape. We thought we could save a lot of time and money if we slit the tape as it was made.'[28] Volin's first prototype of a solution for this problem was jerry-rigged using his kid's Tinker Toys. Since Volin didn't have a lot of lab space at 3M, he recalls, 'my "lab" was a couple of sawhorses in the hallway leading to the garage in my unfinished house. When I needed a vacuum source, I used my home shop vac.'[29] Two years after he conceived his initial idea, in 1988, the first production machine was released. By 2002, 3M had seven of these machines in use around the globe. Each machine is estimated to save the company $1 million annually. If you are offered the chance to participate in the experimentation process as part of your normal job responsibilities, you should seize the opportunity – practical experience with experimentation will teach you things you cannot learn simply by observing others.

Experimentation is natural; we all conduct experiments, and we do so more often than we are conscious of. However, most employees without a doctorate or research degree lack an understanding of the process of conducting experiments and hence do so in a manner that is not rigorous, effective, or efficient. Thus, employees should practice integrating experimentation into their routine work and decision-making processes. A basic model for conducting experiments is outlined in the next section.

Methods for Experimentation

Most of us know something about the *scientific method* (see figure 5.1). The process starts with an interesting problem of current value and lasting significance. First, you review the literature about the problem (articles in academic and popular journals, market research reports, conference proceeding, etc.) to determine whether a solution for the problem has already been found. At this point, either inquiry ends or your research findings help you refine your understanding and formulate a hypothesis about a possible solution. Next, you design empirical tests of the hypothesis, collect and analyze data, and evaluate the results. The results may indicate that you need to carry out more tests, redefine your problem, or do more research. Eventually, you will document your process and communicate your results, usually in a scientific paper. Your work will then be judged by your peers, who will assess the scientific rigor of your methods to determine whether your results are valid.

Prototyping is essential to employee experimentation. Prototyping can involve creating working models that can be used to see how your idea tests out under a variety of conditions. Prototyping used to be complicated but now can be done early and inexpensively using rapid prototyping (RP) methods or low-cost tools such as Google's Sketchup to quickly convert computer-generated designs into three-dimensional models, so that hands-on modeling now occurs very early in the experimentation process. For example, 'Sony Ericsson has a policy

Figure 5.1: The scientific method

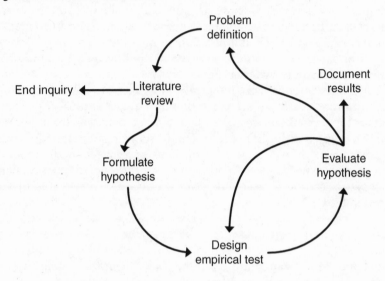

where they don't want their designers to work more than a few hours before they build their very first physical model.'[30] The basic steps in prototyping include (1) creating a concept/prototype, (2) documenting it, (3) experimenting with it, (4) generating and analyzing results, (5) refining the concept or the experiment, if needed, and (6) repeating the process until satisfactory outcomes are reached.

Simulation of a product or service is another form of experimentation. Crash simulation and modeling at BMW München provide good examples of gains from using modern simulation tools. Early simulation models at BMW, using about 3,000 finite elements, ran for nearly three months and were unable to make any significant impacts on design decisions. Thanks to advances in computational modeling techniques and computing power, however, in 2002 the simulation model of the new BMW X5 used roughly 700,000 finite elements, ran for less than thirty hours, and drove important design decisions.[31] Simulation tools provide fast visual data processing and other sensory aids. VirTra Systems, a simulation training company, offers a simulation tool that not only provides a learning experience to trainees but also lets them experience the consequences of their decisions in real field operations.[32] With these technical advances, experimentation through simulation will enhance individual learning as well as collaborative knowledge construction.

Information and communication technologies (ICTs) can streamline and optimize the process of collaboration, design, and testing. Consider the case of DreamWorks Animation SKG (DWA).[33] A film production company that produces acclaimed computer graphics animation (such as that used in *Shrek*), DWA uses virtual collaboration technologies, utility computing, and open-standards technologies to extend its innovation capabilities. Computer graphics animation requires creative collaborations and tremendous computer resources. Despite these difficulties, DWA made a decision in 2001 to produce two films per year. To achieve this goal, the company needed to overcome a number of difficulties. For example, geographically distributed teams needed to collaborate very deeply yet couldn't do so through person-to-person interactions. Because traditional electronic communications such as e-mail, instant messaging, conference calls, and videoconferencing didn't capture the non-verbal nuances that are a large part of creative collaboration, DWA developed a system called Virtual Studio Collaboration (VSC). The system allows people in two different studios (Redwood City, CA, and Glendale, CA) to engage in interactions that include many visual cues. VSC has large screens that display images and data in different studios simultaneously. These life-size screens capture behavioral cues from the collaborators – smiles, shrugs, smirks, and laughs. VSC helps people feel as if they are working together in the same room. The success of VSC spurred Hewlett-Packard to develop Halo, a commercialized version of VSC. Early users of Halo include PepsiCo, AMD, Proctor and Gamble, Novartis, and Hewlett-Packard.[34]

Experimentation can also be used to test ideas for non-products and services such as a new marketing strategy. Say, for example, you would like to introduce a new sales promotion. Instead of launching the newly conceived strategy based only on the usual data from sound market research, analysis of past promotions, and information gleaned from customer surveys, you could experiment with a series of promotions, seeing how customers react, refining the promotions based on this feedback, and repeating the process until the most effective promotion is identified. Simulation techniques can also be used to understand the interplay between variables being considered for a decision.[35] For example, at one boutique consulting house, two employees had different views about the best office layout to facilitate knowledge flow among employees in order to enhance creativity and innovation. One employee argued that the standard setup, with employees segregated by department (e.g., all accountants sitting near each other in the same section) was efficient and effective. Another argued that such a layout, though more efficient on a micro-level, fostered silo-based thinking that undermined effectiveness at the global level. To encourage more 'big picture thinking,' he argued, it would be best to mix up people and have individuals from different units sit near one another. Doing so would help employees appreciate the diversity of the organization's interests. Moreover, since individuals still predominantly communicated via e-mails, productivity clearly did not depend on physical proximity.

Which one of these options would you have favored? Would you have proceeded with an office reorganization project with just hunches or strong arguments? The decision to change office designs is non-trivial. To determine which strategy might promote innovation, the two solutions were tested by building an agent-based model. Agent-based models are computational techniques that allow you to simulate complex problems, especially those for which a solution is non-linear and emergent and cannot be easily computed.[36] In the above case, the model built simulated a group of employees each of whom had distinct knowledge, tasks that needed completion, and costs associated with information flows. The model enabled the organization to study how a change in the cost of information flows affected the efficiency and effectiveness with which different types of tasks were performed, from simple tasks (e.g., structured problems) to complex ones (e.g., unstructured problems). (For example, the cost of transmitting complex information using electronic communication would be greater than the cost of transmitting simple information, as a large number of e-mails would be required for the message to be understood). Through the analysis, the organization realized that neither of the original proposals was ideal and went on to construct a hybrid solution – in which only personnel who worked on complex tasks where cross-functional information and knowledge flows were critical were co-located.

Experimentation Simplified

At places like Amazon, data-based evidence trumps intuition and promotes the ability to innovate quickly and effectively through an efficient experimentation platform. Think of the problem of redesigning a web page – how would you know which of several competing designs is best? One way is to let a test group try out the new page, measure results, and compare them against a control scenario. Amazon often tests scenarios in different 'live' settings. For example, a portion of customers might see a website where coupons for purchases are presented on the first page. Another portion of customers could receive their coupons via e-mail and be presented with click-through links directly to the products that interest them. Amazon then determines which set of customers has responded more favorably. Not all organizations can experiment with the same amount of ease, but most employees can conduct experiments effectively and efficiently. Some general guidelines to consider include the following:

- Try different modes of experimentation. For example, switch between prototyping and simulation, between individual and group scenarios, and between different locations.
- Be wary of the cost of experimentation and ensure that costs don't exceed the expected benefits.

SPECIFIC STEPS IN THE EXPERIMENTATION PROCESS

Below is a description of the steps in the experimentation process (definitions of the terms used to describe each step are given in the Appendix at the end of this chapter).

1 *Select a problem.* Develop a clear problem statement; how it is worded can affect outcomes. Define the who, what, when, why, and how of the problem to establish initial boundary conditions (although boundaries might shift as experimentation progresses). Be clear about what kind of experiment you are running: *descriptive, exploratory, associative, predictive, control,* or *hypothesis testing.* Develop baseline measures of what is currently being done in order to understand causation and correlation.

2 *Define the dependent variable.* The *dependent* variable is the one you expect to change. The *independent* variables are those that you are going to manipulate to see changes in the dependent variable. Sometimes there are direct links between the independent and dependent variables. You can also have *moderating* and *mediating* variables. You need to be selective in the choice of variables. In the

best models, the fewest number of variables can account for most of the behavior.

3 *Determine the independent variables.* These are the ones you will change (or that might differ across two samples, if you are not engaged in experimental design). Determine the number of levels and see the possible combinations (interactions) among the variables.

4 *Determine the number of observations.* You need to determine whether random or purposive sampling is required. Also, you need to consider how many test subjects are required and how to select your subjects.

5 *Determine the method for data collection.* Researchers must maintain objectivity and exercise caution against manipulation. In designing surveys you need to follow best practices, such as avoiding leading questions, getting a diverse sample, and doing adequate simulations.

6 *Carry out testing.* Carry out the identified steps needed to test your hypothesis.

7 *Analyze the data.* Analyze how well the results support the hypothesis. Note that detecting change is very important when you are conducting experiments. You should evaluate how an intervention changes the outcomes or behavior among variables. Look for correlation between variables (when two variables seem to move together) and for evidence of causation (when one variable causes the other). Your goal is to tease out the true effects of one variable on another variable and deal with the issues of noise and confounding effects.

8 *Interpret the results.* Draw conclusions about the results.

9 *Communicate the results.* Prepare and disseminate your findings and conclusions.

10 *Evaluate your findings and identify areas for future research.* Outline the effectiveness of your experiments. Suggest modifications to the experiment and indicate areas for further research.

In analyzing and interpreting your results, it's important, first, to be aware of the pitfalls and opportunities associated with findings you weren't expecting, and second, to find effective ways to evaluate as many potential solutions as possible.

Accounting for Randomness and Outliers. Unintended results need to be investigated. Actually, if you think about it, results that don't confirm to expectations have a greater *information* value. If someone told you the sky was blue, you probably wouldn't give that piece of information even a second of your attention because it confirms your expectations. However, if someone told you that they found the sky was green, at the very least you would take a second to see if you heard them correctly. Similarly, when running experiments it is important not to discard or ignore results that don't conform to our expectations. A striking example of unintended consequence is 'Pasteur's demonstration that airborne microbes were responsible for beer turning bad.'[37] Pasteur's discoveries eventually led to a theory on germs and the field of microbiology.

Unexpected results can be valuable. For example, one organization was trying to arrive at a new customer retention strategy, so an employee experimented with the idea of signing up customers to multi-year rather than single-year contracts. He selected a few clients and offered them a multi-year option with a sizable discount; many clients signed up for the deal, but they were low-volume customers of the firm. The clients who had a sizable amount of business with the organization, including two of the firm's top-tier 'gold clients,' didn't take the offer. The employee didn't investigate why these loyal customers avoided long-term contracts, so the results he presented to his manager (using the law of averages) showed that a large percentage of his test clients had accepted his strategy – with the anomalous response of the gold clients buried in the data. After the firm implemented the new strategy, a manager decided to offer one of the multi-year contracts to a gold client. The firm lost the gold client because the client felt insulted that the relationship was being commoditized. The client felt that the offer of a three-year contract meant the firm was only interested in the volume of transactions and did not want to negotiate new deals every year to respond to business changes that might occur in the client's organization. Had the employee taken the time to investigate why the gold clients in his sample didn't go for his idea, he would have discovered these attitudes.

Thus, unexpected results may point to new spaces for discovery and more fruitful ideas, or to areas requiring further investigation and reflection – or to the need to modify your methods of experimentation. For example, as a report on the recent concern about stuck accelerator pedals in certain Toyota models noted, 'the tests described by Exponent did not appear to duplicate the sophisticated methods that automotive engineers say are needed to ensure that electromagnetic interference does not cause failure of the hardware or software of engine controls.'

In other words, the tests, although conducted by an outside firm and supported by Toyota, were insufficient to diagnose a complex and intractable problem.[38] When conducting experiments, you may also have to consider the many different facets of the organization's operations. You may then become aware of conditions that need attention before your idea can be deployed effectively. For example, during your experimentation with a new process design for a factory, you might discover that the factory is underperforming because employee motivation is low and/or because existing equipment is not being used to its full capacity. Based on this information, you might want to investigate ways to increase employee productivity using current processes before trying a complete redesign.

Managing the Solution Space. At the heart of experimentation is the desire to find the optimal way to achieve your objective. That is, you want to identify the 'correct' solution from within the search space (the set of all possible solutions). As you experiment, the search space expands or shrinks. Eventually, you'll home in on a particular section of the space and abandon areas where the solutions don't meet requirements. Through repeated experiments you'll eliminate a number of possible solutions until only the appropriate one remains.

The notion of a search space gives you a way to organize all possible solutions based on their key features. Think of a square with each line representing a dimension of a solution – for example, cost (low to high), or risk (high to low) – or, to take a more complex example, in the case of a technology solution the dimensions might include the operating system or programming language to be used. All possible solutions fall somewhere in the square.

The process of experimentation involves both *exploration* and *exploitation*. As you begin to experiment with an idea, you *explore* the search space for all possible solutions that might be of interest. Then, through repeated experiments and refinements, you move your attention to *exploitation*. Here, you focus in depth on a few solutions and continuously refine and update them to select the most appropriate one.

In the figure below, each star represents a candidate solution in the search space. Note that several candidates have been abandoned between the first and second spaces. In the third space, not only are there fewer solutions but they are clustered in fewer areas of the space.

Figure 5.2: Evolution of the solution space

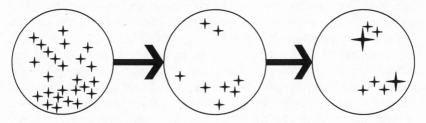

When we actively manage the search space, a success (or failure) leads to abandonment of a portion of the search space. The objective is to be efficient in the design of experiments, but not get caught up in local optima. In figure 5.2, you can see that the focus seems to be shifting to the bottom half of the search space. These candidate solutions appear to be the most promising and have withstood testing through repeated experiments. The solutions at the bottom of the space have more similarities with each other. *Since in most cases it is impossible to test all possible solutions in the search space, we normally investigate only a sample* – focusing on a handful of solutions to see how well they meet our needs. We then decide whether to explore solutions within the same space, or to move on to other areas. As you can see from the figure there might be a number of candidate solutions in the top half of the solution space. But if you shifted attention away from that part of the space after sampling and rejecting a few solutions in the area, you might not discover them and might miss some potentially interesting solutions.

As you experiment, you should constantly revisit the entire search space and compare your local optima solution with other options that might be available in other parts of the search space. While there is no foolproof method for ensuring you don't get stuck in local optima, do take steps to avoid this pitfall as you maneuver in the search space.

Getting Help from Your Friends

Experimentation requires a certain level of discipline and persistence. Not all of us are good experimenters, but everyone should know the basics of experimentation. It's important to recognize that the best idea experimenter may not be the person who came up with the idea or advocated for it. In any case, there is no shame in asking for help. Sometimes, organizations leave it to the discretion of the idea creator to involve other people in the experimentation process. In other cases, an organization might require an employee to involve others; for example, it might arrange for a rookie employee to team up with a mentor who can provide guidance. I strongly recommend that you build a team of people who can help you get the most out of experimentation. The best team comprises individuals who bring complementary skills to bear on the experimentation process. Some might be good at data analysis, while others are good at running the various experiments and collecting data. Some might have domain expertise in the idea, while others bring years of experience in conducting experimentation. As with any project, clear articulation of roles and responsibilities for each team member and good communication and coordination will enhance the experimentation effort.

Experimenting outside the Organization

Sometimes, despite your best efforts to find opportunities, for a number of reasons your organization may not be the best environment for experimentation. For example, (1) the idea is too radical and may provoke opposition within the organization; (2) the expertise needed to experiment with an idea is not available within the organization; (3) the resources needed to experiment with an idea are not available within the organization; or (4) the idea requires collaboration with external parties who may feel uncomfortable collaborating within the organizational confines. Under these conditions, it may be best to find alternative environments for experimentation. Some organizations choose to collaborate with think tanks and academic institutions. I have had the pleasure of working with organizations through the Institute for Innovation in Information Management at the University of Washington on such efforts, and it is from this vantage point that I provide some suggestions for how to proceed.

1 *Understand the limitations of your organization.* Most organizations have built-in constraints of one type or another; trying to experiment within these constraints, even if feasible, might not be optimal. Instead, try to find partners who (a) have appropriate experience with experimentation, (b) understand your organization, and

(c) have a reputation for managing intellectual property (IP) with care and integrity.

2 *Understand the nature of the idea you are thinking about experimenting with.* Highly sensitive ideas may require experimentation within the confines of the organization because experimenting externally could result in loss of intellectual property. Other ideas – for example, ideas about emerging problems that require new thinking – may benefit from outside input. Problems that are not unique to your own organization may also be best solved in partnership with external entities.

3 *Get to know the universities in your area and seek ways in which you can collaborate with them on research projects.* Universities are good places to look for collaborators and fresh thinking. Bring them ideas for which you don't have the time, resources, energy, or (possibly) capability to experiment on.

4 *Work toward a mutually beneficial partnership.* Remember that you don't want to nickel and dime during experimentation; what you want is to share your problems, collaborate to find solutions, learn from and share knowledge with your partners, and enrich the knowledge base of all parties.

5 *Start small with low-risk ideas and then scale up to higher-risk ideas.* Working with ideas that are low risk will allow you to get used to the experimentation process and develop trust and effective communication with the research partners.

6 *Understand the various IP issues.* Establish a clear understanding of who owns the idea, who owns the data generated from the experimentation process, how the results will be communicated, and to whom you will report results. These may be difficult conversations, but they should be conducted before any work is done, to provide the basis for a good working relationship.

Conclusion

The goal of experimentation is to develop new knowledge and test ideas in new settings. The organization's task is to create an environment in which employees are motivated to engage with the process of testing ideas and are able to learn from both their failures and their successes. To create such an environment, the organization must extend experimentation beyond its R&D labs, to invite all employees into its culture of active inquiry. In this environment, employees are encouraged to try out their ideas, build prototypes, and gather data rather than simply going with their gut feelings. Though the organization provides guidelines for the process of experimentation, it also recognizes the need to develop and continuously refine this process.

Every employee within an organization should be trained in the basics of experimentation. The objective is to develop a workforce that is knowledgeable about the science of experimentation, able to develop innovative and cost-effective ways to conduct experiments, and enthusiastic about participating in the experimentation process. The organization should find ways to inculcate the behaviors that drive good experimentation and establish mechanisms for capturing the knowledge generated by the experimentation process and for sharing it across the enterprise.

The outcome of the experimentation process is a set of ideas that are ready to be instantiated into tangible products, services, or practices; in other words, they are ready to be commercialized. As the next chapter explains, the process of commercialization calls for figuring out how best to package solutions, communicate their value, and promote their adoption.

Appendix:
Definitions of Terms Used in the Description of the Research Process

Term	Description
Independent variable	A variable that is manipulated or changed to gauge the effects on some outcome or dependent variable – it is the 'force' that is hypothesized to cause change in the outcome of the experiment.[39]
Dependent variable	The experimental variable that is measured to determine the effects of an independent variable (e.g., experimental treatment) on selected subjects during a research experiment. Sometimes referred to as the *dependent measure, criterion variable,* or *Y variable.*[40]
Exploratory research	Broad-ranging, intentional, systematic data collection designed to maximize discovery of generalizations based on description and direct understanding of an area of social or psychological life.[41]
Descriptive research	Research that provides a detailed account of a social setting, a group of people, a community, a situation, or some other phenomenon.[42]
Hypothesis	A tentative statement of belief based on the expert judgment of the researcher. This hypothesis must be subject to falsification; that is, the research needs to be set up in such a way that the scientist is able to conclude logically that the hypothesis is either correct or incorrect.[43]
Reliability	The dependability, consistency, and/or repeatability of a project's data collection, interpretation, and/or analysis.[44]
Validity	A research investigation is said to have *internal validity* if there are valid causal implications and is said to have *external validity* if the results are generalizable.[45]
Moderator variable	An independent or predictor variable, $Z,$ that interacts with another independent or predictor variable, $X,$ in predicting scores on and accounting for variance in a dependent or predicted variable, $Y.$[46]
Mediator variable	A variable that transmits the effects of an independent variable to a dependent variable. Mediator variables are common in disciplines such as psychology, sociology, management, education, political science, and public administration.[47]
Simple random sampling	A method of drawing a sample of some fixed size n from the population of interest, which ensures that all possible samples of this size (n) are equiprobable (i.e., equally likely to be drawn).

(Continued)

Appendix: (*Continued*)

Term	Description
	(A *sample* is a subset of a population, and *sampling* refers to the process of drawing samples from a population.)[48]
Purposive sampling	The use of expert knowledge of a population to select in a non-random manner a sample of elements that represents a cross-section of the population.[49]
Correlation	A statistical measure of the relationship or association between two or more variables.[50]
Causation	The relationship between an event (the *cause*) and a second event (the *effect*), where the second event is a consequence of the first.[51]

6 Idea Commercialization

No idea is ready for mainstream adoption and implementation without a commercialization strategy. Even if it has obvious merit and potential tangible benefits, it must be translated into a product or service with convincing appeal for end users. At this point in the intrapreneurship process we turn from 'ideas' to 'solutions.' A solution can represent a product or service meant for either internal or external consumption. It could also be a new business process or a refinement to an existing business practice of the organization. In general, consumers are receptive to solutions that can either fix a specific problem they are experiencing or extend their capabilities so that they can achieve something they desire.

To start commercializing an idea, you need to consider the price – either in real dollars or opportunity costs – that a customer would be willing to pay. You also need to think about the most appropriate target group to pitch the product to initially. Who would be most capable of documenting results and proselytizing to create a 'bandwagon effect'? Once you have achieved success with this key group, you can package the idea to promote its widespread adoption and to integrate it into users' consumption patterns and work practices.

Apple Inc.'s products have been adopted at a revolutionary rate, disrupting entire industries. By paring down a new product to achieve simplicity of form and function, building on its core technology, and launching it as the 'Next Big Thing,' they show instead of tell customers what their new products do.[1] Consider the launch of the iPod in 2001, where 'at the end of 2001, only 128,000 people had iPods. At the end of 2009, Apple ha[d] sold somewhere near a quarter-billion iPods . . . The century-old music industry reordered itself around the iPod . . . The iPod became a permanent fixture in the social and political culture.'[2]

Unlike the previous stages in the intrapreneurship process, where the organization took a backseat to its employees, here the organization takes control. It's rare for an individual or a team of employees to drive the commercialization process; most idea creators lack expertise or even interest in the administrative, marketing, legal, and accounting aspects of commercialization. For example, academic research institutions such as the 'Carnegie I' universities each have dedicated 'technology transfer' units that take the results of research and transform them into products and services that can actually be used by various groups of consumers. These units work with the researchers who have taken new ideas from conceptualization to proof of concept (the outcome of the experimentation stage), helping them find venture capital, build a business case, do market analysis, work out pricing and promotion details, and even identify a management team to oversee the commercialization process. The ideal technology transfer office will facilitate the commercialization of ideas by providing value-added services in a consultative manner that frees the researcher from the burden of bureaucratic details such as developing intellectual property agreements, analyzing markets, and so on. Successful units make the process easy and transparent for researchers, who seldom have the skills or interest to commercialize on their own. Most universities see significant returns from their investments in these centers.[3]

The example of academia's technology transfer offices can be useful to organizations looking for ways to build their capacity for commercialization. The good news is that the literature on how to commercialize products and services is vast and that all organizations already have experience with the commercialization process (after all, if an organization couldn't commercialize its products and services, it wouldn't exist!). The focus of this chapter is not on the commercialization process in general (about which a great deal of literature is already available)[4] but on the often ignored yet important challenge of commercializing solutions that have an *internal* focus and need to be deployed within the confines of the organization. This less glamorous aspect of the process is central to realizing the promise of intrapreneurship. An idea creator needs the expertise of a cross-functional team and support from the company's infrastructure just as much when attempting to commercialize ideas within an organization as when launching a new product in the outside world. Ultimately, the organization will only see returns from its investment into intrapreneurship if it is able to commercialize solutions both internally and externally.

Organizational Perspective

Most organizations already have commercialization processes for their signature products and services; simple economics dictate that the organization can't invent a new commercialization process for every product or service it develops. For solutions intended for external markets, the use of existing/traditional commercialization processes will suffice. For both incremental ideas and radical ideas, the commercialization strategy will most likely be based on the regular product launch strategy. Ideally, an organization facilitates commercialization through plug-and-play templates and tools that can be used with minimal customization. The discussion that follows focuses on an area in which organizations are less likely to have a tried-and-true commercialization strategy in place – the category of *internal* solutions, which can be much more difficult to implement than other kinds of intrapreneurial ideas.

Creating the Commercialization Team

The idea will be taken from concept to adoption by the commercialization team, or 'guiding team.' Members of this team should be carefully chosen to include people who have experience in bringing products to market, even if the idea in question is an internal one. Normally, these cross-functional teams include representatives from marketing, public relations, engineering (if applicable), legal, and any other units in which the idea needs to be launched. The organization should choose a project manager with skills that can help the team work as a cohesive unit and collaborate effectively. The commercialization team is akin to a SWAT team or a Navy SEALs unit. The ideal team will have the right mix of skills and good collaboration and the agility to take advantage of opportunities as they arise. Team members will have deep domain knowledge in the areas relevant to the solution and a network of relationships (social capital) that enables them to draw on relevant knowledge sources and make deals. Since team members usually have 'day' jobs, resources need to be put in place to allow them to focus on the task at hand.

The commercialization team for an internally focused solution must include members from all sectors in which the idea will be implemented. After all, they're the customers and are positioned to provide valuable feedback. By including them in the process, the organization communicates that it is serious about understanding their work processes and environment. Solutions based on radical ideas – for either internal or external implementation – need external players on the team. They may be strategic consultants, academic partners, or representatives of major customers. These players give the team diversity and the fresh perspective needed to avoid 'groupthink.' In some cases, they may serve as trusted partners who can help to implement the solution and recruit customers. Consider a Boeing program, CREATE, that aims to commercialize externally oriented solutions.[5] Through this program, Boeing works directly with its business partners on the defense side of its business to commercialize advanced military applications. The strategy not only produces tangible benefits such as the development of new products and solutions but also helps enhance Boeing's brand image and deepen its business relationships.

Conversation with the Idea Creators

Once the team convenes, the next step is to give the idea creators a chance to voice their opinions about how involved they would like to be in the commercialization process. It would be unwise to try to move the idea through the process without the originators' input. In my experience, most idea creators want to be kept abreast of overall progress but not burdened with the nitty-gritty of marketing, legal, and communication strategies. Nevertheless, the team should give idea creators the option of being as involved as they would like to be. In an ideal world, idea creators would participate and see the commercialization process unfold, gaining a new perspective on the challenges of transforming experimentation outputs into commercial solutions that people will adopt. This exposure would give creators an appreciation of the behind-the-scenes work of commercialization, and would also help develop an understanding of the intrapreneurship process across the organization.

It is important to establish early on how the team will communicate with the idea creators, especially how they will be kept updated through the remaining stages of the process. Lack of timely communication from the commercialization team can be frustrating for inventors and can hamper the development of an intrapreneurial culture within an organization. Regular check-ins and progress updates are vital to reduce any apprehension and anxiety felt by idea creators. It may be worthwhile to designate one person of the commercialization team to take on this role.

Give the idea creator the option of getting involved in important decisions (e.g., related to pricing, packaging, promotion, etc.). When the idea creators are happy about their working relationship with the commercialization team, the image of intrapreneurship across the organization is enhanced. Conversely, if idea creators are inconvenienced or shunted aside during the commercialization process, the intrapreneurial spirit of the organization can suffer.

Recognition and Compensation for Idea Creators

As ideas are moved into the commercialization process, it is essential to recognize and compensate the idea creators. For every idea that has made its way to being a *solution* for experimentation, there are hundreds, possibly thousands, of ideas that have not. There may also be quite a number of intrapreneurs who have had to abandon their ideas at an earlier stage. Hence, because successful ideas are relatively rare, the organization needs to reward idea creators who have persevered and succeeded against the odds. Doing so serves two important purposes: first, it provides idea creators with the necessary jolt of energy that comes from having their achievements recognized; second, it lets the rest of the organization know that success is possible and helps to sustain belief in the intrapreneurship process.

Forms of compensation will vary, sometimes dramatically, given the range of ideas and organizational contexts. Reward structures can be based on outcomes (i.e., end results that contribute to the financial bottom line) or processes (i.e., control-based rewards that measure how well an internal process was followed), and can be monetary or not. If an idea has an external customer, the organization often rewards the employee with a percentage of the revenues received from net sales or compensation based on gross margins. For radical ideas that have the potential to open a new business venture or operational focus for the organization, the employee may be rewarded with management responsibility to oversee the new venture as well as stock options that give an incentive to grow the venture. If the idea causes efficiency gains and new modes of working internally, employees may be granted a lump sum bonus to compensate them for their time and effort.

When designing rewards you should consider employees' personalities and motivations. Monetary rewards, no matter how enticing, don't appeal to everyone. Sometimes, public recognition in front of peers and managers is just as pleasing. Respect from peers, greater responsibility, and opportunities to do interesting work are all powerful motivators.[6] On the other hand, some employees prefer to work behind the scenes and not be the center of attention. A manager must communicate with employees to determine what sort of rewards would suit them best. Based on my experience, the best compensation packages have a combination of monetary and non-monetary incentives. Monetary rewards can come in the shape of royalties, bonuses, or pay raises, while non-monetary rewards can take the form of public recognition, time and resources for training and development, or even discretionary resources to pursue the next set of ideas. By all means publicize the non-monetary rewards as examples of what the organization wants all employees to aspire to, but be aware that broadcasting the amount of a monetary reward is not always desirable.

Most employees will not have thought about the rewards they want. They may come to this conversation unprepared. The ideal organization will not take advantage of their inexperience, but will provide them with resources such as books and articles and even contact with other inventors who can help them think through these vital issues. Remember, your long-term goal is to develop evangelists for intrapreneurship by ensuring that each innovator feels fairly compensated and treated professionally and courteously. Organizations that are just beginning to set up their intrapreneurship programs should be especially generous when constructing rewards for idea creators as this draws the attention of other employees to the value of intrapreneurship.

Identifying Resources and Assets

When building a commercialization strategy, it is important to identify the resources and assets needed to move the idea to market. Resources can be categorized as *'must have'* and *'nice to have.'* If essential resources can't be secured internally, the commercialization team must evaluate whether to acquire them from the outside, hold off on the commercialization process, or abandon commercialization of that particular idea altogether. If 'nice to have' resources aren't readily available, the commercialization effort can begin without them. If these kinds of resources are already tied up, consider doing without them or leveraging them later.

Three categories of complementary assets are normally considered during commercialization – generic, specialized, and co-specialized.[7] Generic assets are those that already exist within the organization and can be used, as is, to leverage the idea. For example, an existing piece of equipment may be used to mass produce the new product. A specialized asset is one that is specific to the innovation in question; there is a direct and necessary connection between the new product/service and the asset. For example, an organization might need to purchase a new piece of equipment specifically to produce and commercialize an item. Finally, a co-specialized asset is one that both furthers and benefits the innovation. An example would be the very valuable 'gold clients' of the organization. Convincing them of an idea's benefits and getting them to use it, if done properly, can increase the idea's popularity and impact and also enhance the organization's relationship with the client.

Categorizing assets in these ways will help the team develop strategies for acquiring necessary resources that are not currently available within the organization. When the assets are available internally, the organization needs to calculate the opportunity cost involved in having these resources diverted from their current function to support the innovation. If the assets need to be acquired, the organization needs to identify the 'useful life' of the innovation, and then see how much of the cost of the asset (especially, if the asset is very expensive to acquire) can be amortized over the life of the innovation.

The commercialization team first decides how to situate the new idea in the context of resources and assets that are available to the organization. Next, the team constructs strategies to share revenue and rewards with departments that own complementary resources. For example, ideas that originate in one department will need cooperation and know-how from other departments that can enhance the reach of an idea (or, alternatively, that can limit the idea's potential if not consulted). It's important to gain the support of other departments and motivate them to join the commercialization plan. Alternatively, the team will need to justify the cost of acquiring new complementary resources. Sometimes an idea that requires resources beyond what is currently available cannot be taken further because the returns from the idea might not warrant investing in a new set of complementary assets. In some cases, the organization needs to consider whether it is feasible to transport either the idea or the complementary assets from one location to another. For example, if there are geographic or functional distances between the place the idea was created and experimented with and the place where the complementary resources are located, the team must decide whether the idea can be moved to the space where the complementary resources exist, or vice versa.

For incremental ideas and those that build on existing products and services, complementary assets will usually already be present. But for radical ideas and internally focused ideas that are being launched for the first time, special arrangements may be needed to procure the complementary assets. It is also essential to give people ample time to implement the idea. People may need training in the type of work involved in developing the idea or access to experts with relevant skills and knowledge. Or you may need to bring in temporary help during the initial launch phase of the idea to lower the workload of regular employees.

Markets

Your commercialization strategy should define the characteristics and size of the target market. Market research to explore the idea's potential zone of influence will be needed. It's important to identify immediate markets that can be tapped into right away and potential future markets for the longer term. The resources invested in the commercialization strategy and approach will be dictated by the likely size of the market. Small markets should have targeted and very low-cost initiatives since you don't want the marketing expense to exceed potential revenues. The commercialization strategy should also identify the path to market by including product launch plans and plans for moving from initial market entry to market saturation or full exploitation. Develop these plans early, but be prepared to revise them as necessary as you work through the stages.

Accurate market definition is critical for internal ideas: unrealistically high expectations can lead to disappointing outcomes. Defining your primary market will help you tailor your messages about the commercialization plan and attend to details such as how to provide incentives to a specific group.

In devising a commercialization strategy, you will need to ensure that you have calculated a reasonable and accurate amount of time for bringing the idea to market. Your 'time to market' may range from a few days to a year or more. Collaboration with external customers and partners can help cut down on time to market and can provide organizations with a bridge over 'the so-called "valley of death" by connecting their creative technologies with leading companies who have access to markets.'[8] Some ideas may not be ready to go to market because of poor market conditions. Nagesh Challa has repeatedly encountered this situation with his innovative ideas. For instance, 'in the early 1990s, he invented the Media Stick, a 2-megabyte storage device for PCs and mobile phones,' but people did not know what to do with that much storage space.[9] Challa found himself ahead of the curve again when he founded Ecrio in 1998. He pitched his idea for a multimedia device to a number of mobile phone companies who gave him feedback that they 'were looking for something simpler.'[10] In these cases, it may be best to wait for a change in market conditions before introducing your idea.

Time to market may also depend on how quickly the organization can get approval from external entities – for example, from regulatory authorities (think of the FDA's role in the drug approval process) or other bodies that the organization can influence but not control. Choosing the best time to launch the solution is also important. The best choice is a time when there is little else competing for your customers' attention. Itera's first viable bicycle made out of plastic composite instead of metal was a genuine innovation.[11] Itera had a strong marketing campaign and newspaper support for the bicycles, but the product ultimately failed because it looked and felt 'different'; the bikes were heavier than their metal counterparts. Furthermore, a competitor released similarly priced, standard bikes at the same time.[12] Had the competitor not introduced a product at the same time, Itera would have had a better chance (albeit a small one) of success. Consider the movie industry's calculus regarding release dates. The major studios consult the National Research Group (NRG) Competitive Positioning report before they finalize the all-important opening date for a movie. The report lets them know 'when one of [its] films is on a collision course with a competitor's film that appeals to the same herd . . . and the losing studio can reschedule its opening to a different weekend, even if it's a less advantageous time period (i.e., not the summer and not the holidays).'[13]

It's also important to consider time to market in terms of *attention management*. You must take a global view of how many new ideas are being introduced within (or across) the organization. Even though the idea may be ready to be released, holding back might be a good option when there are many other ideas competing for people's attention. Again, in the case of the movie industry, the NRG helps movie studios to 'rethink their entire business models by examining movies' declining share of the public's "wallet" and "clock" as they compete with music, DVDs, cable TV, and other forms of home entertainment.'[14] Sometimes product commercialization fails not because there's anything inherently wrong with the idea but because it came out at the wrong time.

Packaging, Pricing, and Promotion

A commercialization strategy, like any marketing strategy, needs to be based on the 'three Ps': packaging, pricing, and promotion.[15]

PACKAGING

First, an idea must be *packaged* into a product, service, or business practice in order to be commercially viable. In my experience, the single most important packaging decision is whether to create a new stand-alone offering or to piggy-back the idea onto an existing solution. Each option has its pros and cons. Creating a new product, service, or practice can be a significant undertaking, but it may pay off if the organization clearly differentiates the idea and uses it to signal a departure from how things are currently done. However, the organization must understand that it's much easier to get existing customers – whether internal or external – to accept and use add-ons and incremental improvements.

Think of the decisions related to packaging in terms of a two-by-two matrix (see table 6.1). Along one dimension is the type of idea – for example, radical or incremental. Along the other dimension is the type of market – existing or new. An existing market is one where the organization has already established channels for product distribution and brand recognition. New markets are unexplored spaces where the idea provides an entry-point for the organization.

As the table shows, for incremental ideas that serve existing markets, the optimal strategy is to try and find ways to place the solution as an *add-on* to existing offerings. Incremental ideas that are aimed at new markets will find it difficult if not impossible to go it alone. Hence, the development of sound business relationships with existing

Table 6.1
Packaging different types of ideas

Type of Idea	Type of Market	
	Existing	New
Incremental	Add on to existing solutions, as this is the lowest-risk approach and adoption rates are likely to be higher.	See what business partnerships you can forge: who might find the idea of value and whose customers and channels you could use to enter the market (e.g., business partners could purchase rights to provide the idea to their existing customers, for which they would pay you royalties).
Radical	Develop new packaging to clearly differentiate the offering.	Launch the idea as a new, stand-alone offering.

players in the market becomes critical. These organizations already have the customers and channels developed. Partnering with them will help you plug the idea onto an existing solution that customers understand. This is especially true of ideas for internal consumption. Each unit of the organization has deep relationships that can be leveraged by other units within the firm when commercializing ideas. It would be foolish, and costly, for a department to make a separate approach to existing customers of a peer unit in the organization. When packaging radical ideas for existing markets, it's important to create a package that clearly differentiates the solution from other offerings. Existing relationships with customers can be leveraged as long as the packaging makes it easy for customers to see what is revolutionary about the solution. When packaging radical ideas for new markets, a substantial investment may be needed to build the relationships that will make potential customers receptive to the idea.

For internal ideas, the critical packaging issue is one of framing and placement. Is the idea going to be part of a new human resources policy directive, a new incentive system, a new legal mandate for how work should be done, or a new operational approach such as how projects should be managed and mandated? The packaging of the idea tells a lot about how the idea is perceived and valued in the organization. An idea packaged as a legal mandate will be received differently from a casual suggestion about how to improve productivity. Similarly, ideas that are packaged as part of an internal technology rollout will be viewed differently from ideas that are framed as part of a new human resources incentive system. It is important to gain an understanding of how users will perceive and respond to the packaging of the internal idea.

The packaging of internal solutions requires as much care and attention as the packaging of an external product. Internal solutions have to compete for the attention of employees who may be overloaded with information from many other sources. Hence, one of the critical attributes of a good packaging is its ability to capture employee attention.

It is also important to present the solution in an accessible and readily usable form. Internal ideas are usually designed to improve business processes either directly (by increasing the effectiveness and/or efficiency of a business process) or indirectly (by introducing a new product/service into an existing process). The customer will be more receptive to the solution if you can integrate it into the work process with minimal disruption. Some disruptions can't be avoided, and here the focus should be on explaining why the costs to be incurred are justified. Once you capture employees' attention, you want to ensure that that attention is focused more on the benefits of the idea than on any inconveniences attached to its introduction.

Finally, the packaging should provide information about what the solution does, who should use it, and what are the intended outcomes (benefits) of its use. It's essential to think through exactly what you want to highlight about the idea, and how this relates to the employees who are its intended customers. Consider how you would design an advertisement for the solution that could go on a web page, be shrunk down to the size of a business card, or blown up to the size of a poster. Use focus groups to design and evaluate this artifact through multiple lenses. And remember, best marketing practices teach us to err on the side of caution and avoid overselling the solution.

PRICING

How much will it cost customers to adopt and implement the idea? Costs may be actual monies they need to shell out, opportunity costs (if they have to divert attention from other activities), or even psychological costs (if they have to overcome mental blocks and fear of change). Understanding the costs is critical to determining the right price. This is especially important for artifacts that are going to be consumed *within* the organization rather than by *external* customers. It is often easier to price an idea for external consumption; most of the time you have at your disposal one or more of the following: (1) historical information about previous product introductions in the marketplace, (2) information about how other organizations are pricing similar offerings, and (3) the need to quantify the price into real dollars (or rupees, or whatever). These conditions are seldom present when you are determining the cost of internal ideas. Ideally, the costs of adopting the idea should be less than the intended benefits. However, even when this isn't the case, there may still be a business need to adopt the idea. For example, changes to business processes to comply with legal or regulatory requirements may be costly and often do not produce direct economic benefits, but organizations still have to implement them.

There is a tendency to get 'soft' when thinking about the right price at which to commercialize internal ideas because issues such as profit margins and the like do not apply. Nevertheless, taking too casual an approach to the pricing of internal ideas can be dangerous. Inappropriate pricing could cause the idea to be ignored. As well, when marketing and advertising the idea, the organization needs to explain why the cost of adoption is justified. For example, the idea may produce savings in the long run or produce benefits that will far exceed the initial costs.

Questions to consider regarding the costs and benefits of an idea include the following: (1) Who is going to bear the cost? (2) Will costs differ among the various user groups and if so how? (3) Where will individuals look for the resources to pay the costs (remember costs may be cognitive and/or psychological as well as monetary)? (4) How can benefits be realized in a manner that is tangible and visible? (5) What resources are required to make adoption of the idea viable at a given price point? You must also consider traditional pricing issues such as whether there is a need to differentiate pricing by customers and/ or develop a promotional pricing scheme. A promotional pricing scheme, for example, might offer early adopters the chance to implement the solution for free, thus allowing the organization to 'test drive' the solution and build a base of users who endorse the product and support its eventual adoption throughout the organization.

PROMOTION

Advertising and communication strategies will need to be developed to promote the idea. How will the idea (via the artifact in which it is

Figure 6.1: Customer bull's-eye

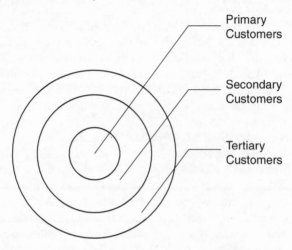

instantiated) be communicated to the intended target consumers? The first things to consider are: *who are the primary customers of the idea* and *how are you going to turn them into believers and evangelists*? For every idea with commercial potential there are primary, secondary, tertiary, and other customers. The dartboard image in figure 6.1 may help you visualize how important it is to target the right group of customers:

Trying to communicate the idea to all customers at the same time will be costly and often fruitless. A better strategy is to identify your primary customers: those for whom the idea will make the most impact and who will become the true believers in the value of the idea. Once these customers are identified, design a communications strategy to engage them. You may want to tailor your marketing and promotion messages to their requirements. If you are successful, your customers will love the idea so much they will spread the word and urge others to try it out. As their influence makes itself felt, other parts of the organization will embrace the idea. In effect, success will make the bull's-eye larger. These high-priority internal customers are normally called the *lead users*.

Lead users are customers who are thinking about the next generation of products and who are using your current products and services in advanced ways and may even be extending them by building

Table 6.2
Communicating with customers

Element	Description
Benefits to customers	Provide a concise, clear statement of the idea's value, describing its expected outcomes and how the idea will benefit its intended customers.
Costs to customers	Describe the potential costs, including the cost of not adopting the idea.

add-ons.[16] Research has shown that the pressing needs of lead users will become the requirements for other users in the marketplace within months or years.[17] Lead users have foresight that can help an organization plan product improvements and guide both incremental and radical innovations. Lead users are most likely to try out new products and services. Lead users are also the most mature users when it comes to exploiting current offerings; they already realize the limitations of these solutions and are waiting to try out new ideas that address these weaknesses. They work well with ideas that extend a current offering in the marketplace.

In addition to lead users, you should also focus on targeting early adopters, hobbyists, and opinion makers. Since they're risk takers, these are ideal candidates to bring a radical offering to the marketplace or get attention for an offering in a new marketplace. Identify opinion makers, such as bloggers and new technology enthusiasts who have vast social networks and can easily get the word out about your solution (the presumption being that you have something good to offer and that they will have positive things to say).

In developing a communication plan, it's vital that you deliver a clear and compelling message about how the idea is going to *benefit* the intended customers. Most of the time, you will be expecting customers to bear some cost for adopting the idea. This cost can take different forms: it might require them to change their current way of working, or to add new steps to an existing process, or even to abandon their current work practices in favor of new ones. In developing your communication plan, you may find the points outlined in table 6.2 helpful.

Remember that change is difficult, and that unless communication is clear, people won't adopt the idea. Therefore, a clear communication strategy is essential. The best communication strategies have a simple, jargon-free 'elevator pitch' that, at a minimum, engages the customer to seek more information. Avoid technical words and acronyms (the Common Craft video series contains some useful tips about how to communicate ideas simply and clearly).[18] Consider using stories and case studies to demonstrate the value of ideas, show customers how they can be used, and describe how much better their personal or professional lives will be when they adopt the idea. Another approach is to write a value proposition from the perspective of the intended customer to show the benefits of adopting the idea. The value proposition should clearly identify: (1) who the idea is for, (2) why the idea is important, (3) how the idea is going to make a difference in the customer's life, and (4) why ignoring the idea could be costly. In the case of Apple's iPad, the value proposition is an intelligent and simple-to-use device that provides a large display. In contrast, Dell's tablet computer provides a different value proposition to business users: 'a promise that its tablet won't just be a coffee-table device, but instead a powerful productivity tool.'[19] Positioning the idea – pitching the idea to attract the attention of your intended customers – is also important. For example, as a product leader, Apple's 'challenge [was] ensuring successful launch . . . and being first to market.'[20]

Your commercialization strategy should also chart out the life cycle of the artifact (product, service, or practice) that embodies the idea. How will the artifact be managed through the stages of introduction, growth, maturity, and (finally) decline? This analysis should also include strategies to keep the idea relevant by adapting to changing conditions in the market in order to 'keep your innovation fresh, responsive, and ideally suited to the needs it was designed to meet.' Thinking through the lifecycle of the artifact will help your organization put in place necessary marketing, advertising, and communication programs from launch to eventual removal from the marketplace. For instance, when thinking of the introduction stage, the organization should clearly identify (1) the initial adopters for the artifact, (2) their likely reasons for adopting it, (3) how the organization can learn from the experiences of early adopters in order to bring other users on board, and (4) how to structure pricing so as to get the most important customers to adopt the idea.

Implementation Plans

The organization needs to create a plan to support the initial users in their adoption of the idea. Initial users are bound to run into trouble during implementation, so support mechanisms to help them through the early stages will be critical (this issue is explored further in the next chapter). Once you attract people to the idea, you want to ensure they get the best possible experience with it. The last thing you want is for customers to flock to the new idea only to walk away disappointed. For example, *Toys R Us* made a disastrous misstep when it first launched Toysrus.com in 1999. After significant investment in the customer-facing e-commerce infrastructure, the company failed to 'meet promised shipping deadlines'[21] during the holiday season. Toys R Us 'drew heavy fines from the U.S. Federal Trade Commission (FTC),'[22] but more significant damage may have been loss of customers' trust. In 2000, the company corrected its fulfillment issues by opening two new distribution centers and 'revamping its customer service software to help it through the holiday shopping season.'[23]

Performance Measurement

Performance measures such as key performance indicators (KPIs) are an important part of the commercialization strategy. How will you know if you've received adequate returns on the effort you put into developing, experimenting with, and commercializing an idea? Failure to earn adequate returns from your efforts to date will jeopardize the future of intrapreneurship. Bear in mind that for every idea that has come this far in the process, there are several dozen (or in the case of large organizations, several hundred) that did not. The organization has gambled that the ideas that made it through to commercialization will generate sufficient returns to support an infrastructure to leverage ideas going forward. Now it needs to determine how well the gamble has paid off.

Calculating your expected return on investment (ROI) is very important at the commercialization stage. ROI is a function of how much has been invested to date and how much more has to be invested for the idea to reach its full potential. When an organization has limited resources, it usually promotes the idea that can get the highest ROI. Other metrics, such as the payback period (how quickly the organization can recoup its investment) and the internal rate of return, are not germane to this discussion (and are covered in any accounting textbook), but every organization needs to calculate and document them systematically. The return on internal ideas isn't normally calculated in terms of 'real' earnings. Instead, it is calculated in terms of cost savings achieved, new business opportunities generated, or new customers signed up. Ideally, the commercialization strategy would outline the steps to capture these internally generated savings, efficiencies, and opportunities.

Accurately measuring the resources saved, gained, or developed through innovation projects can be quite challenging and requires some creativity. Applying traditional measurements such as ROI to intrapreneurship activities may not be very helpful. These measurements, taken in isolation, are notoriously bad at uncovering the true business value of intrapreneurship.[24] ROI evaluates the resources allocated to a project and the return upon those resources, but the returns on innovation can be hard to quantify. Innovation often affects many aspects of a business; it can cause perceptual shifts, improve efficiency, and sometimes confer competitive advantages. Yet innovation projects involve a degree of uncertainty: they revolve around promises, risks, and opportunities rather than concrete outcomes or assurances. For these reasons, the mechanisms for capturing value for innovative projects need to be carefully negotiated so as to encourage intrapreneurship while maintaining objectivity and rigor around the evaluation process. It is always a good idea to use a combination of measures, including quantitative and qualitative and short-term and long-term measures, to capture the returns on an innovation assignment.

Metrics to evaluate a phenomenon normally fall into two categories: process metrics and output metrics. Process metrics evaluate the steps required to move from inputs to outputs. Output metrics are those that evaluate the finished product. Output evaluations are conducted by the customers of the product or service, whereas process evaluations are conducted by the producing organization. Output metrics are more subjective and may be highly variable depending on the perspective of the customer answering the questions – but they do give us a sense of how those who are outside the production process view the product and whether the product meets the demands of the customer.

THE MEASUREMENT PROCESS

First, define the measurement process. Without an adequate definition of the process, you might be inclined to measure different things at different points in time. The various components of what you are measuring must also be defined: what indicators will you look for to determine the idea's impact on your business? Both first-order (direct) and second-order (indirect) impacts should be defined.

Once we define the process, the second step is to articulate the attributes to be measured. For example, in weight training we can measure body fat, stamina, muscle strength, and a whole slew of other indicators of fitness. We can also look at composite indicators that show the combined impact of several individual indicators. In the case of intrapreneurship, we must be clear about what each indicator of commercialization success is measuring, and how each indicator relates to other indicators. For instance, we must specify if individual indicators can be combined to arrive at a composite score. It's common to measure attributes such as the time taken to complete the process, or the number of problems that arise during the conduct of a process. Output-based KPIs are derived from an understanding of what the customer wants. In the case of intrapreneurship, we can have both internal and external customers. If we are launching a solution for the human resources functions of the organization, such as payroll processing and the administration of employee benefits, the customers of interest are the employees of the organization. If we launch a new service (or process) for a call center, the customers of our products and services who call the center are the customers we are interested in. Developing good output measures calls for the identification of customers and their needs. We normally have multiple categories of customers for an idea. While all customers may share certain characteristics, differences in their experiences and needs can be used to segment them. Long-standing customers have different needs from new ones; similarly, repeat customers will have different needs from occasional customers. It's always a good idea to seek feedback from all customer segments to get a better grasp of the range of customer expectations. Getting this feedback through surveys or other instruments is the second step in measuring outputs. Here, the overriding rule is the KISS principle – Keep it simple, stupid! Nothing is more certain to dissuade customers from providing input than a long and cumbersome survey. Customers must be polled routinely and frequently for their opinions, yet they must not feel imposed upon. Also, customers will get frustrated very quickly if they feel that their opinions are being ignored or are making no difference to how the product or service is being delivered.

The third step involves analyzing the measures – in essence, trying to answer the question 'What do the indicators tell us?' For scores to be meaningful, we need to understand them within a given context. Context normally involves two items: (a) the history of the process, and (b) outsider response. The history of the process tells us how we are doing currently compared to how we were doing in the past, and we look for improved scores on positive indicators and lower numbers on negative indicators. Developing a historical context for evaluating metrics requires time and experience. We can't expect comparisons over short time periods (i.e., today versus yesterday) to be significant; however, comparing how we did today against the average performance over a month will provide us with some useful insights.

Unlike historical indicators, outsider information provides a more immediate sense of the impact of an innovation. Through external benchmarking, these indicators allow you to compare results with those obtained by other organizations in similar situations. Two types of benchmarking are common: (1) comparison with the average performance of organizations in the industry, and (2) comparison with industry leaders. The first kind of benchmarking is most useful in the early stages of designing an intrapreneurship capability. If there is no previous history of similar efforts to use as a basis of comparison, it is best to gauge commercialization success relative to rest of the industry. The latter type is more suitable once we've gained more experience with the process and are looking to move up in the standings and reach higher goals.

The fourth step involves devising interventions to improve performance in targeted areas. Interventions can serve as positive or negative reinforcements. Positive reinforcements involve understanding and continuing to do what worked well in order to make the process stronger. Negative reinforcements entail uncovering what went wrong, determining how to correct it, and then implementing the correction to improve the process. For example, if we know that our idea screening process is satisfactory and sound based on customer receptivity during the launch, we must make sure that all successive projects follow the same methodology so as to gain the same positive results. On the other hand, if we uncover shortcomings in our attempts to shorten time to market, corrective alternatives should be devised and implemented. The fourth step feeds back into the second or third steps, depending on whether we need to calibrate new measures. If new measures are required, we go back to the second step; otherwise, we go ahead to the third step and analyze the measures.

DEVELOPING KPIS

Choosing the right key performance indicators (KPIs) depends on the nature of the idea and its commercialization zone. Radical ideas that are being deployed externally might call for metrics on the number of customers that adopt the idea, the revenues earned, the increase in market share, and the changes in the organization's position in the industry. For an incremental externally focused idea, the organization might look for KPIs that show how customers adopt the idea or the extent to which complaints decrease or positive reviews increase among those that adopt the idea. For incremental ideas that are commercialized internally, the KPIs may range from process metrics (such as reduction of process defects) to a reduction of time to complete the process and/or to improvements in employee satisfaction with the new process.

When devising KPIs, identify what the *baseline* measures are before commercialization, so you can accurately gauge the idea's contribution. For example, if the error rate of a process was 18 percent before an idea was implemented and 10 percent after implementation, you can measure the significance of the 8 percent drop in the context of the investment in the new intervention, the time it took to deploy it, and the impact on the bottom line. It's also important to clearly communicate the KPIs to stakeholders. KPIs are too often 'kept secret' or are only known to a few people in the organization. Accordingly, problems arise when *evaluative* decisions are made about the idea's performance because people don't have a common understanding of the criteria being used to evaluate the idea. This leads both to confusion and to evaluation based on subjective measures rather than hard facts.

Employee Perspective

If you are an employee and have reached this stage of the process, the first thing you should do is take a moment to enjoy your achievement. You have progressed where most have not. The odds of making it this far in the process are low. Most employees rarely get to commercialize their ideas, and repeated success is even rarer. Take a moment to smell the roses and enjoy the progress you've made.

Working through the commercialization process is as much an art as a science. Much of the art comes from having to navigate the politics and battle organizational inertia. The help of your idea advocate was critical during the screening process; now the commercialization team is your new best friend. Its members have been around the block multiple times and are well versed in dotting all the 'I's and crossing all the 'T's. Equally important, they understand the politics of idea adoption within your organization and how to make concepts stick in the minds of the audience. They are a great resource to help you navigate the complexities of your organization.

Appreciate the Commercialization Process

Employees should trust that their organization has a vast body of knowledge about commercialization. After all, unless an organization can successfully commercialize products and services, it will underperform or even cease to exist. Major successes in the commercialization of ideas, such as the iPod or the iPhone by Apple or the Windows operating system by Microsoft, are anomalies. Most organizations hope for blockbuster success stories but are content with more humble outcomes. Commercialization, especially when launching blockbuster and game-changing products and services, is very difficult. You should not compare your organization's commercialization track record to that of outliers like Apple. Most organizations consider commercialization a success if they attain the goals set during launch: the number of customers, the revenue expectations, the adoption rates, and the lifespan of the product or service.

Employees should recognize that, with the exception of new startups, the commercialization process in an organization has evolved over years or even decades. This process is not easy to change, and trying to do so may be a losing battle. A more viable strategy is to work within the process. In most organizations I've studied or worked with, attempts to make drastic modifications to the commercialization process guarantee one thing – a barrage of meetings with the legal department, the public relations team, and more. The bottom line is that unless you have an urgent and compelling reason to disrupt the existing commercialization process, your best strategy is to (1) get to know the commercialization process, (2) identify how to utilize the expertise and know-how that is built into the process, and (3) work collaboratively with the individuals who control the various components of the process in order to get your idea commercialized. A good understanding of the commercialization process will help you get better at developing ideas that will succeed in your intended market; you will see how the idea you have developed is viewed from an external, value-added perspective. How is value ascribed to this idea? How is it communicated? How will the value be captured? Finally, how is the value going to be realized by your customers? Studying and observing this stage of the process is immensely valuable; in order to do it right, however, you need to develop some objectivity about your idea and view it from a more detached perspective.

Employees also need to understand that while their efforts were essential in bringing the idea this far along in the intrapreneurship process, the next few steps require that they give up much of their control over the idea and turn it over to a team of specialists who have deep expertise in the commercialization process. Patience is key in commercialization. Remember, the team often doesn't have the same knowledge or level of understanding of the idea as you do. Their questions may seem naive, and they may challenge you to communicate the idea's merits and value more clearly. This could also be a good time for you to take a much-needed break from your idea. Allow others to play with it and enhance its potential. The commercialization team wants success; they want to make sure your idea can be deployed in its marketplace and the necessary returns secured. To this end, they're trying to enhance, refine, and even design the various artifacts that will make your solution a winner in an often very congested marketplace. This takes time and diligent work – often as much time and effort as you spent experimenting on the idea.

Working with the Commercialization Team

Have faith that the commercialization team, working on the organization's behalf, is trying their best to get the most out of your idea. At times, I have seen intrapreneurs get irritated about how the marketing team is presenting their idea, or question why legal takes so long to work out an agreement. The commercialization process needs to play out, even if it seems more structured and formal than the stages of the intrapreneurship process you've already passed through. This structure is necessary for an organization to gain economies of scale. Hence, at times, it may come across as a rigid process that isn't being tailored specifically for your idea.

Play an active supporting role in the development of the commercialization strategy. Try and check in on the progress, give your opinions at key decision points, and engage in the dialogue around the strategy as much as possible. One of the key outcomes of doing this is that you will not be surprised when the final commercialization strategy is about to be implemented.

Negotiating Compensation for Idea and Effort

A crucial aspect of your involvement will be to negotiate the compensation you receive for your idea. This is an item you need to think about carefully. Begin by estimating how much time and energy you invested in the idea; this is normally a good indicator of the amount of 'sweat equity' you should claim. If you worked with a team, each of you needs to consider your respective 'sweat equity' investments and arrive at a ratio to share the returns. A team can arrive at this distribution by itself, or the commercialization team can participate in these discussions in order to help calculate what is fair based on the amount and type of effort involved.

You need to explore the value of the idea not just from your perspective but also from the customer side. This will be where the commercialization team provides you with the numbers. The numbers should show various targets: how many people (employees, customers, etc.) are going to adopt the solution, what the customer will pay for the idea, what the cost of delivery will be (the costs of actually creating and handing off the solution to the customer), and so on. For internal ideas, the expected cost savings or revenue from new business opportunities should also be determined. These numbers need to be carefully studied. If necessary, seek more information and even ask if you can bring in an advisor. The focus of these conversations should be to understand the value proposition of the idea, get a reasonable understanding of its scale and scope, and calculate your expected returns on that basis.

Using this information, you can now think about how you would like to be rewarded. Options could include (1) getting a lump sum payment up front, (2) getting fixed payments over time, or (3) choosing a variable payment depending on the performance of the solution. As you can imagine, each of these has its pros and cons, so it's important not only to do a financial analysis but also to understand your own needs. For example, a lump sum payment will normally be smaller than the total value generated by the idea, whereas a fixed annuity gives you less money up front. If you choose variable pay based on the performance of the solution, you are assuming some risk; if the idea does well you could become very rich, but if it doesn't your financial payoff could be quite modest. Remember, too, that while most ideas won't make you rich, there are other kinds of rewards. There is the satisfaction you gain from seeing your idea being implemented. In cases without a significant financial return, don't despair. There may be opportunities to negotiate more independence in the kinds of projects you work on or better access to resources for training and learning new skills. These may all be possibilities for one of the few who has succeeded in getting an idea this far. You need to think about what might motivate you to pursue more ideas, and seek rewards accordingly.

Finally, begin the conversation, but be realistic. You do want to see a genuine effort to support and reward you, but unless you've created a blockbuster, it's unlikely that the organization will open the floodgates in terms of access to resources and other opportunities. Over time, however, as you build a track record and history of intrapreneurship, you'll be in a stronger position to negotiate for the things you want.

Conclusion

This chapter covers the key elements needed to develop a successful commercialization strategy: establishing the guiding team; identifying and prioritizing the required resources and assets; and developing a marketing plan that addresses packaging, pricing, and promotion. It also describes key components of a communication plan, including how to target the primary customers or lead users and how to time the product release. Finally, it discusses the use of performance measures, including the development of KPIs and output metrics.

The next chapter covers the diffusion and implementation stages, including the life cycle of the idea as it moves from early adopters to wide acceptance, and how to assist users in maximizing the potential benefits of the idea. As in the commercialization stage, the organization takes the lead in diffusing and implementing the idea. This final stage of the intrapreneurship process requires resources and infrastructure that far exceed the capabilities of individual employees. Thus, an enterprise-wide commitment is vital.

7 Diffusion and Implementation of Ideas

The final stages in the intrapreneurship process are (1) diffusing the idea to the farthest corners of the identified markets, and (2) helping customers use the commercialized artifact successfully. Diffusion and implementation are two sides of the same coin; diffusion is the process of generating buy-in and acceptance for the solution, while implementation is the process of setting up the structures, maintenance, and resources to allow it to be produced or brought into effective use.

Good *communication* is the key to success in these last stages. The organization needs to communicate effectively with its intended customers; it also needs to encourage communication between customers as they interact with the solution. The focus is on communication with stakeholders outside the domain where the idea was originally developed. This normally involves identifying the intended audience – a complicated and challenging process but one that sometimes has the benefit of revealing other audiences you may not have thought of. For instance, an organization might think it is deploying a product for stakeholder X, but in fact an unexpected group Y grabs hold of the product and gets excited about it.

During the implementation stage, communication continues to be paramount. Specifically, the organization will need to monitor channels for feedback, both positive and negative, as customers begin engaging with the solution. Real-time data will need to be collected on how the solution is performing in the marketplace in order to track its performance and compare it with expectations outlined in the commercialization strategy. Feeding customer input back into the organization facilitates and stimulates the intrapreneurship process to begin again by allowing the organization to learn about unmet opportunities for new products and services that another part of the organization might be able to serve. This last stage does not 'end' the intrapreneurship process, therefore, but cycles back to the beginning stages – idea generation and mobilization.

As in the previous stage, the organization (rather than the individual idea creator) drives this stage of the intrapreneurship process. The organization needs to be prepared to communicate the value of the idea beyond its initial target audience. There is plenty of literature about how to diffuse and implement solutions (just about any marketing book deals with this issue in some form).[1] The good news is that a lot of the practices and mechanics of how to diffuse and implement solutions externally also can be deployed when dealing with internal ideas. Hence, rather than repeating what has been covered in other texts, I will highlight some key issues you will want to consider in the context of intrapreneurship.

Organizational Perspective

Diffusing ideas is a necessary preparation for implementing the commercialization strategy. The strategy is a flexible and spontaneous plan that you must be prepared to revise and rework based on how things play out on the ground. All plans are theoretical and subject to revision to respond to changing circumstances. Diffusion begins when the organization makes a conscious decision to 'go live' with the solution, moving beyond theory and the process of refining and improving the idea, and putting it on view to see how the market embraces it.

Diffusing Ideas

Before the solution goes live, the organization needs to acquire a clear picture of the culture of the market in which the solution will be deployed in order to frame its messages in ways that will be most relevant to its audience.

CULTURAL INTELLIGENCE
Solutions are relevant within an *environment*. Environments are defined in part by expectations about behavior, norms, and values. Many solutions fail because they are introduced in a manner that is not in step with the cultural expectations of the environment. Cultural attitudes and expectations can significantly shape the customer response

to an innovation. They are relevant to everything from how you communicate with customers to how you introduce solutions and even how you handle clients. Consider the example of a law firm in the Northwest. The chief information officer at the firm had been on the job for only six months when he arrived at a breakthrough solution for managing cases and building a client referral networking platform. As he was going to roll out the solution, he made a big blunder! He had enlisted the support of the senior leaders of the firm but had neglected to talk to the firm's most seasoned (and highly regarded) lawyers. This misstep, while small, led to a complete failure in terms of solution acceptance. When the junior lawyers and secretaries did not see the personnel they held in high esteem using the solution or advocating its use, they ignored it because they did not want to upset their superiors and/or weaken their chances of promotion.

Examples such as this are not rare! The organization needs to take the necessary time to understand the cultural realities of the environment in which it will deploy the solution – the expectations, values, and behaviors of its identified customers. It needs to determine whether the idea is aligned with, or at least does not run counter to, these expectations. To give a very simple example, the colors for advertising materials need to be chosen based on whether they will be seen as appropriate by customers or employees located in different geographical regions. The wrong color choice may alienate users. If you have multiple sets of customers, it becomes even more critical to understand each customer group, so as to be able to tailor the diffusion to each of the customer segments. Today, we are in the business of building 'markets of one.'[2] Markets of one call for tailoring solutions to every individual (the one). While this level of fine tuning may seem to be overzealous, advances in information technologies have made it possible. Consider the case of firms such as Amazon, which can tailor communications, including product recommendations, to each customer based on the customer's preferences, purchase history, and browsing behavior. The bottom line: do not take things for granted when it comes to cultural expectations. If you don't do your homework, you are inviting disaster.

COMMUNICATION AND CONVERSATIONS

The previous chapter discussed the creation of a communication plan as part of the commercialization strategy. Now it is time to put that plan into action. Often, we use the words *communication* and *conversation* interchangeably. However, while related, they are not the same. Communication is the flow of information from a source to a recipient, while conversation is a dialogue between two people, groups, or entities. During the diffusion of solutions, an organization should both *communicate* and also serve as a platform for *conversations*.

Communication involves getting the message out. Communication should focus on making the relevance of the innovation clear to its audiences. Ideally, the organization will take advantage of the rich variety of media through which the target customers process information. For solutions that are being deployed internally this is especially important, as people are usually quite busy enough just keeping up with the communication requirements for their 'day jobs.' Therefore only communications that they can receive and process with minimal inconvenience will be successful. In organizations that have internal cafeterias, for example, it could be effective to produce an enticing visual display of ideas and important communications for people waiting in line. The goal is to have each plug for the solution stimulate employees to do more research on the solutions as they arrive back at their desks. In addition, supervisors or division heads can publicize new solutions and suggest their adoption to bring them to employees' attention. PNC Bank, for example, marketed innovative online learning courses for employees by tying them to specific job skills.[3] Employees could go online to see what skills were necessary for their current job and for job opportunities, and could tailor their online learning to meet those clear objectives.[4] In this way, employees saw how the innovative course offerings applied directly to their situation and could then decide how to invest their time. Without such efforts, entrenched behaviors and institutional barriers may make employees resistant to change and unwilling to seek out resources or knowledge that would assist with diffusion and implementation. For internal and external ideas, any good book on how to launch a targeted and effective marketing campaign will be immensely valuable to ensure that you cover all important bases.[5]

In addition to communicating the value of the solution and making employees aware of it, the organization must also invest in building a platform on which *conversations* can take place about the innovation. Conversations are important means by which the idea creators get to interact directly with potential consumers, whether internal or external, and demonstrate the idea to them. For example, Samsung creates internal initiatives like its Patent Expo, which allows different departments to show off patent ideas at a single large gathering.[6] The Patent Expo is designed to allow scientists to interact and collaborate about ideas, and it works: more than 200 patent ideas were submitted to be shown at the expo, and additional ideas were generated during the event.[7] During the expo, researchers leave comments, converse, and collaborate, not just within their specific fields but also on interdisciplinary technological topics, and this process encourages breakthrough ideas.[8] To get ideas diffused, one must go beyond simple one-way communication; conversations are essential to foster dialogue. Include platforms for conversation in your communication plan. Platforms enable the development of communities by bringing together individuals who share common interests.

Organizations also stand to gain by helping their customers connect with each other through communication technologies. Both current and potential customers can engage in dialogue about their experiences with an organization and its products and services. These communities, especially those that are active and vocal, can play a major role in influencing customers' purchase decisions by shaping their opinions on key issues. For example, take the case of a recent wiki (software that allows users to create, remove, and edit content on web pages with ease) introduced by eBay. Customers are encouraged to develop shared product reviews and recommendations on the eBay wiki. By facilitating this interaction, eBay (1) attracts the attention of customers to its portal, (2) provides an experience of ownership and control among its customers, and (3) taps into the insights and ideas of its customers. Organizations are even sponsoring user-developer conferences to encourage customer communities to interact with each other. Such conferences let the customers engage with each other to develop new product ideas and brainstorm new delivery models. In effect, they increase the company's visibility and create wealth for all stakeholders.

America Online's AOL Watch has had a negative impact for AOL because it surfaces negative opinions and complaints from former AOL customers. On the other hand, the Harley Davidson User Community has helped the company secure sales based on the 'initiative of passionate customers.'[9] Sales generated by referrals from current Harley riders are estimated to be as significant as those from the organization's paid advertisements. The Harley community helps riders share routes and driving tips, organize riding excursions, exchange knowledge, and interact with fellow riders. Potential Harley customers are able to send questions to seasoned riders and learn about their biking experiences.

This positive activism helps Harley retain its brand image and attract new customers. Potential buyers for motorcycles like the fact that when riding a Harley they are not just riding a bike but are joining a community of bikers with whom they can connect.

Physical platforms could take the form of presentations, town halls, or even a booth in the cafeteria. Electronic platforms are easy to deploy as well. These foster conversations and build a sense of community by taking advantage of Web 2.0 technologies and social media. Examples of these include blogs about the solution, forums and discussion boards that allow for interactions between the idea creators and those using the solution, and even videos about the solution. These days, social media platforms are integral to the launch of external products and services. However, when setting up such platforms – whether they are external or internal – many organizations forget to make a plan for their maintenance. Keeping conversations flowing requires ongoing attention from individuals who spend time stimulating discussion and who respond to queries quickly and appropriately. Bear in mind, however, that precautions need to be taken to avoid the various pitfalls (e.g., trolls) of social media.[10]

THE POWER OF NETWORKS

As humans, we love to connect. We seek out connections with our friends, our co-workers, our families, and the people we interact with at our favorite restaurant or pub. Today, with the rapid development of social networking technologies (e.g., Facebook, LinkedIn, Twitter, blogs), people are more connected than ever before. Many of us maintain profiles on a number of social networking sites. Furthermore, it is not uncommon for people to be connected with their co-workers on these platforms. While most of these sites are *social* in nature, it would be a mistake not to take them seriously when you are considering how to diffuse ideas. Consider the recent paradigm shift: whereas a top ranking on Google's search engine results page was once the key to success, now the goal is to 'go viral' through Facebook and Twitter, where information acquisition has been personalized and humanized by one's peers.[11] There are entire books written on how to leverage the power of social networks toward business ends, and I urge you to consult them for in-depth coverage of social networking issues.[12] Here I will cover a few basic principles.

First, identify the *central connectors* – people who attract connections from all over the organization. These are like the popular kids in high school. Within organizations, they are often individuals who (1) are approachable and have significant formal authority, (2) have significant informal authority because of their tenure or expertise, or (3) are likable individuals whose company is enjoyed by all. They often have significant social capital, including deep networks, personal charisma, and a fund of goodwill within the organization. These are the people you want to help you diffuse the solution. (And if they do not like your solution, you will have a significant uphill battle!) Mars, the candy company, used a novel approach to map out social network interactions. At a conference for its employees, the company gave everyone a nametag with RFID components that lit up when they passed near someone they did not know.[13] Social networks were mapped out on a huge overhead projection that changed in real time as employees met new people.[14]

Second, identify the *boundary spanners* – people who have communication capabilities that transcend organizational boundaries (e.g., geographic boundaries, functional domains, and even hierarchical levels).[15] Boundary spanners are invaluable for diffusing ideas across the organization, especially when an idea that originates in one unit of an organization must be implemented in other sectors that are considered 'foreign' by the idea creating unit. Managers need to consider two principles in particular related to boundary spanning and bridging across networks: (1) how to structure and sustain the practice of boundary spanning, and (2) how to maintain efficient and effective boundary roles (for both boundary spanners and boundary objects). These are not mutually exclusive aspects of boundary spanning. Rather, they are two different sides of the same innovation practice. For example, at Leo Burnett, managers maintain a well-structured model of boundary spanning in innovation. They assign lead teams for each project and encourage collaboration across the vertical silos within the lead team. The lead team comprises senior managers from across all the vertical silos (such as account management, creative, design, media). These teams are responsible for coordinating efforts within each unit and also across units. In this way, Leo Burnett has established clearly defined boundary roles that are supported by flexible and efficient mechanisms of boundary spanning.

Boundary spanning may be instituted both across the organization and at subunit levels. Hargadon and Sutton examined the innovation work of IDEO at both the company and the subunit levels and found that IDEO has become successful because of its unique innovative culture.[16] In part, IDEO's success across geographies – including consulting offices in Palo Alto, Boston, Chicago, London, New York, and Tokyo – comes from its consultants' ability to act as idea brokers. IDEO has been very effective in creating products for its clients with new combinations and novel applications of existing individual technologies that IDEO designers have identified on previous client engagements. This reflects IDEO's practice of encouraging its designers to transfer ideas across their projects and across project team boundaries. This culture of innovation through collaborative communication is enhanced by IDEO's reward systems, which are largely based on informal reputation among fellow designers and on peer reviews. It also characterizes IDEO's unique position as a boundary spanner, or 'technology broker.'[17] IDEO, as an organization, seems to serve as a boundary spanner and introduces ideas, concepts, and methodologies from a wide array of industries and environments to further its projects and address client needs.

Third, identify the *gatekeepers* of information – the entities that allow for, or restrict, the flow of information to a particular environment. Gatekeepers are most often people, such as managers who want to screen information before it is shared with staff. But they can also be devices. For example, corporate intranets are often gatekeepers to the information that employees have readily available. In many organizations, if information is not displayed on the homepage of the corporate intranet, it is unlikely to get much attention. Understanding the nature of these gatekeepers is critical to diffusing solutions. Gatekeepers who are too busy can become bottlenecks that slow the diffusion process, and relevant interventions (e.g., finding ways to free up more of their time) will be needed. If the gatekeepers are overly protective of information, then implementation teams will need to get them on board with the solution and get them to approve communication messages before they are broadcast to employees. If there are technical mechanisms that act as gatekeepers, permission must be obtained in order to securely use these information channels.

Fourth, identify other types of network elements – such as cliques – that will help you understand how information flows in the organization. Cliques are made up of individuals who are in frequent communication with one another but are detached from the rest of the organization. Cliques may operate within or across defined organizational units. They can help you identify the informal information-sharing structures in the organization and also where cutoffs are in terms of how information flows. You will need to think through engagement strategies to include these groups in the communication plan.

Analyzing the social network map of the organization will enable you to identify the effectiveness and efficiency of various communication strategies. For example, if the social network map indicates that an organization of a thousand employees has forty central connectors, and if the solution being diffused is relevant to the entire organization, you are better off personalizing the initial communication so as to make it relevant to the forty 'connector' individuals. You can then get them talking to each other about the solution and use their feedback to determine how to communicate with the rest of the organization.

Implementing Ideas

As the solution is diffused, individuals will begin to incorporate it into their routines. Throughout implementation you should ensure that the solution is being used to its full potential, and you should also work to enhance the solution on an ongoing basis. For internal ideas, employees will begin implementing the solution into their work practices. For ideas aimed at external audiences, the solution will be used by customers. It is critical that the organization remain alert and responsive during this period – keeping help desks open and support functions ready, communicating promptly and effectively, and ensuring that the organization is able to capture value from the solution. These activities are the same regardless of the type of solution being deployed, and are covered in great detail in other sources. Again, in this section, I focus on issues that are poorly understood or that are unique to implementing internal solutions within organizations.

TRAINING AND DEVELOPMENT
Training and development are critical components of the implementation process. Training can range from providing a handbook about how to use a solution to delivering in-depth programs such as workshops or training courses for employees who will be using it. The nature of training should depend on the solution. At a minimum, simple documentation should be provided covering details such as who created the solution, for what purposes, how it is supposed to be used, what the expected outcomes are from using it, and who should be contacted should issues arise during its use.

For some solutions, especially those that have risks associated with their use or that require specific usage guidelines to be followed, a more formal training and development program may be needed. For example, when one global manufacturing organization implements a new solution that includes major changes to their business processes, employees are required to complete online modules or attend brief workshops describing the change before they can use the new process. For some innovations, employees may require outside certification or relevant experience – certification by a government authority, for example, or a prescribed number of years of relevant work experience. In other cases, innovations may pose significant risks if misused or used incompetently. Industries that are heavily regulated (e.g., healthcare, financial services) may need to invest substantial resources to ensure that appropriate training is provided when new procedures are introduced. Ideally, the organization will attempt to introduce new ideas at defined intervals or in batches rather than in a continuous stream. Introducing innovations in batches allows the organization to synchronize and combine training initiatives to achieve economies of scale.

TRACKING VALUE

When launching external solutions, organizations carefully build in the steps to capture value. They draft legal contracts to protect intellectual property and create risk-reducing pricing schemes to protect themselves. Otherwise, they would run out of resources and capital to support their activities. Unfortunately, this level of care is often missing for ideas launched internally: the organization may fail to gauge the impact of intrapreneurship accurately, making it difficult to be precise in allocating rewards and incentives to intrapreneurs. As was mentioned in the previous chapter, it is important not to get 'soft' on devising metrics to capture the returns from internal ideas. In the implementation stage, the commercialization strategy should guide how value is captured from the solution. In the diffusion and implementation stage, the focus is on tracking the value of the solution as it goes 'live.' The goal at this stage of the process is to develop a well-defined monitoring and reporting mechanism for tracking the value being captured.

One value-capturing mechanism is an internal account that tracks the use of the solution, the purposes for its use, and the impact of its use on the organization. In one global technology organization,

solutions are tracked based on the number of times they are implemented. Every time a given solution is used, employees must fill in a
short electronic form giving details of what it is being used for, who is
using it (which client), how it is being used, and what added value is
being sought (what outcomes and impacts are desired). It can also be
useful to capture the level of clients' interest in the solution. For example, if a client finds the solution interesting but does not want to pay
extra for it, the organization may decide to bundle the solution within
an existing contract or procedure, choosing to forgo new revenue in
order to preserve an existing relationship. In that case, a portion of the
existing contract's value should be allocated to the solution.

ENGAGING FEEDBACK

As the solution makes its way to customers and customers engage with
it, it elicits a variety of reactions. Some reactions will be positive, while
some, naturally, will be negative. Be extremely worried if there are *no*
reactions to the solution (as this might mean that people are ignoring it
and not using it!). Listening to customers and observing their behavior
is important for successful innovations. Customer feedback may touch
upon an organization's products and services, reveal customer trends
and future needs, or suggest ideas for further product innovations.
Such ideas often come from end users and customers of the products
rather than from within the organization. The organization must
actively seek out external feedback and use it to enhance products and
develop innovations. It is better to design, manufacture, and sell a product that customers want than to try to convince them that they need a
particular product or service after it has been developed. For example,
Hewlett-Packard (HP) added handles to its Laser Jet V printer design
after observing that more than 30 percent of its customers moved printers routinely. In some offices, HP noticed that women most often
moved the printers, so they made the handles big enough to allow
women to move them without breaking their fingernails.

At times, however, an organization will need to push the boundaries in terms of expectations – creating a product that redefines rather
than merely meeting customer expectations. Most likely this will be
done in artistic, design, architecture, and technology firms, where the
goal is not to meet customer needs but to exceed them through a focus
on what *amazes*. Consider the work of Frank Gehry, whose marvelous
structures include the Guggenheim Museum in Bilbao, Spain. While
Gehry had to work within the constraints of what the space was

expected to be (a museum) and stay within a given budget and time, he pushed the boundaries on defining what was possible.

Person-to-person communication is needed to elicit knowledge from customers and get at novel ideas. Information from customers is not always straightforward or easily interpreted. Engaging with it calls for rich interactions between the sources and the recipients. Most organizations try to promote a variety of rich personal interactions to get at customer knowledge. Procter and Gamble (P&G) believes that the 'consumer is boss' – a motto repeated in almost every article about the organization.[18] The consumer is boss, and market research is neither a luxury nor an affectation, but is usually used to improve 'the everyday lives of our consumers.'[19] P&G focuses on customer needs in every element of its business: Researchers spend time with young mothers to research diapers. Research is conducted to identify the behavior and attitudes of young Chinese girls vis-à-vis tampons and cold-water shampoos.[20] This approach to research has allowed P&G to innovate with packaging (such as crinkle-free tampon wrappers that can be opened silently), with new products (such as the Swiffer® mop, based on a product in Chinese markets), and with marketing and design campaigns (such as one for diapers that stay wet for two minutes to aid potty training). There's even an internal reward, the North Star Consumer Fellowship, which recognizes employees with exceptional customer focus and designates them as mentors for others in the company.[21]

Ethicon Endo-Surgery, a creator and supplier of medical devices, established an idea center, a website open to the general community where people can post their ideas. The company also uses ethnography as one of its main tools to capture innovative ideas. It sends its teams on 'field trips' to observe procedures in order to come up with novel ideas. Sometimes, employees even visit non-medical sites such as hardware stores to pick up ideas for new medical devices.

While there is no substitute for going out to customers and seeing how they use the solution, it is not always possible to observe customers in their own environment. Simple economics dictate that only boutique enterprises can really interact closely with all of their customers. Organizations must segment their customer base to identify which customers should be polled for their knowledge. It would be wise for a company to expend proportionally more resources to listen to high-volume customers and repeat customers rather than one-time or occasional customers. Customers who have repeated interactions with a product will be more aware of the product features, their current value propositions, and the need for future improvements.

Organizations also struggle with ways to tap into customer information; customer knowledge is 'sticky' and therefore difficult to articulate. Customers' words for their tasks usually differ from the technical jargon of the engineer who created the product. To address the challenges of understanding feedback from customers, you may need to go beyond traditional mechanisms such as collecting information through surveys or forums (e.g., comment and suggestion boxes, either physical or online). You should try to provide customers with the means to use their reactions and information about the solutions to *enhance the solution*. Many organizations have deployed user toolkits that enable customers to innovate directly, modifying and customizing products to meet their particular needs and preferences. For example, Bush Boake Allen allows clients like Nestlé to develop their own specialty flavors using an Internet-based tool, and then have the new flavor design sent to an automated machine that will manufacture a sample within minutes. After tasting the flavor, the clients can make changes or request additional samples. After finalizing their preferred formula, clients can order their customized flavor through the manufacturer. Using toolkits in this manner reduces the experimental burden on the manufacturer to find the right flavor, reduces design cycle time, and utilizes customer knowledge. The organization deploys one artifact that can be customized by an entire community rather than trying to create individual solutions to meet the differing needs of particular customers.

Organizations have begun to host user conferences for the specific purpose of learning how their customers utilize, customize, or modify products to meet their individual needs. As products become more sophisticated, customers rarely use them in a uniform way. Most software organizations tap into their lead users to discover new routines, methods, and enhancements that have been adapted to the technology. These modifications, if they have a broad appeal, can be made part of upgrades or newer versions of the software. Some companies, including SPSS, an analytical and decision-support software producer, have begun to host customer workshops, where they bring together the 'super users' of their products in order to learn from them. Other organizations have product research centers where they monitor subjects as they interact with products and services: both are attempts to co-create value with the customers. Some software development firms purchase add-ons, scripts, and other artifacts created by their customers during the course of using their products. These artifacts are then introduced in future versions of the products and services. For example, Twitter bought Tweetie, a very popular iPhone and Mac application, from Loren Brichter.[22] Brichter had created Tweetie in his spare time to remedy what he thought were deficiencies in the current Twitter offerings. Brichter initially began selling Tweetie on the App Store for $2.99.

When implementing new solutions, you need to pay particular attention to how customers use your innovation and be prepared to modify the offering to enhance its ability to meet customers' needs. TGI Friday's, a restaurant chain, used knowledge about its customers to redefine its food offerings. The restaurant managers changed their menu when they observed that customers were seeking more healthy options. For example, they gave customers the option to replace french fries with baked potatoes or green vegetables. The restaurant conducted data-mining analysis on their point-of-sale data to uncover the patterns and combinations in how their patrons customized the standard offerings. The results of this study led to the creation of diet menu items. TGI Friday's signed an agreement with the creators of the Atkins' Diet to offer low-calorie meals for the health-conscious customer. TGI Friday's innovation would not have been possible if customers' food choices and customizations had not been captured and analyzed.

CONFRONTING FAILURES

As solutions move from the theoretical to the practical, things often do not go as planned. While no one expects that plans and concepts will be perfectly executed, rarely does one expect massive disasters. However, even the so-called most innovative companies get it wrong sometimes! Google, a poster child for innovation, has suffered a series of high-profile product failures. Most recently, Google announced it would close down its investment in Google Wave.[23] Google Wave was launched in September 2009 with initial access given to 10,000 users in beta form, and was billed as a tool that would transform online communication and collaboration.[24] Just under a year later, Urs Hölzle, senior vice-president of operations and a Google Fellow, announced that 'Wave has not seen the user adoption we would have liked. We don't plan to continue developing Wave as a standalone product, but we will maintain the site at least through the end of the year and extend the technology for use in other Google projects.'[25] Interestingly enough, although the company did end up failing, they focused on how to learn from the disappointment. The same blog post from Hölzle noted that 'Wave has taught us a lot, and we are proud of the team for the ways in which they have pushed the boundaries of computer science. We are excited about what they will develop next as we continue to create innovations with the potential to advance technology and the wider web.'[26] Not all implementations will be stellar successes, so it is critical to accept setbacks, learn from failures, and infuse this hard-won knowledge back into the intrapreneurship process. Building the capacity to learn from each solution that gets implemented is critical. As was discussed in the chapter on experimentation, learning needs to become a natural component of the organizational fabric.

Blockbuster and instant success stories are few and far between. Procter and Gamble became profitable in Japan fourteen years after expanding there, and in China six years after entering the region. CEO A.G. Lafley explained P&G's thinking in both of these global expansions as follows: 'failure is learning. If we can fail early, fast, and cheap, and learn from it, then it's okay.'[27] The goal is not to get caught up with failures and become too risk averse or kill the program too hastily. Since many ideas are initially ill-adapted or unsuccessful, the ability to quickly cycle through possibilities and incorporate learning into the next iteration can be a major competitive advantage.

CELEBRATING SUCCESS

Since true success stories are rare, especially those of blockbuster or game-changer status, it is important to celebrate each success. The organization can *instill belief in the power of intrapreneurship* by documenting successes and telling stories. At the same time, it must emphasize that intrapreneurship will require a significant and challenging cultural shift. The chances are slim (really slim!) that an employee will make it past the 'Valley of Death' and reach the diffusion stage. This is not meant to discourage employees but to make them aware of the effort and care needed to move their ideas ahead. But the rewards, especially in the longer term, make up for the difficulties.

In order to develop a culture of idea generation and mobilization, the organization should highlight for employees that intrapreneurship is a priority and that intrapreneurial behavior and results will be rewarded. This message should align with the mission and goals of the organization. For example, Hewlett-Packard has taken concrete steps to communicate the value and process of innovation to its employees, hosting an expensive 'Power-UP' event (think roadshow!) to showcase its cutting-edge work on innovative ideas and projects across the enterprise. HP makes it clear to every employee that though coming up with innovative ideas is hard work, it is well worth the effort to do so.

Employee Perspective

At this stage of the process, you can focus on enjoying your success. You have made it this far and are moments away from seeing your solution go live. While most employees feel anxious and excited and may even lose sleep the night before their solution debuts, they also feel fulfilled. They know that they have made a difference to their organization; they have realized the promise of intrapreneurship. Even while you celebrate, however, your job is not quite done. You have an opportunity to see how your solution is being used by customers, seek out ways to enhance the solution, and perhaps enjoy the serendipity of discovering new problems and opportunities for innovation.

Diffusing Ideas

As the organization works to get the solution to the intended customer, you are likely to be in high demand to answer questions about communicating appropriate messages, and to participate in conversations about the solution. It's important for you to be accessible and continue to be engaged with your solution. A solution with an enthusiastic support system and a zealous idea creator behind it will lead to greatness.

JOINING THE CONVERSATION

As the organization begins to engage customers in conversations about the solution, it is important for you, the idea creator, to be part of those conversations. You are a valuable source of knowledge about the details of the solution and also one of its most passionate champions. Most employees express some degree of apprehension when it comes to giving presentations, especially when they deal with large audiences, or audiences they do not know well. This apprehension is natural, but you should try to overcome it. Successful intrapreneurs understand the value of having – and using – good communication and persuasion skills.

Even the best public speakers have had to work to hone their presentation skills. Don't be reluctant to seek training in public speaking. Training can include taking classes or participating in public speaking forums such as Toastmasters International (http://www.toastmasters.org). In most cases, your organization will gladly help cover the cost of such professional development. In addition to seeking training, take the time to rehearse your presentation. The organization, especially the marketing and communication professionals, will gladly help you prepare PowerPoint slides and even draft the speech, but you still need to deliver it. Practice makes perfect. In one organization, I knew of an employee who was so petrified at the thought of giving a presentation that he practiced it well over a hundred times with six of his closest colleagues as an audience. Each time he practiced, he recalls, 'I felt calmer. I cannot explain it, maybe it was because I was eventually speaking in cruise control mode, but I did feel a sense of calm . . . knowing that I could speak to an audience, even if it was just one person, was refreshing . . . I eventually did not sweat or run through my slides.' Practicing your presentations with friends can be invaluable, and the feedback and questions you get during these dry runs will help you anticipate future questions. Other common strategies that will enhance the effectiveness of your presentations include creating note cards, making eye contact, and even doing mock question-and-answer sessions to prepare for the real thing.

It is also important to make yourself accessible through online platforms. The organization might set up a website to showcase the solution, encourage readers to post their questions and comments, and share general feedback. You have a role to play on these platforms. The role is one, first, of information sharing, answering questions as they arise, and, second, of sharing your thinking about the feedback received and how it might be used constructively. Getting comfortable with the various social media platforms will be a wise investment of your time.

If the organization calls upon you to be a resource during training and development, do not hesitate to help out. Not only will your involvement help your organization make the solution more accessible to its intended audience, it will also help you advance your name and reputation in the organization, extend your social networks, and learn new things. The bottom line: do not be just a spectator. Take every opportunity to engage with the 'contact sport' of diffusing solutions.

LEVERAGING YOUR NETWORK

Employees have deep social networks within their organization. Your network is made up of people you associate with on a daily basis, individuals you trust and look to for counsel, and even friends with whom you enjoy going to the pub and sharing a few pints. When it is time to diffuse the solution, these connections need to be leveraged. These are the first go-to people you should connect up with to share the story of your solution – for two reasons: first, these are the people who you know have your best interests at heart, and second, it is easy for you to talk with them. In their turn, they can ask difficult questions, give you candid feedback on how to sharpen your pitch, and even help you in the diffusion process. As an example, consider the case of a novice software engineer working for a mid-sized IT firm. The intrapreneur had developed a novel module that would enable programmers to embed documentation more easily into programs as code was written. During the diffusion process, the programmer got eight people in his network to try out the solution and share feedback about it on a daily basis, not only with him but with other people they knew and trusted. Within a matter of two weeks, more than 80 percent of the programmers (the intended market) had heard of the solution and tried it at least once. This type of bottom-up communication and diffusion works well in conjunction with the top-down approaches that the organization will take. The two are complementary, and both are essential.

In addition to leveraging your existing network in order to diffuse the solution, you should also work to extend your network. During the diffusion process, it is quite likely that you will meet new people – people you never thought were relevant to your line of work and people whose acquaintance you have always wanted to make. This is an opportunity to build new connections, strengthen old ones, and even reprioritize existing connections. To build new connections, you need to be part of the diffusion process. Being able to make presentations about your solution and/or answer questions in an online forum connects you directly with your audience (and minimizes the need for middlemen). At this time, as you mobilize your most valuable contacts to help get the message out, you have an opportunity to evaluate who is ready to step up to help you. (Of course, some of those who say they will help promote your idea will be more effective than others; you need to use your judgment and intuition to select the best candidates.) This is also a good time to 'segment' your network, analyzing or 'profiling' the people in it. For example, some may be more likely to take risks while others are better at helping to connect you with people you did not know, and still others have persuasive skills that can help you turn a 'no' into a 'yes.' Segmenting your network will enable you to take a more effective and efficient approach to mobilizing people to help in the diffusion process.

Implementing Ideas

As the solution goes live, and customers are using it, you have an opportunity to start thinking about how to make it still better. No solution is perfect. Customers will find ways to ask for more, or perhaps to point out drawbacks in the features the designer considers most important. Being part of the direct stream of feedback that customers share is an invaluable experience; there is no substitute for hearing directly from customers. During the implementation process, opportunities arise to think beyond the specific solution that is being launched. Many times, intrapreneurs are burnt out by this stage and have maxed out their thinking about the solution. They find it refreshing to spend time exploring new spaces that represent opportunities (or problems) for innovation. Having the spotlight on you and access to the customers gives you a perfect opportunity to do just that.

LOOKING FOR ENHANCEMENTS AND THE NEXT BIG THING
Observe, make notes, ask questions, and be curious. The implementation stage is an opportune time to seek out information to help you evaluate how your solution is performing and making the lives of your customers better. Here are some tips for getting the most out of this process.

First, do not expect to get only rave reviews and positive feedback. Chances are high that you will hear responses such as 'If only the solution could do this . . .,' 'Maybe you could have changed this . . .,' and 'I like it, *but* . . .' instead of 'I love it,' or 'This is the best thing since . . .' This is only natural – your masterpiece, like all solutions, can still be improved, so do not despair or get frustrated. First-time intrapreneurs need to take a deep breath and understand that criticism is a normal part of the process.

Second, collect and analyze feedback from as many different sources as possible. Invest in a pocket-sized notebook to jot down feedback as you get it. Remember to write about the source from which the feedback came and what triggered it. Was the customer using a particular feature, or using the solution in a particular environment? If you do not have time to explore the issue further with customers right away, try to contact them later for a more in-depth conversation. As you aggregate feedback, you will begin to see patterns emerging. Is the feedback converging on a few major themes? Are there things about the solution that a significant portion of customers find valuable (or, alternatively, useless)? Study the feedback carefully to see if you have reached *saturation* in terms of the information you are receiving from customers – that is, you are hearing just about the same thing from every customer. Remember that interactions with customers are valuable and such opportunities should not be wasted. However, do not keep on polling if you are hearing the same thing from everyone.

Third, if the feedback signals a need for incremental improvements to the solution, work with your commercialization team to chart out a plan to make the necessary enhancements. Depending on the nature of the enhancements, these may be introduced quickly (especially if they signal fixes to major problems that customers are experiencing) or may be rolled out after the solution has gotten a foothold in the market (if the fixes are minor enhancements to the solution and can wait).

Fourth, if the feedback inspires you to think of new ideas and problems to explore, jot them down. If you are a rookie intrapreneur, it is natural but not wise to focus on your solution rather than looking beyond it for new ideas. However, jumping too hastily into exploring a brand-new problem is also unwise. To address the first issue, keep an open mind as you analyze the feedback and consider bringing in a few external eyes to help you parse out the information that you receive. These can be the peers you trust, your idea advocate, and even members of the commercialization team. To deal with the second issue, there is no substitute for holding yourself back a bit and being disciplined. You need to take time to reflect on the current experience before you begin a new endeavor.

When conditions are right for exploring new ideas, you still need to take a few precautions.

- Check your energy level. Think back to how much energy it took to reach this stage. Do you have it in you to go through this again, or do you need time to recharge your batteries?
- Do not compromise your day job. You have a job to do, and you need to do it well. Do not sacrifice quality in the work you are paid

to do. During the intrapreneurial pursuit, you may have had colleagues who covered for you, or excused you from meetings, and
so on, to give you time to pursue your idea. Now is a good time to
repay those favors so that your colleagues stand ready to help you
out in the future.

• Do not try to skip steps in the intrapreneurship process. Skipping
any step in the process is dangerous. The success you have had on
the idea is directly related to the effort you spent going through
each and every step, from working through the idea, to finding an
advocate, to getting the idea through the screening and experimentation processes, to working with the commercialization and implementation teams.

• Have realistic expectations. As you know by now, intrapreneurship
is difficult, and success with one idea does not guarantee a similar
success in the future. One reason why some intrapreneurs remain
'one-hit wonders' is that they fail to set realistic expectations their
second time through the process and end up disappointing themselves. (It's the intrapreneur rather than the organization that suffers
in this case; the organization is for the most part still celebrating the
good results from the initial solution.) So, view this as a time when
'all the pressure is off.' Do not think that you need to prove something. Take the time to be choosy about your next effort.

REFLECTING ON THE PROCESS

It's essential for you to take time to reflect on the *process* of intrapreneurship. You have come full circle and are thinking about going
through the process again with another idea (either related to the
first one, or a brand-new effort). Thinking through the steps of the
process is critical, for a number of reasons. For one thing, you do not
want to make the same mistakes or face the same struggles again.
Seasoned intrapreneurs discipline themselves to learn from experience, not in order to assign blame or make excuses but to improve
their performance. As you think about the learning you have come
away with, share this with the people who worked with you during
the process. Interview your idea advocates to get their perspective
on the process; talk with your peers who helped you in commercializing and diffusing ideas; re-examine the experimentation process.
Document your findings from this period of introspection and reflection, and design relevant interventions to help you deal with challenges or hurdles you faced last time. These reflections and insights

will be part of a continuous improvement process. You want to be like an athlete who does not just win one race or game but who is constantly winning championships. You want to build a legacy of success. So train yourself to keep honing your skills and perfecting the art and science of intrapreneurship. The bottom line: do not begin another intrapreneurial effort before completing this reflection step, no matter how sexy and slam-dunk – like the opportunity might seem.

Conclusion

The U.S. Transportation Security Administration (TSA) launched its Idea Factory, a secure intranet, in 2007, to give employees the opportunity to submit ideas for improving agency operations and processes. By the end of January 2009, more than 7,800 ideas had been contributed, resulting in over 69,000 comments.[28] Guess how many were implemented: a thousand? a hundred? No. A meager thirty-nine! Imagine the waste of human energy and creative potential. Implementing ideas is never easy, and organizations need to take this final stage of the process very seriously. Many of the challenges in implementation can be traced back to a lack of diligence in previous stages of the process. For example, in the case of the TSA, they collected ideas without a solid plan for how to experiment with and commercialize them.

The diffusion and implementation stages are driven more by the organization than the employee. The organization's role is to capture value and feedback from the process. Initially, feedback will be used to correct problems that arise while the implementation process is underway. Later, feedback will be used to stimulate the generation and mobilization of new ideas. Idea creators should consider shadowing the personnel who are involved in the diffusion and implementation of the idea. In this way, they can gain direct access to the feedback that is being received on the solution and can use this information to generate new ideas and innovative solutions. All employees should have access to the feedback so they can use it in the development of the idea. The idea creator, especially, should use the last stage as a source of input on how to refine and develop the solution. In addition, the idea creator should talk directly to customers who are using the product and get a better understanding of how the solution is incorporated into their daily lives. The intrapreneur needs this period of reflection to identify lessons learned and calibrate interventions, and to take a moment to savor the experience of success.

We have seen the intrapreneurship process come full circle. The feedback generated by the implementation and diffusion stages can now be used to kick-start idea development afresh. Now we must consider how intrapreneurship may become not a mere process in the organization but a way of life for all employees, a vital contribution from each member of the organization to the overall health of the enterprise. The next chapter looks at ways to inspire and activate employees to take part in the process – to create a 'network of believers' who are empowered to innovate and encourage their co-workers' ideas as well as their own, thereby creating a living, evolving intrapreneurship process that will give the organization a sustainable competitive advantage.

8 Intrapreneurship from Concept to Sustained Competitive Advantage

Intrapreneurship extends beyond the R&D lab and encompasses the entire enterprise. An organization may face resistance when introducing intrapreneurship because it embraces open practices, relies on the strength of networks to move an idea forward, and focuses on merit. An idea can come from anywhere in the organization and be rewarded and promoted through formal processes and informal channels. It takes time, energy, and dedication to build a culture where intrapreneurship is valued. Success is almost never immediate, but it will come eventually, so the results will be well worth the slog. Intrapreneurship calls for a change in mindset on the part of both the organization and the employees. Throughout this book, I have outlined the necessary steps that the organization and the employee have to take as they move through stages of the intrapreneurship process. This concluding chapter describes how you can take intrapreneurship from a concept to a source of sustainable competitive advantage for your organization.

Open Up a Dialogue

Begin a discussion to get employees excited about the concept. Not everyone will have had exposure to intrapreneurship or will have committed time and energy to a thoughtful examination of its relevance to their work, their ideas, or their team and units. Based on the experiences of several dozen individuals who have started a dialogue that eventually led to successful intrapreneurship programs in their organizations, here are some suggestions for getting started:

- *Be prepared for skepticism.* Don't expect people to love the concept at first; if even 10 percent of employees are excited, take this as a positive sign, and charge ahead. Acknowledge that people have been burned before. They have heard the buzzwords come and go and have experienced promises for organization-wide change that were never delivered on, from knowledge management to business process re-engineering and total-quality management.
- *Do not build up the concept as the next best thing since sliced bread.* In your excitement to convince people about the value of intrapreneurship, you might get a bit carried away and oversell the concept. Ultimately, a good salesperson can sell anything, and you don't want people to buy into intrapreneurship with false hopes and overblown expectations. The end result of overselling is disappointment all around and loss of credibility.
- *Keep it simple.* Avoid jargon and buzzwords when communicating the concept. Frame it in language that others in your organization are comfortable with. Use case histories to illustrate key points. A common strategy is to build sketches of what the organization will look like if employees are intrapreneurial and supported by the organization. Construct scenarios and hypothetical cases that people can relate to, so they can visualize their role and get excited about it.

The goal of opening a dialogue is to ensure that people are thinking about the concept. Encouraging dialogue opens up avenues for people to share their reactions and feedback. If possible, use existing mechanisms and platforms to begin dialogue. For instance, instead of calling a 'special' meeting to discuss the concept, ask for a ten- to fifteen-minute slot on the agenda of an existing meeting to introduce it. In this way, you're not asking people to make special accommodations for you but are using the times and spaces that people have already set aside. You don't want people to associate the idea with an inconvenient interruption to their work or an added burden.

Create a Network of Believers

Unless you are the CEO or have accumulated vast social and political capital, you won't be able to drive organizational change on your own. Organizations are socially, politically, and psychologically complex entities. Recruit and create alliances with as many people as possible who share your vision and passion for intrapreneurship. Remember, getting people to engage in intrapreneurship requires that they understand and internalize the mechanisms of the process when it's first introduced to the organization. You must identify the central connectors and 'boundary spanners' who can help you spread the message, and the advocates and sponsors who will support and develop ideas. Try to recruit people with complementary skills, expertise, and networks to fully develop the intrapreneurship culture. Bringing diverse perspectives creates healthy tension – and even disagreements – early in the process; these will guard against premature consensus when what is needed is vigorous debate and critical scrutiny of ideas. As you recruit individuals and form alliances, your initial understanding of how to situate intrapreneurship in the organization will evolve. This is an important time for reflecting on and refining the concept. I have yet to meet anyone whose concept of intrapreneurship doesn't undergo significant modification as he or she engages in early dialogue. Openness and support for change are essential to moving the campaign forward and building relationships with potential allies.

Take a Community Approach

Intrapreneurship is not a one-person show or a one-team activity. You need a community approach to get the concept off the ground and to hold it together. You will need to give up control and involve others in the process. The community – that is, the organization – must drive the process and take ownership of it.

Assemble a cross-functional team to sketch out the blueprint for intrapreneurship in your organization. A cross-functional team will be able to avoid a 'silo perspective,' and increase your chances of getting organization-wide backing for the process. Moreover, because the team will bring knowledge from several units to sketch out how the stages of intrapreneurship will be made operational, they will be able to spell out how people's roles across departments and even geographies will be affected by the process.

You'll need to request resources to build this cross-functional team by tapping into corporate-level budgets that can be used to charge time for exploratory and strategic efforts. These budgets are not charged against departmental resources, and they allow employees to be compensated for work on projects that fall outside their day-to-day operational responsibilities. You will need to find an executive sponsor who will grant you access to these funds. If you can't secure executive sponsorship or the budget to form an organization-level cross-functional team, don't despair. You can always begin from the bottom up! The bottom-up approach involves proving the process locally, working out the kinks, and then seeing how to scale it across the organization.

Many intrapreneurship programs grow from bottom-up efforts. In these scenarios, local champions of the concept mobilize people within their units to develop, refine, and improve a process for intrapreneurship that would serve the needs of their own units/departments. When the process goes live, the unit commits time and energy to communicate the success of its program, not only to increase the energy of members within the unit but also to gain recognition and seek resources from senior executives. Units that work closely with the initiator of an intrapreneurship program are often inspired to build their own intrapreneurship processes. Over time, as units need to share ideas across boundaries, intrapreneurship processes are reconciled and standardized, and an organization-wide process emerges. At this point, with many in the community convinced of the need to invest in the effort, the organization will be more likely to dedicate resources to support and manage intrapreneurship.

Learn, Unlearn, and Relearn

It would be naive to assume that you could get the intrapreneurship process 'right' on the first try. Often the initial design will have to be tweaked, reworked, or even scrapped and redesigned. You will only construct a viable intrapreneurship program through constant learning, and that learning needs to be done *scientifically* to be useful. Feedback collected at regular intervals and analyzed effectively will help you gain insights that can be used to improve the process. Once you've had a chance to implement interventions, you will need to evaluate their effectiveness yet again. Learning is not a one-time deal; it should be built into every stage of the process and promoted at all levels, from individuals, to groups, to the organization as a whole. The sections that follow outline ways to build learning mechanisms into your process.

Build Multiple Avenues

Provide multiple avenues so people can share feedback on their interactions with the intrapreneurship program. Ideally, feedback mechanisms should be present throughout the process. When an employee is interacting with any aspect, whether submitting an idea or trying to advocate for one, he or she should be able to provide feedback, both positive and negative, about the experience. Feedback mechanisms should span both the physical and virtual environments. Within physical environments, feedback can be collected through drop-boxes, suggestion boxes, or a help desk. In the virtual environment, feedback can be collected through online submission forms, internal blogs and discussion groups, or e-mails to designated representatives. Global and multilingual organizations should enable employees to send information in their native languages. In several global organizations I know of, feedback is collected in native languages through physical drop-off locations. This feedback is then aggregated and translated at the local level before it is analyzed at the organizational level.

Keep Feedback Mechanisms Simple

Mechanisms for capturing feedback should be one click (or the physical equivalent) away from the person interacting with the intrapreneurship program. The easier it is for employees to submit feedback, the greater the chance that they will do so. In the Internet space, Amazon has set the standard with its 'one-click' shopping – you can purchase anything you want on the site with one click as long as you have an existing account. This single-click option should be available to employees for submitting ideas or implementing solutions. If they need help solving a problem, employees should be pointed to a solution or a person who can help resolve the issue. An employee will not be interested in logging out of the system and then logging in to another system to submit the feedback. Similarly, in physical environments, you have to make it very easy (almost a no-brainer) for the employee to submit feedback: for example, place suggestion drop boxes strategically throughout the offices or send targeted surveys to employees.

One Fortune 100 organization collects intrapreneurship process feedback during quarterly staff meetings. Employees are given a five-question survey to fill out: How do you feel about the intrapreneurship process? What are the three major challenges you faced when using it? Whom did you go to to seek help with the challenges you faced? What are three changes you would like to see? Would you be willing to give thirty minutes to talk to us about your feedback? During the first two years of collecting survey responses to the program launch (using these exact survey questions), the intrapreneurship team was bombarded with suggestions for improvement. But, over time, as feedback was carefully incorporated into the process, participation in the intrapreneurship increased and the nature of the comments changed. Common sentiments eventually included, 'I love the system,' 'Jack's idea was adopted by our group last week and we have scheduled Jack to come and talk to us,' and 'Of course, there are places to improve it . . . but for now, just leave it as is, as it works for us.'

Collect Feedback with a Plan in Mind

As noted in the chapter on idea advocacy and screening, simply collecting ideas for the sake of collecting ideas is a mistake. Collecting feedback only for show is also a mistake. Unless you actually have a plan in place to analyze and respond to the feedback, it might be better not to collect any at all! A sure-fire way to destroy an intrapreneurship process, or any change management initiative for that matter, is to allow feedback to languish in the proverbial black hole. Your plan should specify how often and for what purposes the feedback will be analyzed, by whom, and how the results will be communicated. When collecting feedback, your intention should be to engage in reflection and learning not to evaluate the performance of individuals or units. People won't share their feedback in an honest and open manner if they think the feedback may negatively influence their performance evaluations or eligibility for rewards and incentives.

Communicating Feedback

Plan regular intervals when feedback will be analyzed and results communicated to the stakeholders. Remind users that their feedback leads to new interventions and innovations in the intrapreneurship program. Employees need to know not only that their feedback is being analyzed but that it can actually have an impact. Communicate results through multiple channels by publishing reports or having intrapreneurs present the findings (which can be recorded for asynchronous delivery to those who can't attend the event in person). Be honest, clear, and appreciative: honest in presenting the good, the bad, and the ugly; clear in how the feedback is going to inform future activities; and appreciative of the effort that people have put in to share their opinions. If possible, when employee opinion is split among alternatives, you need to make it clear why a given alternative was chosen and how its effectiveness will be gauged.

Schedule forums where feedback can be discussed; once you arrive at conclusions and identify action points based on the feedback, give employees a chance to share feedback on the feedback. In one organization, senior executives hold 'office hours' after key decisions have been made based on employee feedback. All senior executives give up a three-hour slot on their calendar, during which employees can come by and share their feedback in person or schedule a phone or video conference to get their voices heard. Simply having this personal avenue puts a 'face' on the decision-making process, thereby reducing much of the apprehension about feedback.

Technology Doesn't Drive the Process

Too often organizations get caught up in thinking that technology alone will drive intrapreneurship. From intranets, to social network analysis studies, to new forms of video and web conferencing, they rely on the latest and greatest inventions. Often, these organizations have been swayed by persuasive consultants who show them a utopian view through the lens of technology. Technology pitches can be sexy, but without a sound organizational setup they will not deliver any value. The bottom line: before you invest in any technology to achieve intrapreneurship, ask yourself three questions: (1) What is the current state of affairs? (2) What issues are we facing that are holding us back? (3) What are some non-technology solutions that can be deployed to address these issues? Only after you have tried several non-technical approaches should you consider technology solutions. Technology solutions can help you take a good process and make it better, but they can't help you go from a nonexistent process to an optimal one! For example, if you have trouble organizing ideas for easy retrieval, the first step will be to craft a taxonomy that classifies ideas by type, source, focus, cost, risks, and other criteria – not to immediately purchase a technology like Microsoft SharePoint.

The Human Factor

You and your employees are responsible for making intrapreneurship a success story and a capacity builder in your organization, so invest in the human capital needed to make the process work. Of course, use traditional mechanisms such as pay raises, bonuses, and promotions; but also invest in strategies for building connections among employees, especially among peers who seldom interact. It's through these interdisciplinary and 'weird' encounters that some of the most radical, game-changing ideas arise. Much of the innovation that will change the face of business in the next few years will come from the edges of disciplines, so organizations should facilitate connections around these edges. Rewarding people for looking beyond their immediate horizons for ideas will make them more willing to share ideas with colleagues they do not see or work with daily.

Intrapreneurship works only if people believe in themselves and their potential to make a contribution that goes beyond the performance of day-to-day tasks. Only through dedicated efforts on the part of the organization – perhaps through such mechanisms as structured retreats or mentoring arrangements – will employees be able to discover their latent talents. Employees need to know that their ideas are valued and respected – that they will be listened to and not rejected out of hand. Employees also need to experience novel situations and activities outside their comfort zones. For example, in one large technology organization, highly skilled software engineers were asked to spend a week delivering classes on the value of engineering practices to employees from the business side of the firm. This put the software engineers in an uncomfortable place; they were most comfortable dealing with complexities in the artificial world of 1s and 0s, bits and bytes. However, this opportunity provided them with a chance to reflect on their professional practices and uncover what made them great programmers. They were able to draw conclusions about the way they solved problems, how they structured their work assignments, and how they could improve their skills. Several realized that they needed to be more flexible in looking at problems, addressing customer requests, and communicating the limitations of the technology. Through this effort, the firm was able to show that individuals who were not technically 'peers' could both teach and learn from one another. When they believe that they have a contribution to make beyond the specific job for which they have been hired, individuals are empowered to take a global view of their role and their potential impact within the organization.

If You Can't Measure It . . . You Can't Manage It

Management requires measurement. Without metrics we won't know how good (or bad) a job we're doing or how we can improve our efforts. Too often, intrapreneurship programs lack metrics to gauge

Table 8.1
Building metrics

Issue	Implementation Steps
Know what you are measuring	Be clear about what you want to measure and why. Anything that you are going to measure has to have a business motivation to justify its cost. Expending resources to measure without clear guidelines will lead to wastage of resources.
Ensure that the measurement you are using is valid	Ensure that the method of measurement is actually capturing the data you want: if you want to know the temperature of a room, use a thermometer, but if you want to know the size of a room, find a different instrument.
	Many times executives fail to tie indicators back to the things they want to measure, so their rationale for why a given measure is indicative of a given behavior or state is unconvincing. For example, in the corporate world, stock price has been used as a surrogate measure of how well firms are doing. The recent financial crises and several other crises in the past (e.g., the bursting of the Internet bubble) have shown us that stock price may not be the best indicator of a corporation's health. Yet, because it is easy to measure, we continue to use it. Steer clear of the 'easy road' and make sure that the measurement is connected to the behavior or outcome that you want to assess.
Develop and publish baseline measures	Ensure that you have baseline measures in place. To know how well you are doing, you must first know your starting point. Many organizations lack baseline measures for the management of ideas, yet such measures are essential for assessing the progress of an intrapreneurship process.
	Collect baseline measures by observing, sending out surveys, and talking to people. Then publish them. Having a clear understanding of the starting point can help people orient themselves to a change of direction.
Select a mix of measurements	Try to develop a balanced scoreboard with both quantitative and qualitative measures, and choose strategic, productivity, or profitability measures that match your goals. Qualitative measures (such as

(Continued)

Table 8.1   (*Continued*)

Issue	Implementation Steps
	stories and case studies) are good at capturing details and people's perceptions of the program. Quantitative measures are useful in gauging the impact on the firm's bottom line and in linking outcomes that are used to evaluate other investments (i.e., the real cost in dollars and cents).
Measure the results of interventions	After implementing interventions, measure the gains or losses; these measures then need to be synthesized and analyzed to arrive at knowledge you can act on.
	Do not worry if the first measurement actually shows that performance is worse than before you invested any resources. It is natural to see a time lag between the deployment of new interventions and results. It also takes time for individuals to fully adopt the new interventions.
Communicate results	Communication of measurement data is essential to inform the various stakeholder groups about progress (or lack of progress). Results should be communicated both laterally and vertically, to reach the broadest possible audience.
	Tailor the message to the interests and needs of the audience. Executives may be more interested in the big picture, whereas employees on the front lines may prefer to see metrics specific to their unit and group and to how their performance compares to that of other employees. Today, many organizations are constructing 'dashboards' to capture metrics in a manner that is easy to visualize, with different levels of detail provided to different groups depending on their roles within the organization.

performance. Metrics are important for several reasons: (1) they help us see what is working well and where there are 'weak links' that need resources; (2) they help us benchmark how we are doing compared to our external peers, and even compared to other groups and units within the organization; and (3) they reaffirm that our investment in a course of action is justified.

As was discussed earlier, two types of metrics – process and output – may be used to measure success. Process metrics, as the name implies, evaluate the process by gauging its efficiency and effectiveness. Efficiency indicators may measure *how quickly ideas are being screened, how many ideas are being experimented on,* and *the cost of experimentation.* Effectiveness indicators will show *which reviewers are the most competent.* Output metrics gauge the end results, such as *the number of ideas diffused and implemented,* or *the revenues gained from an idea.* Both types of metrics have their place in evaluation. Process metrics help to evaluate what is working and how to continuously improve the process. Output metrics, on the other hand, serve to enlist support for the program by demonstrating why continued investment is important. The basic steps to consider when building metrics are outlined in table 8.1.

Inadequate or ill-communicated metrics can hurt the intrapreneurship program. When times get tough for an organization, programs that can't show direct relevance to the bottom line are the first on the chopping block. On the other hand, in leading companies where intrapreneurship is part of the organizational fabric, executive sponsors use dashboards to capture the key metrics of their programs and take every opportunity to share these metrics with their peers and superiors. Effective metrics make the business case for intrapreneurship much more convincing.

Tracing the Maturity of Intrapreneurship Processes and Linking Them to Business Value

Maturity models continue to make significant contributions to several disciplines: software engineering (the Capability Maturity Model),[1] quality management (ISO Standards),[2] and others. Perhaps the most comprehensive and well-known maturity model to date is the Software Engineering Institute's (SEI) Capability Maturity Model (CMM). Briefly, the CMM is a graduated five-level improvement model of software capability. The levels are arranged in such a manner that capacity at the lower levels forms a strong foundation on which an organization can move to the upper levels. The various levels represent initial, repeatable, defined, managed, and optimized phases of software capability. At the initial level, an organization is characterized as functioning with ad-hoc and chaotic processes. In most cases, no formal procedures and project plans are in place, or, if present, they lack implementation mechanisms. At the repeatable level, the organization has basic project controls in place – such as project management, product assurance, and change controls. Here, the organization demonstrates how to conduct

Figure 8.1: Five-level maturity model of intrapreneurship

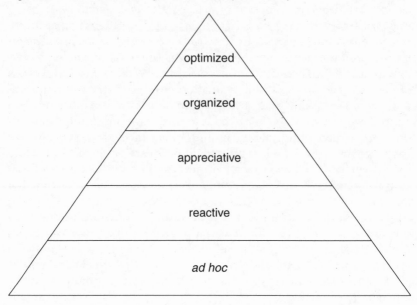

repeatable processes efficiently and effectively but has a tendency to struggle when faced with new problems. At the defined level, the organization has established a foundation for the examination of processes and has devised some initial approaches to improve the process. At the managed level, the organization has established quality and productivity measurements. Finally, at the optimized level, the organization's efforts are solely focused on identifying weak elements and strengthening deficiencies in the process. The SEI CMM model has become the benchmark for evaluating software processes in organizations. It is used for evaluating organizations that bid on software engineering projects and also as a benchmarking tool to aid in process improvement. Movement up and through the CMM model requires improvement in all aspects of the software process – a slow procedure.

As with software development, the development of mature, robust, intrapreneurship processes takes time, resources, and diligent management. Each stage of development (or level of maturity) the organization goes through yields varying results in terms of business value. Organizations can advance through a five-level maturity model toward full intrapreneurship. As shown in figure 8.1, the model describes the levels as *ad hoc*, reactive, appreciative, organized, and optimized.

At the *ad-hoc* level, the organization lacks a defined process for intrapreneurship. If intrapreneurship happens at all, it's due to the efforts of individual employees who care about their ideas, not to any organizational process that rewards or encourages this behavior. The organization might spend significant resources to develop ideas but will see limited returns, if any. The organization will struggle with generating ideas in areas of need, screening and providing feedback on ideas that are proposed, learning from experiments, and even commercializing, diffusing, and implementing ideas. The organization won't be able to maintain sustainable growth and development and will eventually disappear from the marketplace if it can't move to the next maturity level.

At the *reactive* level, 'local' processes exist to support the development of ideas. In many cases, these local processes emerge in reaction to external or internal pressures. For example, one of the first places organizations begin to streamline, collect, and share ideas is in their customer call centers. Pressures from customer complaints cause many organizations to react here first. Or an organization might develop processes around its research and development divisions when it sees competitors taking advantage of its ideas (as in the case of Xerox, described in chapter 1). At other times, companies may react when frustrated employees, unable to leverage their own ideas, leave the organization. At the reactive level, we begin to see local results in terms of business value. For example, we might see increased operational efficiency in departments where intrapreneurship processes are designed and utilized, with a resulting improvement in the rate of resolving customer complaints.

While we might see functional intradepartmental gains from the development of processes in the reactive stage, these local gains are not likely to show up at the organizational level. The reason for this is simple: without coordination *across* units within the organization, radical ideas that cut across departments will never take hold. Cross-functional intrapreneurship processes develop at the next stage, the *appreciative* level. At this stage, units that work closely with each other develop links and connections for transmitting ideas. In most organizations, customer call centers first develop links with engineering and sales units, as these units have the most direct connections to customers. Once these links are developed, the organization can take a broader view of intrapreneurship. Ideas will begin to get mobilized across departments and units, and cross-functional teams may form to participate in the later stages of the intrapreneurship process, such as idea screening and experimentation. Business value outcomes at this level can include not only operational gains but also tactical achievements. For example, instead of addressing customer complaints through Band-Aid solutions, the organization may decide to undertake novel product design and service development to treat the root cause of the problem. In this stage, intrapreneurial business value begins to cut across departments and units with broader impact.

At the *organized* level, an organization-wide framework for intrapreneurship gradually evolves and connects employees across all units of the organization. This stage comes into being as the organization realizes (1) that intrapreneurship is valuable and (2) that idea development is marred by incompatibility and lack of interoperability among the existing processes. The organization takes the lead role here to standardize the processes and help 'connect the dots.'

At this stage, we begin to see truly strategic gains from intrapreneurship. For example, consider the case of a global engineering firm whose profits declined steeply as a result of the global economic slowdown. A significant portion of its U.S. operations was put on hold after the housing bubble burst. In addition, its operations in the United Arab Emirates (specifically, Dubai and Abu Dhabi) were frozen. The firm was struggling to find alternative sources of revenue to sustain it until the economy picked up. A senior manager, an intrapreneur, had a simple idea – find new ways for the firm to deploy its rich knowledge base. The manager began exploring ideas for economic opportunities. He bootlegged resources to fly in four strategic advisors (myself among them) for a half-day meeting. During our meeting, we brainstormed ideas and spoke to employees from across the organization. The idea that bubbled to the surface was rather radical: open up a consulting practice that would help organizations improve their project-management competencies. Why would an engineering firm do such a thing? Leading engineering firms are not only good at building bridges and laying roads; they also have expertise in managing projects. Since projects are the predominant mode through which they get work done, they know how to scope these efforts, allocate resources and tasks, plan for risks and milestones, and ensure that their stakeholders understand the progress being made. These competencies are expected in large engineering firms but are rarer in other disciplines. For example, IT projects commonly go over budget and deadline; in fact, a good percentage of IT projects are either abandoned or escalated with a foolhardy commitment to something that's bound to fail. Recognizing the potential of the idea that came out of our half-day meeting, the manager contacted his personal network within the organization (to garner support and assemble a team who could work on the idea) and in the business community (to secure the first three customers for the firm). Today, the manager leads the consulting arm of the engineering firm, and his division provides the firm with a steady cash flow. The firm has also gained new contacts for its primary business.

The last stage, *optimized*, is more rightly characterized as *optimizing ad infinitum*: we can't simply optimize then stop. Failure to engage in a process of continuous renewal and improvement will cause an intrapreneurship process to stagnate or become obsolete. Organizations that already have a sound organization-wide framework for intrapreneurship must continuously improve their processes. As an organization's experience with intrapreneurship grows, the organization will learn the strengths and weaknesses of the program. For example, an organization may learn that it's very good at generating ideas but weak on idea advocacy and screening – and therefore prone to bottlenecks; it should refine its process accordingly. An organization will also have to adapt its process as internal and external conditions change – for example by increasing process infrastructure as the organization grows. Changes may be required to adapt to new technologies that emerge in the marketplace. Or, using best practices both within the industry and across industries as benchmarks may point to the need for improvements. For example, if an organization learns that a competitor or business partner has discovered a new method for idea experimentation, it should evaluate the technique and incorporate it into its own practice if appropriate. In short, it's helpful to view the intrapreneurship process as a living thing that follows a life-cycle model of learning from experience, adapting, and improving, as it grows to maturity. Learning can occur both from within – through self-learning and correction based on experience – and from the outside – through working with a management consultant, for example.

At the final stage of maturity, the organization witnesses a simple reality – its intrapreneurship process can help it sustain its competitive advantage. The organization needs to develop measures for keeping the intrapreneurship process *intelligent* and *agile* – intelligent enough to recognize opportunities for change and evolution, and agile enough to take advantage of these opportunities. Establishing a culture of intrapreneurship can help counter a tendency to stagnate and lose creative zeal. A continuous focus on improvement through intrapreneurship serves as a stimulus for employees to continue developing new ideas.

Concluding Thoughts

An intrapreneur's job is never done. A final, 'optimal,' or 'best' process doesn't exist. The optimizing and refinement of good practices goes on ad infinitum. Yet complacency can set in even at the most innovative organizations, causing people to 'pull off the pedal.' The result is that intrapreneurship moves from the foreground to the background and eventually disappears. Being intrapreneurial isn't natural for employees; what's natural is to come to work, do assigned tasks, and leave. Hence, if you want to make intrapreneurship stick you'll have to be relentless in your focus and dedication. As such, you need to remain unsatisfied and hungry and be constantly on the lookout for ways to improve intrapreneurship within the organization. Keep an eye out for complacency, and continuously energize and invigorate the intrapreneurship program. In one organization I know of with a robust intrapreneurship process, the executive in charge has a board outside his office called 'the parking lot for new ideas to make a good thing better.' His direct reports have to think of at least one idea to improve the process per month and post this to the 'parking lot.' He also measures which is the 'weakest link' of his organization's intrapreneurship program and then seeks ways to make this the 'star' of the program.

Here are the fundamental rules to keep in mind:

1 Believe in the transformative power of intrapreneurship as a concept and in the value of ideas.
2 Don't expect quick wins, and do expect initial skepticism.
3 Ensure that all stakeholders understand their roles within each component of the intrapreneurship process.
4 Focus on the long-term value of intrapreneurship to the organization, and don't cut corners by trying to push the concept through without buy-in.
5 Work toward a community-driven intrapreneurship process that is leveraged through a wide range of organizational alliances.

6 Invest in human potential and expand and diversify human networks.
7 Measure and communicate progress on a regular basis so as to keep the program in the forefront of all stakeholders' minds.
8 Remember that technology can enable and assist but can't drive your program or its success.
9 You're never done with intrapreneurship; you're on a journey, and every successive effort needs to be better than the last.
10 If you don't love it, get someone else to champion the effort.

I wish you the very best in your efforts to leverage ideas. It is my contention that as we advance through the next few decades of economic competition, societal change, and technological evolution, organizations that are able to build viable intrapreneurship programs will have sustainable competitive advantages. The competition of and for ideas is only going to intensify. Ideas are going to be traded much as physical goods and services are exchanged today. Organizations that can build mechanisms to seek out ideas from their employees and leverage them effectively and efficiently will earn higher returns than their competitors.

On a personal note, I invite you to share your intrapreneurship experiences with others and me. Only through the sharing of experiences and lessons learned can we all increase our intrapreneurship quotient!

Notes

1. Introduction

1 A. Braganza, Y. Awazu, and K.C. Desouza, 'Sustaining Innovation Is Challenge for Incumbents,' *Research-Technology Management*, 52 (4) (2009): 46–56.
2 L.D. DeSimone, G.N. Hatsopoulos, B,W.F. O'Brien, B. Harris, and C.P. Holt, 'How Can Big Companies Keep the Entrepreneurial Spirit Alive?' *Harvard Business Review*, 73 (6) (1 November 1995): 183–92.
3 G.G. Dess, R.D. Ireland, S.A. Zahra, S.W. Floyd, J.J. Janney, and P.J. Lane, 'Emerging Issues in Corporate Entrepreneurship,' *Journal of Management*, 29 (3) (2003): 351–78.
4 R.A. Burgelman, 'Corporate Entrepreneurship and Strategic Management: Insight from a Process Study,' *Management Science*, 29 (12) (1983): 1349–65; R.A. Burgelman, 'Designs for Corporate Entrepreneurship in Established Firms,' *California Management Review*, 26 (3) (1984): 155–66.
5 B. Antoncic and R.D. Hisrich, 'Intrapreneurship: Construct Refinement and Cross-Cultural Validation,' *Journal of Business Venturing*, 16 (5) (2001): 495–527; B. Barringer and A. Bluedorn, 'The Relationship between Corporate Entrepreneurship and Strategic Management,' *Strategic Management Journal*, 20 (5) (1999): 421–44; W.D. Guth, and A. Ginsberg, 'Guest Editors' Introduction: Corporate Entrepreneurship,' *Strategic Management Journal*, Vol. 11, *Special Issue: Corporate Entrepreneurship*, (Summer 1990): 5–15.
6 Z. Block and I. MacMillan, *Corporate Venturing* (Cambridge, MA: Harvard Business School Press, 1993); Guth and Ginsberg, 'Corporate Entrepreneurship'; Barringer and Bluedorn, 'The Relationship between Corporate Entrepreneurship and Strategic Management.'

7 Block and MacMillan, *Corporate Venturing*; S.A. Zahra, 'Predictors and Financial Outcomes of Corporate Entrepreneurship: An Exploration Study,' *Journal of Business Venturing*, 6 (4) (1991): 259–85.

8 R.M/ Kanter, J. North, et al., 'Engines of Progress: Designing and Running Entrepreneurial Vehicles in Established Companies,' *Journal of Business Venturing*, 5 (1990): 415–30; M.H. Morris, D.F. Kuratko, and J.G. Covin, *Corporate Entrepreneurship and Innovation: Entrepreneurial Development within Organizations*, 2nd ed. (Mason, OH: South-Western College Publishing, 2007).

9 A. Tsotsis, 'There's No Success Like Failure: Google's Biggest Product Flops,' *Tech Crunch*: http://techcrunch.com/2010/08/18/is-google-me-nex/.

10 Jena McGregor, 'Outsourcing Tasks Instead of Jobs,' *BusinessWeek*, 12 March 2009: http://www.businessweek.com/magazine/content/09_12/b4124050253173.htm.

11 H. Chesbrough and R.S. Rosenblum, 'The Role of the Business Model in Capturing Value from Innovation: Evidence from Xerox Corporation's Technology Spin-off Companies,' *Industrial and Corporate Change*, 11 (3) (2002): 529–55.

12 J.S. Brown, 'Research That Reinvents the Corporation,' *Harvard Business Review*, 80 (8) (August 2002): 105–13.

13 Ibid.

14 D.S. Alberts and R.E. Hayes, *Power to the Edge: Command, Control in the Information Age* (Washington, D.C.: U.S. Department of Defense, Command and Control Research Program, 2003).

15 E. von Hippel, *Democratizing Innovation* (Cambridge, MA: MIT Press, 2005); E. von Hippel, *The Sources of Innovation* (New York: Oxford University Press, 1998).

16 E. Von Hippel, 'Sticky Information and the Locus of Problem Solving: Implications for Innovation,' *Management Science*, 40 (4) (1991): 429–39.

17 W.M. Cohen and D.A. Levinthal, 'Absorptive Capacity: A New Perspective on Learning and Innovation,' *Administrative Science Quarterly*, 35 (1) (May 1990): 128–52; S.A. Zahra and G. George, 'Absorptive Capacity: A Review, Reconceptualization, and Extension,' *Academy of Management Review*, 27 (2) (2002): 185–203.

18 N. Rosenberg, *Inside the Black Box: Technology and Economics* (New York: Cambridge University Press, 1982).

19 E. Slivka, 'Apple Announces First-year App Store Success: 1.5 Billion Downloads, 65,000 Apps' (14 July 2009). Retrieved 22 July 2010, from *Mac Rumors*: http://www.macrumors.com/2009/07/14/apple-announces-first-year-app-store-success-1-5-billion-downloads-65000-apps/.

20 K.C. Desouza, C. Dombrowski, Y. Awazu, P. Baloh, S. Papagari, S. Jha, et al., 'Crafting Organizational Innovation Processes,' *Innovation: Management, Policy & Practice* (2009): 6–33.

21 B. Iyer and T.H. Davenport, 'Reverse Engineering Google's Innovation Machine,' *Harvard Business Review* (April 2008): 59–68.

2. Ideas, Roles, and Process

1 T. Davenport, *Process Innovation: Reengineering Work through Information Technology* (Boston: Harvard Business School Press, 1993); M. Hammer, 'Reengineering Work: Don't Automate, Obliterate,' *Harvard Business Review*, 68 (4) (July-August 1990): 104–12; M. Hammer and J. Champy, *Reengineering the Corporation: A Manifesto for Business Revolution* (New York: Harper Business, 1993).

2 K.C. Desouza, C. Dombrowski, Y. Awazu, P. Baloh, S. Papagari, S. Jha, et al., 'Crafting Organizational Innovation Processes,' *Innovation: Management, Policy & Practice*, 11 (1) (2009): 6–33.

3 John Mackie, *Problems from Locke* (Oxford: Clarendon Press, 1976); John Locke, *An Essay Concerning Human Understanding*, edited by Peter H. Nidditch (Oxford: Oxford University Press, 1975); John Yolton, 'On Being Present to the Mind: A Sketch for the History of an Idea,' *Dialogue*, 14 (1975): 373–88; Norman Wells, 'Objective Reality of Ideas in Descartes, Caterus, and Suárez,' *Journal of the History of Philosophy*, 28 (1) (1990): 33–61.

4 G.G. Dess, R.D. Ireland, S.A. Zahra, S.W. Floyd, J.J. Janney, and P.J. Lane, 'Emerging Issues in Corporate Entrepreneurship,' *Journal of Management*, 29 (3) (2003): 351–78; R.A. Burgelman, 'Corporate Entrepreneurship and Strategic Management: Insight from a Process Study,' *Management Science*, 29 (12) (1983): 1349–65; P. Sharma, and J.J. Chrisman, 'Toward a Reconciliation of the Definitional Issues in the Field of Corporate Entrepreneurship,' *Entrepreneurship Theory and Practice*, 23 (3) (1999): 11–28.

5 R.C. Wolcott, and M.J. Lippitz, 'The Four Models of Corporate Entrepreneurship,' *MIT Sloan Management Review*, 49 (1) (2007): 75–82. Wolcott and Lippitz examined corporate entrepreneurship programs in general, but their models can be applied at the specific level of intrapreneurship programs.

6 K.T. Ulrich and S.D. Eppinger, *Product Design and Development*, 3rd ed. (New York: McGraw-Hill, 2004).

7 Apple Inc., 'iPhone 4 Sales Top 1.7 Million' (28 June 2010). Retrieved 1 July 2010, from Apple Inc: http://www.apple.com/pr/library/2010/06/28iphone.html.

3. Idea Generation and Mobilization

1 A. Salter and D. Gann, 'Sources of Ideas for Innovation in Engineering Design,' *Research Policy*, 32 (8) (2003): 1309–24.
2 H. Rao, R. Sutton, and A.P. Webb, 'Innovation Lessons from Pixar: An Interview with Oscar-winning Director Brad Bird,' *The McKinsey Quarterly* (April 2008): 1–9.
3 L. Lehr, *Dreaming in Color: The Engineer as an Entrepreneur.* From a speech delivered at University of Nebraska, 2 April 1993.
4 R. Goffee and C. Jones, 'Leading Clever People,' *Harvard Business Review*, 85 (3) (2007): 72–9.
5 T.M. Amabile and M. Khaire, 'Creativity and the Role of the Leader,' *Harvard Business Review*, 86 (10) (2008): 100–9.
6 E.M. Hallowell, 'Overloaded Circuits: Why Smart People Underperform,' *Harvard Business Review*, 83 (1) (2005): 54–62.
7 M. Csikszentmihalyi, *Creativity: Flow and the Psychology of Discovery and Invention* (New York: HarperCollins, 1996); R. McAdam and J.McClelland, 'Individual and Team-based Idea Generation within Innovation Management: Organisational and Research Agendas,' *European Journal of Innovation Management*, 5(2) (2002): 86–97.
8 G. Dutton, 'Innovation Acceleration' (15 January 2010). Retrieved 27 March 2010, from trainingmag.com: http://www.trainingmag.com/article/innovation-acceleration.
9 D. Dougherty and C.H. Takacs, 'Team Play: Heedful Interrelating as the Boundary for Innovation,' *Long Range Planning*, 37 (6) (2001): 569–90; S. Brown, *Play: How It Shapes the Brain, Opens the Imagination, and Invigorates the Soul* (New York: Avery, 2009); M. Statler, J. Roos, and B. Victor, ' "Ain't Misbehavin": Taking Play Seriously in Organizations,' *Journal of Change Management*, 9 (1) (2009): 87–107; K.C. Desouza, 'Strategic Contribution of Game Rooms to Knowledge Management: Some Preliminary Insights,' *Information & Management*, 41 (1) (2003): 63–74.
10 P. Lewis, 'A Perpetual Crisis Machine,' *Fortune*, September 19, 2005 (2005): 58–76.
11 Ibid.
12 M. Ihlwan, 'Camp Samsung,' *BusinessWeek*, 3 July 2006.
13 L. Paige and S. Brin, 'Talks: Larry Paige and Sergey Brin on Google' (February 2004). Retrieved 27 March 2010, from TED: http://www.ted.com/talks/lang/eng/sergey_brin_and_larry_page_on_google.html.

14 T. Brown, 'Talks: Tim Brown on Creativity and Play' (May 2008). Retrieved 27 March 2010, from TED: http://www.ted.com/talks/lang/eng/tim_brown_on_creativity_and_play.html.

15 Paige and Brin, 'Talks: Larry Paige and Sergey Brin on Google.'

16 Brown, 'Talks: Tim Brown on Creativity and Play.'

17 Ibid.

18 Ibid.

19 S. McGrane, 'For a Seller of Innovation, a Bag of Technotricks' (11 February 1999). Retrieved 22 March 2010, from New York Times: http://www.nytimes.com/1999/02/11/technology/for-a-seller-of-innovation-a-bag-of-technotricks.html.

20 P. Rosedale, 'Talks: Philip Rosedale on Second Life' (May 2008). Retrieved 27 March 2010, from TED: http://www.ted.com/index.php/talks/the_inspiration_of_second_life.html.

21 P. Galagan, 'Slash, Burn, and Learn,' T+D (May 2009): 28–31.

22 Ibid.

23 Brown, 'Talks: Tim Brown on Creativity and Play.'

24 Ibid.

25 Ibid.

26 D.N. Sull, A. Ruelas-Gossi, and M. Escobari, 'What Developing-World Companies Teach Us about Innovation'(26 January 2004). Retrieved 22 March 2010, from HBS Working Knowledge: http://hbswk.hbs.edu/item/3866.html.

27 Dava Soberl, Longitude: The True Story of a Lone Genius Who Solved the Greatest Scientific Problem of His Time (New York: Walker & Co., 1995).

28 McKinsey & Company, 2009, 'And the Winner Is . . . Capturing the Promise of Philanthropic Prizes': http://www.mckinsey.com/App_Media/Reports/SSO/And_the_winner_is.pdf.

29 Charles Lindbergh, The Spirit of St. Louis (New York: Scribner, 1953).

30 Centennial Challenges: Descriptions and Resources: http://centennialchallenges.nasa.gov/.

31 J. Hill, 'Eyes on the Prize,' International Herald Tribune, 30 June 2007, 11; J. Hill, 'The Amateur Future of Space Travel,' New York Times, 1 July 2007, 6.

32 Sull, Ruelas-Gossi, and Escobari, 'What Developing-World Companies Teach Us about Innovation.'

33 G. Warwick, 'Advancing Ideas,' Aviation Week & Space Technology, 171 (16) (26 October 2009): 62.

34 W.D. Eggers and S.K. Singh, 'How Innovation Can Help You Do More with Fewer Resources,' Government Finance Review, 25 (6) (December 2009): 14–20.

35 A.B. Hargadon, 'Firms as Knowledge Brokers: Lessons in Pursuing Continuous Innovation,' *California Management Review*, 40 (3) (1998): 209–27; O. Gassmann and G. Reepmeyer, 'Organizing Pharmaceutical Innovation: From Science-based Knowledge Creators to Drug-oriented Knowledge Brokers,' *Creativity and Innovation Management*, 14 (2005): 233–45; M.L. Tushman and T. Scanlan, 'Boundary Spanning Individuals: Their Role in Information Transfer and Their Antecedents,' *Academy of Management Journal*, 24 (2) (1981): 289–305.

36 Marleen Huysman and Volker Wulf, 'IT to Support Knowledge Sharing in Communities: Towards a Social Capital Analysis,' *Journal of Information Technology*, 21 (1) (2006): 40–51; R. Cross, T. Laseter, A. Parker, and G. Velasquez, 'Using Social Network Analysis to Improve Communities of Practice,' *California Management Review*, 49 (1) (2006): 32–60; D. Krackhardt and J.R. Hanson, 'Informal Networks: The Company behind the Chart,' *Harvard Business Review*, 71 (4) (1993): 104–11.

37 M.L. Tushman and D.A. Nadler, 'Information Processing as an Integrating Concept in Organizational Design,' *Academy of Management Review*, 3 (3) (1978): 613–24; Claude E. Shannon and Warren Weaver, *The Mathematical Theory of Communication* (Urbana: University of Illinois Press, 1949).

38 K. Gordon, 'Creating a Haven for Innovation' (1 September 2005). Retrieved from *CMO Magazine*: http://www.cmomagazine.com/read/090105/creating_haven.html.

39 Sull, Ruelas-Gossi, and Escobari, 'What Developing-World Companies Teach Us about Innovation.'

40 P. Lewis, 'Texas Instruments' Lunatic Fringe' (14 November 2006). Retrieved 13 April 2007, from *Fortune*: http://money.cnn.com/magazines/fortune/fortune_archive/2006/09/04/8384732/index.htm.

41 Ibid.

42 R. Austin and R. Nolan, 'Bridging the Gap,' *MIT Sloan Management Review* (2007): 29–36.

43 Ibid.

44 Dutton, 'Innovation Acceleration.'

45 M. Arndt, 'Creativity Overflowing,' *BusinessWeek*; 8 May 2006; F. Warner, 'Recipe for Growth' (30 September 2001). Retrieved from Fast Company: http://www.fastcompany.com/magazine/51/recipe.html; H. Dolezalek, 'Imagination Station,' *Training* (2003): 14; G. Cutler, 'Innovation Mentoring at Whirlpool,' *Research Technology Management*, 46 (6) (2003): 57; K. Melymuka, 'Innovation Democracy,' *Computerworld* (2004): 31–2; M. Arndt, 'Whirlpool Taps Its Inner Entrepreneur' (7 February 2002). Retrieved from

BusinessWeek Online: http://www.businessweek.com/smallbiz/content/feb2002/sb2002027_3066.htm.

46 K.C. Desouza, 'Barriers to Effective Use of Knowledge Management Systems in Software Engineering,' *Communications of the ACM*, 46 (1) (2003): 99–101.

47 Bill McEvily, Vincenzo Perrone, and Akbar Zaheer, 'Trust as an Organizing Principle,' *Organization Science*, 14 (1) (January-February 2003): 91–103; J.D. Lewis and A. Weigert, 'Trust as a Social Reality,' *Social Forces*, 63 (1985): 967–85; J. Coleman, 'Social Capital in the Creation of Human Capital,' *American Journal of Sociology*, 94 (1988): 95–120.

48 B. Iyer and T. Davenport, 'Reverse Engineering Google's Innovation Machine,' *Harvard Business Review* (April 2008): 59–68.

49 M. Granovetter, 'The Strength of Weak Ties,' *American Journal of Sociology* (May 1973): 1360–80.

4. Advocating and Screening

1 Advanced Practices Council (APC), 'Leveraging Emerging Digital Technology at BP: Executive Summary' (June 2007). Retrieved 22 March 2010, from CIOZone: http://www.ciozone.com/index.php/Case-Studies/Case-Study-BP-Uses-VC-Model-To-Pick-Best-Tech.html.

2 Ibid.

3 Ibid.

4 W.D. Eggers and S.K. Singh, 'How Innovation Can Help You Do More with Fewer Resources,' *Government Finance Review*, 25 (6) (2009): 14–20.

5 G. Hamel and G. Getz, 'Funding Growth in an Age of Austerity,' *Harvard Business Review* (July-August 2004): 76–8.

6 Ibid.

7 A. Raman and A.P. McAfee, 'Enterprise 2.0: How a Connected Workforce Innovates (Interview),' *Harvard Business Review*, 87 (12) (December 2009): 80.

8 K. Burnham, 'How Motorola Uses Prediction Markets to Choose Innovations' (27 April 2009). Retrieved 27 March 2010, from CIO: http://www.cio.com/article/490762/How_Motorola_Uses_Prediction_Markets_to_Choose_Innovations_.

9 Morgan M. Shepherd, Robert O. Briggs, Bruce A. Reinig, Jerome Yen, and Jay F. Nunamaker, Jr, 'Invoking Social Comparison to Improve Electronic Brainstorming: Beyond Anonymity,' *Journal of Management Information Systems*, 12 (3) (December 1995): 155–70; P.A. Collaros and L.R. Anderson, 'Effect of Perceived Expertness upon Creativity of Members of Brainstorming Groups,' *Journal of Applied Psychology*, 53 (April 1969): 159–63.

10 M. McLure Wasko and S. Faraj, ' "It is what one does": Why People Participate and Help Others in Electronic Communities of Practice,' *Journal of
Strategic Information Systems*, 9 (2/3) (2000): 155–73.

11 K.C. Desouza and Y. Awazu, 'Constructing Internal Knowledge Markets:
Considerations from Mini-Cases,' *International Journal of Information Management*, 23 (4) (2003): 345–53; K.C. Desouza, Y. Awazu, S. Yamakawa, and
M. Umezawa, 'Facilitating Knowledge Management through Market Mechanisms,' *Knowledge and Process Management*, 12 (2) (2005): 99–107.

12 P.F. Boer, 'Valuation of Technology Using "Real Options," ' *Research Technology Management* (2000): 26–30; M. Amram and N. Kulatilaka, *Real Options: Managing Strategic Investment in an Uncertain World* (Boston, MA:
Harvard Business School Press, 1999).

13 Amram, and Kulatilaka, *Real Options: Managing Strategic Investment in an
Uncertain World*.

14 R.G. McGrath and I.C. MacMillan, 'Assessing Technology Projects Using
Real Options Reasoning,' *Research Technology Management* (2005): 35–49.

15 E.H. Bowman and D. Hurry, 'Strategy through the Option Lens: An Integrated View of Resource Investments and the Incremental-Choice Process,'
Academy of Management Review, 18 (4) (1993): 760–82.

16 R. Adner and D.A. Levinthal, 'What Is Not a Real Option: Considering
Boundaries for the Application of Real Options to Business Strategy,' *Academy of Management Review*, 29 (1) (2004): 74–85.

17 Hamel and Getz, 'Funding Growth in an Age of Austerity.'

18 D. Rigby, K. Gruver, and J. Allen, 'Innovation in Turbulent Times,' *Harvard
Business Review*, 87 (6) (June 2009): 79–86.

5. Idea Experimentation

1 J.H. Dyer, H.B. Gregersen, and C.M. Christensen, 'The Innovator's DNA,'
Harvard Business Review, 87 (12) (December 2009): 60–7.

2 D.D. Sackett, 'When We Began, We Were Almost Pariahs. Interview by
André Picard' (30 October 2009). Retrieved 15 April 2010, from *The Globe
and Mail*: http://www.theglobeandmail.com/life/health/when-we-
began-we-were-almost-pariahs/article1344833/.

3 G. Linden, 'Early Amazon: Shopping Cart Recommendations' (25 April
2006). Retrieved 15 April 2010, from Geeking with Greg: http://glinden.
blogspot.com/2006/04/early-amazon-shopping-cart.html.

4 D. McCann, 'Testing, Testing: The New Innovation Game' (15 March
2010). Retrieved 15 April 2010, from CFO: http://cfo.com/article.cfm/
14482988.

5 B. Gleba and L.Cavanaugh, 'Applying the IKEA Values to Improving the Intranet,' *Strategic Communication Management*, 113 (10) (2005): 30–3.
6 Ibid.
7 J. Barthélemy, 'The Experimental Roots of Revolutionary Vision,' *MIT Sloan Management Review*, 48 (1) (Fall 2006): 81.
8 Ibid.
9 C.L. Hodock, 'Honest Innovation,' *Marketing Management*, 18 (2) (March/April 2009): 18–21.
10 T. Goetz, 'Freeing the Dark Data of Failed Scientific Experiments' (25 September 2007). Retrieved 24 April 2010, from *Wired*: http://www.wired.com/science/discoveries/magazine/15-10/st_essay#ixzz0mBSZdopH.
11 M. Warman, 'It May Not Be as Polished as Apple, but Google Has a Way of Beguiling,' *The Daily Telegraph* (London), 9 January 2010.
12 T. O'Brien 'Encourage Wild Ideas' (30 April 1996). Retrieved 15 April 2010, from *Fast Company*: http://www.fastcompany.com/magazine/02/ideosec.html.
13 Dyer, Gregersen, and Christensen, 'The Innovator's DNA.'
14 C. Prather, 'Use Mistakes to Foster Innovation,' *Research Technology Management*, 51 (2) (2008):14–16.
15 P.J. Schoemaker and R.E. Gunther, 'The Wisdom of Deliberate Mistakes,' *Harvard Business Review*, 84 (6) (June 2006):108–15; Dyer, Gregersen, and Christensen, 'The Innovator's DNA.'
16 Dyer, Gregersen, and Christensen, 'The Innovator's DNA.'
17 Prather, 'Use Mistakes to Foster Innovation.'
18 A. Hargadon and R.I. Sutton, 'Technology Brokering and Innovation in a Product Development Firm,' *Administrative Science Quarterly*, 42 (December 1997): 716–49.
19 Ken Starkey, Sue Tempest, and Alan McKinlay, *How Organizations Learn: Managing the Search for Knowledge*, 2nd ed. (London: Thomson Learning, 2004); Barbara Levitt and James G. March, 'Organizational Learning,' *Annual Review of Sociology*, 14 (1988): 319–40.
20 Dyer, Gregersen, and Christensen, 'The Innovator's DNA.'
21 Schoemaker and Gunther, 'The Wisdom of Deliberate Mistakes.'
22 A. Tugend, 'The Many Errors in Thinking about Mistakes' (24 November 2007). Retrieved 29 April 2010, from the *New York Times*: http://www.nytimes.com/2007/11/24/business/24shortcuts.html.
23 Hodock, 'Honest Innovation.'
24 K.C. Desouza, T. Dingsøyr, and Y. Awazu, 'Experiences with Conducting Project Postmortems: Reports vs. Stories,' *Software Process Improvement and Practice*, 10 (2) (2005): 203–15.

25 S. Laidlaw, 'Drug "Reports" Found to Be Faked; Firms Misrepresented Some Research Results, Slew of Cases Suggest,' *Toronto Star*, 22 June 2009.

26 Warren M. Bodie, *The Lockheed P-38 Lightning: The Definitive Story of Lockheed's P-38 Fighter* (Hayesville, NC: Widewing Publications, 2001, 1991); Ben Rich and Leo Janos, *Skunk Works: A Personal Memoir of My Years at Lockheed* (New York: Little, Brown & Company, 1994).

27 Hodock, 'Honest Innovation.'

28 3M Company, *A Century of Innovation: The 3M Story* (St. Paul, MN: 3M Company, 2002), 37.

29 Ibid.

30 K. Patel, 'Need to Know: Rapid Prototyping,' *Creativity*, 17 (4) (1 June 2009): 73.

31 S.H. Thomke, *Experimentation Matters: Unlocking the Potential of New Technologies for Innovation* (Boston: Harvard Business School Press, 2003).

32 D. Duffy, 'Briefing: The Sting of Virtual Warfare,' *CSO* (April 2005).

33 E. Leonard, 'IT Gets Creative at DreamWorks' (1 April 2006). Retrieved 18 October 2010, from *InformationWeek* (originally available at Optimizemag.com): http://www.informationweek.com/news/software/open_source/showArticle.jhtml?articleID=185300380.

34 Ibid.

35 Michael J. Prietula, Kathleen M. Carley, and Les Gasser, eds, *Simulating Organizations: Computational Models of Institutions and Groups* (Menlo Park, CA: AAAI Press /The MIT Press, 1998); Kathleen M. Carley and Michael J. Prietula, eds, *Computational Organization Theory* (Hillsdale, NJ: Lawrence Erlbaum Associates, 1994).

36 Robert Axelrod, *The Complexity of Cooperation: Agent-Based Models of Competition and Collaboration* (Princeton, NJ: Princeton University Press, 1997).

37 C. Bereiter and M. Scardamalia, 'Teaching How Science Really Works,' *Education Canada*, 49 (1) (Winter 2009): 14–17.

38 K. Bensinger and R. Vartabedian, 'Toyota Calls in the Big Guns; California Engineering Firm Exponent Inc.,' *Los Angeles Times*, 18 February 2010.

39 N. Salkind, 'Independent Variable.' In *Encyclopedia of Measurement and Statistics*, Vol. 2 (Thousand Oaks, CA: Sage Reference, 2007), 453–4.

40 N. Salkind, 'Dependent Variable.' In *Encyclopedia of Measurement and Statistics*, Vol. 1 (Thousand Oaks, CA: Sage Reference, 2007), 249–50.

41 L. Given, 'Exploratory Research.' In *The SAGE Encyclopedia of Qualitative Research Methods*, Vol. 1 (Thousand Oaks, CA: Sage Publications Inc., 2008), 327–9.

42 N. Salkind, 'Descriptive Research.' In *Encyclopedia of Measurement and Statistics*, Vol. 1 (Thousand Oaks, CA: Sage Reference, 2007), 250–3.

43 B. Strickland, 'Scientific Method.' In *Gale Encyclopedia of Psychology*, 2nd ed. (Detroit: Gale, 2001), 562–3.

44 L. Given, 'Reliability.' In *The SAGE Encyclopedia of Qualitative Research Methods*, Vol. 2 (Thousand Oaks, CA: Sage Publications Inc., 2008), 753–4.
45 P. Lavrakas, 'Validity.' In *Encyclopedia of Survey Research Methods*, Vol. 2 (Thousand Oaks, CA: Sage Publications Inc., 2008), 938–9.
46 N.J. Salkind, 'Moderator Variable.' In *Encyclopedia of Measurement and Statistics*, Vol. 2 (Thousand Oaks, CA: Sage Reference, 2007), 624–6.
47 N.J. Salkind, 'Tests of Mediating Effects.' In *Encyclopedia of Measurement and Statistics*, Vol. 3 (Thousand Oaks, CA: Sage Reference, 2007), 995–9.
48 N.J. Salkind, 'Random Sampling.' In *Encyclopedia of Measurement and Statistics*, Vol. 3 (Thousand Oaks, CA: Sage Reference, 2007), 816–19.
49 P. Lavrakas, 'Purposive Sampling.' In *Encyclopedia of Survey Research Methods*, Vol. 2 (Thousand Oaks, CA: Sage Publications Inc., 2008), 645.
50 P. Lavrakas, 'Correlation.' In *Encyclopedia of Survey Research Methods*, Vol. 1 (Thousand Oaks, CA: Sage Publications Inc., 2008), 154–6.
51 'Causality' (26 October 2010). Retrieved 26 October 2010, from Wikipedia: http://en.wikipedia.org/wiki/Causality.

6. Idea Commercialization

1 J. Gruber, 'Apple's Constant Iterations,' *Macworld*, 27(4) (April 2010): 100.
2 A. Hesseldahl, 'Apple's iDecade' (1 January 2010). Retrieved 1 June 2010, from *BusinessWeek Online*: http://www.businessweek.com/technology/content/dec2009/tc20091231_183323.htm.
3 E. Rasmussen and O.J. Borch, 'University Capabilities in Facilitating Entrepreneurship: A Longitudinal Study of Spin-Off Ventures at Mid-Range Universities,' *Research Policy*, 39 (5) (2010): 602–12.
4 Vijay K. Jolly, *Commercializing New Technologies: Getting from Mind to Market* (Boston: Harvard Business School Press, 1997); Donna L. Hoffman and Thomas P. Novak, 'Marketing in Hypermedia Computer-Mediated Environments: Conceptual Foundations,' *The Journal of Marketing*, 60 (3) (July 1996): 50–68; Dale S. Rogers, Douglas M. Lambert, and A. Michael Knemeyer, 'The Product Development and Commercialization Process,' *International Journal of Logistics Management*, 15 (1) (2004): 43–56.
5 Junu Kim, 'Maintaining the TECH Edge,' *Boeing Frontiers Online*, 1 (3) (July 2002). Retrieved from http://www.boeing.com/news/frontiers/archive/2002/july/cover.html.
6 Bruce Kogut and Anca Metiu, 'Open-Source Software Development and Distributed Innovation,' *Oxford Review of Economic Policy*, 17 (2) (2001): 248–64; Josh Lerner and Jean Tirole, 'Some Simple Economics of Open Source,' *Journal of Industrial Economics*, 50 (2) (June 2002): 197–234.

7 D.J. Teece, 'Profiting from Technological Innovation: Implications for Integration, Collaboration, Licensing and Public Policy,' *Research Policy* (1986): 285–305; D.J. Teece, 'Reflection on "Profiting from Innovation,"' *Research Policy* (2006): 1091–9.

8 C.J. Brez, 'Open Innovation and Technology Transfer,' *Baylor Business Review*, 28 (1) (Fall 2009): 20–1.

9 E. Svoboda and C. Dillow, 'The Mad Scientist of Mobile Phones,' *Fast Company*, 126 (June 2008): 48–9.

10 Ibid.

11 J. Hult, 'The Itera Plastic Bicycle,' *Social Studies of Science*, 22 (2) (1992): 373–85.

12 Ibid.

13 E.J. Epstein, 'Hidden Persuaders: The Secretive Group That Helps Run the Movie Business' (18 July 2005). Retrieved 14 June 2010, from *Slate*: http://www.slate.com/id/2122934.

14 Ibid.

15 Information about basic marketing principles is available in a wide range of textbooks and online sources. See, for example, Philip Kotler and Gary Armstrong, *Principles of Marketing*, 11th edition (Upper Saddle River, NJ: Prentice Hall, 2006); for online resources see http://www.knowthis.com/, including Principles of Marketing tutorial series.

16 E. Von Hippel, *Democratizing Innovation* (Cambridge, MA: MIT Press, 2005).

17 E. Von Hippel, 'Lead Users: A Source of Novel Product Concepts,' *Management Science*, 32 (7) (1986): 791–806; G. Urban and E. von Hippel, 'Lead User Analyses for the Development of New Industrial Products,' *Management Science*, 34 (5) (1988): 569–82.

18 See Common Craft's explanation regarding developing communications 'in Plain English': http://www.commoncraft.com/about/who.

19 P. Ganapati, 'Dell's Tablet Aims to Stick It to Apple's iPad' (24 February 2010). Retrieved 12 June 2010, from *Wired*: http://www.wired.com/gadgetlab/2010/02/dells-tablet-aims-to-stick-it-to-apples-ipad/.

20 M.B. Beverland, J. Napoli, and F. Farrelly, 'Can All Brands Innovate in the Same Way? A Typology of Brand Position and Innovation Effort,' *Journal of Product Innovation Management*, 27 (1) (2010): 33–48.

21 J. Weisman, 'Toysrus.com Rebounds after 1999 Stumble' (5 January 2001). Retrieved 12 June 2010, from *ECommerceTimes*: http://www.ecommercetimes.com/story/6478.html.

22 Ibid.

23 Ibid.

24 G.F. Mechlin and D.Berg, 'Evaluating Research – ROI Is Not Enough,' *Harvard Business. Review*, 58 (5) (September-October 1980): 93–9.

7. Diffusion and Implementation of Ideas

1 See, for example, P. Kotler, *Marketing 3.0: From Products to Customers to the Human Spirit* (Hoboken, NJ: Wiley, 2010); P. Kotler and G. Armstrong, *Principles of Marketing*, 11th ed. (Saddle River, NJ: Prentice Hall, 2009).

2 J.H. Gilmore and B.J. Pine, II, eds, *Markets of One: Creating Customer-Unique Value through Mass Customization* (Boston: Harvard Business School Press, 2000); Paul Nunes, Diane Wilson, and Ajit Kambil, 'All-in-One Market,' *Harvard Business Review* (May/June 2000): 19–20.

3 M. Gold, 'Banking on Enterprise E-learning: Part 5,' *T + D*, 57 (8) (1 August 2003): 48–55.

4 Ibid.

5 See, for example, David Meerman Scott, *The New Rules of Marketing and PR: How to Use Social Media, Blogs, News Releases, Online Video, and Viral Marketing to Reach Buyers Directly* (Hoboken, NJ: Wiley, 2010); Shama Kabani, *The Zen of Social Media Marketing: An Easier Way to Build Credibility, Generate Buzz, and Increase Revenue* (Dallas, TX: BenBella Books, 2010).

6 D.J. Sohn and J.Y. Kwak, 'Facilitating "Knowledge Clashes" at Samsung,' *Knowledge Management Review*, 8 (2) (2005): 6–8.

7 Ibid.

8 Ibid.

9 D. Hinchcliffe, 'Twelve Best Practices for Online Customer Communities' (25 July 2008). Retrieved 22 June 2010, from ZDNet: http://www.zdnet.com/blog/hinchcliffe/twelve-best-practices-for-online-customer-communities/190.

10 Shel Israel, *Twitterville: How Businesses Can Thrive in the New Global Neighborhoods* (New York: Portfolio, 2009); Charlene Li and Josh Bernoff, *Groundswell: Winning in a World Transformed by Social Technologies* (Boston: Harvard Business School Press, 2008).

11 F. Vogelstein, 'Great Wall of Facebook: The Social Network's Plan to Dominate the Internet – and Keep Google Out' (22 June 2009). Retrieved 21 June 2010, from *Wired*: http://www.wired.com/techbiz/it/magazine/17–07/ff_facebookwall#ixzz0rYfHM2bl.

12 See, for example, several books by Robert Cross, et al., including: *Networks in the Knowledge Economy* (New York: Oxford University Press, 2003); *The Hidden Power of Social Networks: Understanding How Work Really Gets Done in Organizations* (Boston: Harvard Business School Press, 2004);

and *Driving Results through Social Networks: How Top Organizations Leverage Networks for Performance and Growth* (San Francisco: Jossey-Bass, 2009).

13 S. Patton, 'Who Knows Whom, and Who Knows What?' (15 June 2006). Retrieved 22 June 2010, from CIO: http://www.cio.com/archive/061505/km.html.

14 Ibid.

15 M.L. Tushman, 'Special Boundary Roles in the Innovation Process,' *Administrative Science Quarterly*, 22 (4) (1977): 587–605; M.L. Tushman, and T.J. Scanlan, 'Boundary Spanning Individuals: Their Role in Information Transfer and Their Antecedents,' *Academy of Management Journal*, 24 (2): (1981): 289–305.

16 A. Hargadon and R.I. Sutton, 'Technology Brokering and Innovation in a Product Development Firm,' *Administrative Science Quarterly*, 42 (December 1977)): 716–49.

17 Ibid.

18 K. Dedker, 'Reward the Inventors of Our Future,' *Brandweek*, 47 (25) (2005): 16–18.

19 S. Khosla, 'It's Ideas That Add Real Muscle,' *Knight Ridder Tribune Business News*, 27 April 2006.

20 D. Teather, 'Financial: Profile of a Giant: Five-bladed Razors, Billion-dollar Budgets and Chinese Cold-water Shampoo: The $57bn Marriage of Gillette with Procter & Gamble – the Best a Brand Can Get?' *The Guardian*, 27 October 2005, 28.

21 Dedker, 'Reward the Inventors of Our Future.'

22 Jason Kincaid, 'Twitter Acquires Tweetie,' *TechCrunch,* 9 April 2010: http://techcrunch.com/2010/04/09/twitter-acquires-tweetie/.

23 J.D. Sutter, 'Google Plans to Drop Wave' (4 August 2010). Retrieved 30 August 2010, from CNN Tech: http://articles.cnn.com/2010–08–04/tech/google.wave.end_1_google-plans-google-senior-vice-president-google-maps?_s=PM:TECH; U. Hölzle, 'Update on Google Wave' (4 August 2010). Retrieved 30 August 2010, from The Official Google Blog: http://googleblog.blogspot.com/2010/08/update-on-google-wave.html.

24 J.D. Sutter, 'Google Wave to Be Released to 100,000 Testers Wednesday' (30 September 2009). Retrieved 22 June 2010, from CNN Tech: http://articles.cnn.com/2009–09–29/tech/google.wave.beta_1_lars-rasmussen-google-maps-beta-testers?_s=PM:TECH.

25 Hölzle, 'Update on Google Wave.'

26 Ibid.

27 'Procter & Gamble CEO A.G. Lafley: A.G. Lafley on Developing Markets' (n.d.). Retrieved 24 April 2010, from ChiefExecutive: http://www.chiefexecutive.net/ME2/Audiences/dirmod.asp?sid=&nm=&type=Publishing&mod=Publications%3A%3AArticle&mid=8F3A70274218

41978F18BE895F87F791 &tier=4&id=CED125AFBE694D6DA879ABA5
BAE6276D &AudID=ae720e7de3fe473693930869a5157c27.

28 William D. Eggers and Shalabh Kumar Singh, *The Public Innovator's Play-
    book: Nurturing Bold Ideas in Government* (Winnipeg, MB: Deloitte Research,
    2009): see http://www.deloitte.com/assets/Dcom-Global/Local%20As
    sets/Documents/dtt_ps_innovatorsplaybook_100409.pdf.

8. Intrapreneurship from Concept to Sustained Competitive Advantage

1 M.C. Paulk, B. Curtis, and M.B. Chrissis, *Capability MaturityModel for Soft-
    ware* (Technical Report, CMU/SEI-91-TR-24, ADA240603) (Pittsburgh:
    Software Engineering Institute, Carnegie Mellon University, 1991).

2 ISO, 'International Organization for Standardization' (n.d.). Retrieved
    21 January 2010, from ISO Online: www.iso.org; E. Naveh and A. Marcus,
    'When Does ISO 9000 Quality Assurance Standard Lead to Performance
    Improvement?' *IEEE Transactions on Engineering Management*, 51 (3) (2004):
    352–63.

Acknowledgments

This book draws on the wide range of experiences with which I've been blessed, and which I cherish. It's not the outcome of my individual efforts. Its pages contain the essence of my interactions with the many talented individuals I have been fortunate to collaborate with over the years and without whose support, tireless work, and counsel this book would not have come to fruition.

I would like to thank the numerous executives, managers, innovators, inventors, scholars, writers, and students who have opened their doors to me. I want specifically to thank George Kraft, Margaret Kraft, Roberto Evaristo, Yukika Awazu, Scott Paquette, Chen Ye, Tobin Hensgen, Sandeep Purao, Sumit Roy, Peter Baloh, Mike Eisenberg, Annie Searle, Mike Crandall, Miha Škerlavaj, Nelson Del Rio, Peter Trkman, Aleš Groznik, and Chris Rivinus. Each of these individuals has been a longtime collaborator and friend. I've learned a lot from each of them.

A university is only as good as the students it enrolls, and I've had the chance to interact with some of the best young minds. My current and former students Subramaniam Ramasubramanian, Kristen Lau, Jared Keller, Tim Moon, Sam Dichupa, Yuan Lin, Akshay Bhagwatwar, Nick Sweers, Peter Ellis, Bryce Smart, and Nina Yuttapongsontorn have been wonderful collaborators and sources of ideas. They enriched my thinking, and never hesitated to ask me to explain myself more clearly.

This book documents lessons from a wide range of research and professional experiences. I would like to express my sincere gratitude to all the employees, business partners, and customers I worked with for more than five years when creating and directing the Engaged Enterprise. In the pages that follow, I use examples and concepts I learned from you. I thank you for taking time to enrich my thinking about how to leverage ideas within and across organizations. This book also draws on work I did at the University of Washington from 2005 to 2010. I learned a lot from my peers at the Information School, the College of Engineering, and the Daniel J. Evans School of Public Affairs. I've had the pleasure of leading two research centers during my time at the University of Washington: the Institute for Innovation in Information Management and the Institute for National Security Education and Research. These institutes afforded me the opportunity to collaborate with leading thinkers and practitioners on a wide assortment of organizational innovation challenges. Since June 2009, I've been involved in designing the X-Prize Lab at the University of Washington. The X-Prize Lab has given me the opportunity to collaborate with bright minds to develop prize concepts that encourage innovative solutions to the grand challenges facing our world. My gratitude goes to Sandy Archibald and Ann Bostrom, who have been invigorating peers to collaborate with on this effort. In 2011, I decided to make the cross-country move to the Washington, D.C., area (leaving one Washington for another) to join Virginia Tech to direct the Metropolitan Institute. I want to thank all those who worked behind the scenes to make the move painless, thereby giving me the necessary time to put the finishing touches on this book.

During the writing of this book, I was fortunate in having opportunities to present my research at a number of leading organizations across the globe, in locations as diverse as Poland, India, Slovenia, the United Kingdom, France, South Africa, Thailand, and the United States, among others. I thank the attendees at these various forums who were gracious with their time, ideas, and hospitality.

Numerous individuals and organizations supported my research for this work. The Institute for Innovation in Information Management (I3M) at the University of Washington Information School, and the American Productivity Quality Center in Houston, Texas, provided resources for studying innovation programs in global organizations, for which I am thankful. In addition, I'm grateful to the University of the Witwatersrand, the London School of Economics and Political Science, the University of Ljubljana, and the Montpellier Business School, each of which provided visiting positions for me during the writing of the book. Sections of this book were written in Spain, Portugal, India, Slovenia, and South Africa. I want to thank all the hosts of the various residences at which I stayed during the writing process.

Matthew Daniels, Orchid Magd, Tim Moon, Michael Fors, and Seaton ('Chip') Daly read the entire manuscript and provided valuable feedback from the perspective of employees and managers. I extend my thanks to them, as well as to the anonymous reviewers who commented at various stages in the process. I want to thank Marissa Lavelle, my graduate assistant, for working with me on the manuscript. Marissa spent numerous hours working through drafts, challenging my thinking, and forcing me to be clear and direct when describing complex ideas. Brian Le Blanc did a wonderful job reading several chapters and providing valuable feedback. James Wilson and Adam Taplin did an excellent job turning my thinking, random collections of notes, and ramblings into lively prose that you can understand.

I also want to thank the team at the University of Toronto Press for believing in the concept of this book and seeing it through to publication. Special thanks are due to my editor, Jennifer DiDomenico, who has been pleasant, kind, and generous with her feedback and handling of the manuscript.

My family has always been supportive of my endeavors, even the ones that seem random or farfetched. I'll always be thankful for the sacrifices that my parents, Priscilla C. Desouza and Michael J. Desouza, made to afford me a world-class education and the opportunities that come with it – I hope that I have done my part to make you proud. My brother, Kenneth Desouza, and sister, Karishma Desouza, are wiser and smarter than me; they are also much more patient. I thank them for their patience and support over the past few years of my writing.

My work on this manuscript has coincided with meeting a new family: the McLurgs. I thank them for their understanding as I have taken time to write the book, which on many occasions has kept me, and their wonderful daughter, from visiting them. This is the first book I have written with a significant other in my life. Sally is a wonderful and loving person. She has been compassionate and kind during these last two years as I have worked on various aspects of research and writing. I can honestly say that, at times, I was a crankier writer than I would like to admit! Sally has been a source of calm, energy, and focus throughout. She's read every chapter, sometimes multiple times, and has done so thoughtfully and without concern for the added workload.

Winston Churchill put it best when he said, *'my most brilliant achievement was my ability to be able to persuade my wife to marry me.'* I dedicate this book to you, Sally, and I look forward to spending the rest of my life with you.

Kevin C. Desouza
Seattle, Washington

About the Author

Dr Kevin C. Desouza is the director of the Metropolitan Institute and an associate professor at the Center for Public Administration and Policy at Virginia Tech. Before joining Virigina Tech, he was an associate professor at the University of Washington (UW) Information School and held adjunct appointments in the UW's College of Engineering and at the Daniel J. Evans School of Public Affairs. At UW, he co-founded and directed the Institute for Innovation in Information Management (I3M); founded the Institute for National Security Education and Research, an interdisciplinary, university-wide initiative, in August 2006, and served as its director until February 2008; and was an affiliate faculty member of the Center for American Politics and Public Policy. He holds a visiting professorship at the Faculty of Economics, University of Ljubljana. He has held visiting positions at the Center for International Studies at the London School of Economics and Political Science, the University of the Witwatersrand in South Africa, the Groupe Sup de Co Montpellier (GSCM) Business School in France, and the Accenture Institute for High Business Performance in Cambridge, Massachusetts (U.S.A.). In the private sector, he founded the Engaged Enterprise and its think tank, the Institute for Engaged Business Research. The Engaged Enterprise was a global strategy consulting firm with expertise in the areas of knowledge management, crisis management, strategic deployment of information systems, and government and competitive intelligence assignments.

Dr Desouza has authored, co-authored, and/or edited eight books and has published more than 125 articles in prestigious practitioner and academic journals. His work has also been featured by a number of publications such as *Sloan Management Review, Harvard Business*

Review, BusinessWeek, Washington Internet Daily, Computerworld, KM Review, Government Health IT, and *Human Resource Management International Digest.* He has been interviewed by the press on outlets such as *Voice of America, Manager* (Slovenia), among others. He has been invited to edit special issues of several prominent journals such as *Technology Forecasting and Social Change, Information Systems Journal,* and the *Journal of Strategic Information Systems,* among others. In addition, he serves on a number of editorial boards, including the board of the *Journal of Strategic Information Systems,* and has reviewed research for government agencies such as the Research Council of Norway, the Finnish Funding Agency for Technology and Innovation, the National Research Foundation of South Africa, and the Qatar National Research Fund-Qatar Foundation, among others.

Dr Desouza has advised, briefed, and/or consulted for major international corporations and government organizations on strategic management issues ranging from management of information systems to knowledge management, competitive intelligence, government intelligence operations, and crisis management. He is frequently an invited speaker on a number of cutting-edge business and technology topics for national and international, industry, and academic audiences. He has given more than sixty invited talks in a wide assortment of venues. Dr Desouza has received over $1.4 million in research funding from both private and government organizations.

Index